Sexuality, Religion and the Sacred

Sexuality, Religion and the Sacred is a thoughtful collection of bisexual, polysexual and pansexual scholarship on religion and spirituality. It examines how religious and spiritual traditions address sexuality, whilst also exploring the ways in which bisexually-, polysexually-, and pansexually-active people embrace religious and spiritual practice. The volume offers a comprehensive analysis of these prevalent themes by focusing on five main areas of discussion: Christian and Unitarian Discourses; Indigenous and Decolonizing Spiritual Discourses; Feminist Spiritual Discourses; Buddhist Discourses; and Neo/Pagan Discourses.

Sexuality, Religion and the Sacred offers an accessible yet scholarly treatment of these topics through a collection of critical essays by academics of theology, humanities, cultural studies and social sciences, as well as sexology professionals and clergy from various faith and spiritual traditions. It gives readers an insight into the intersection of sexualities and spiritualities, and attempts to disrupt this very dichotomy through its careful consideration of a wide variety of discourses.

This book was originally published as a special issue of the *Journal of Bisexuality*.

Loraine Hutchins teaches inter-disciplinary sexuality studies. Her 2001 Cultural Studies doctoral dissertation documented contemporary U.S. sacred sexualities, particularly those with a queer feminist focus. She co-edited *Bi Any Other Name: Bisexual People Speak Out*, which was awarded a '100 Best LGBT Books of the 20th century' award by Lambda Book Review. She is a national leader in the U.S. bisexual movement, as well as an independent scholar writing on sexuality and spirituality issues.

H. Sharif Williams is a Clinical Sociologist, Sexologist, Educator, and Cultural Theorist, and is the Founder of Black Funk: The Center for Culture, Sexuality, and Spirituality, USA. Under his spiritual name Herukhuti, he is the author of *Conjuring Black Funk: Notes on Culture, Sexuality, and Spirituality, Volume 1*. He is a faculty member at Goddard College, USA. An initiate and practitioner of African wisdom traditions since the age of fourteen, he is spiritual godfather, advisor and teacher to various practitioners around the world and keeper of the Shrine of Sekhmet and Heruhet, USA.

Sexuality, Religion and the Sacred

Bisexual, Pansexual and Polysexual Perspectives

Edited by

Loraine Hutchins and H. Sharif Williams

Routledge
Taylor & Francis Group
LONDON AND NEW YORK

First published 2012
by Routledge
2 Park Square, Milton Park, Abingdon, Oxon, OX14 4RN

Simultaneously published in the USA and Canada
by Routledge
711 Third Avenue, New York, NY 10017

Routledge is an imprint of the Taylor & Francis Group, an informa business

This book is a reproduction of the *Journal of Bisexuality*, volume 10, issues 1-2. The Publisher requests to those authors who may be citing this book to state, also, the bibliographical details of the special issue on which the book was based.

British Library Cataloguing in Publication Data
A catalogue record for this book is available from the British Library

ISBN13: 978-0-415-78304-0

Typeset in Garamond
by Taylor & Francis Books

Disclaimer
The publisher would like to make readers aware that the chapters in this book are referred to as articles as they had been in the special issue. The publisher accepts responsibility for any inconsistencies that may have arisen in the course of preparing this volume for print.

MIX
Paper from responsible sources
FSC www.fsc.org FSC® C004839

Printed and bound in Great Britain by
TJI Digital, Padstow, Cornwall

Contents

Notes on Contributors

Jonathan Alexander, PhD, is Professor of English at the University of California, Irvine. He has worked over fifteen years as an educator, writer, and activist. He co-wrote *Bisexuality and Transgenderism: InterSEXions of the Others* with Dr. Karen Yescavage, and they are currently at work on a new book, *The Future of Sex*.

Ifalade Ta'Shia Asanti is an award-winning writer, poet and journalist. Ta'Shia is the Founder and Director of the World Pride & Power Organization, the National Institute for Indigenous Cultural Studies, the Director of the STAIRS Research Project and Presiding Priestess of Ile Ori Ogbe Egun (I TEACH), a Yoruba/Ifa temple in Denver, Colorado.

Phillip A. Bernhardt-House, PhD, has taught Religious Studies courses at Chapman University and Columbia College, and has also been a Guest Professor in the History Department at the University of Michigan-Ann Arbor. Phillip holds a PhD in Celtic Studies and an M.A. in Religious Studies, and has published widely in academic and non-academic venues, including *Parabola, Journal for the Academic Study of Magic, Celtic Studies Association of North America Yearbook,* and the anthologies, *Queering the Non/Human,* ed. Giffney and Hird, and *Getting Bi*, ed. Ochs and Rowley. His monograph, on werewolves and dogheads in Celtic cultures will be published soon.

Martha Daniels has served as Pastor of MCC Windsor (Ontario) since 2005. She is co-chair of the Service Alliance for Equality (SAFE), a professional gay-straight alliance serving youth in Windsor/Essex County; she is also active in the Windsor Pride Community, serving on the Education/Research Committee and the 50+ Proud support group. Martha enjoys gender theory, both in study and application; theology, and conducting same-gender weddings north of the border. Her favorite book of all time (so far) is a toss-up between *Stone Butch Blues* (Leslie Feinberg), *Soul Mates* (Thomas Moore), and *Coming Out Spiritually* (Christian de la Huerta).

Prof. Dr. Ibrahim Abdurrahman Farajajé is Provost and Professor of Cultural Studies and Islamic Studies at the Starr King School for the Ministry, a seminary whose emphasis is multi-modal/multi-vocational counter-oppressive, multi-religious and Unitarian Universalist thea/ological education in a context of building just and sustainable communities; it is a member school of the Graduate Theological Union in Berkeley, California. Professor Farajajé serves on the Graduate Theological Union's Core Doctoral Faculty in the area of Cultural and Historical Studies of Religions and serves as Senior Research Analyst in the GTU's Center for Islamic

Studies. Professor Farajajé is the architect of a highly innovative anti-colonial/anti-imperialist intersectional epistemology which continues to help provide religious and thea/ological responses to the multiple interlocking oppressions substanding, amongst other things, the global HIV/AIDS pandemic. Performance artist, scholar, author and video- and ritual artist, he works in giving birth to trans-global/trans-religious communities of resistance and is an activist in the realm of bringing burial practices into greater alignment with respect for the body and for the Earth.

Kenneth Hamilton, PhD, is a Lecturer at Notre Dame de Namur University, Belmont, CA and at Graduate Theological Union/Starr-King School for the Ministry, Berkeley, CA. He has been a public speaker and a member of a ministry team with the African American twin priests Charles and Chester Smith, SVD. For over 30 years he has done "rite of passage" work with "at risk" youth, spirituality groups for men and women, etc. His professional goal as a scholar-activist is to be liberated in the struggles of Afro-diasporic people, in their queer erotic spiritualities, in their darker skins, in their oppressed lands, and in the fight to make AIDS that crucible which cannot define us but from which we can find the power to overcome.

Susan Harper, PhD, is a dedicated and passionate educator, researcher, writer, activist, and advocate. She received her PhD in Cultural Anthropology from Southern Methodist University in 2005. Her dissertation focused on the dynamics of conversion and identity formation among NeoPagans in Texas. Her research interests include personal narrative, identity construction, religion, gender, queer studies, media studies, and feminist theology and theory. She is currently pursuing publication of her dissertation and teaching. She resides in Dallas, Texas where she engages in community education around issues of gender equality, gender diversity, and religious diversity.

Lisa Keele is Lecturer of Philosophy in the Department of Humanities at Clayton State University, USA. Her areas of specialization are the philosophy of mathematics and logic. Her areas of competence are ethics, feminist philosophy, and gender studies. Her research is currently focused in the philosophy of mathematics, particularly that of the 19th century and of Charles S. Peirce, and the intersection of religion, ethics, and gender and sexuality studies.

Rev. Stephen Lingwood is the Minister of Bank Street Unitarian Chapel, Bolton, Greater Manchester, UK. He holds a Master of Arts (With Distinction) in Contextual Theology from Manchester University (2008) and a Master of Theological Studies from Boston University (2005). He holds a Bachelor of Science in Geology with Biology (Upper Second Class Honours), from Birmingham University (2003).

Marlon Rachquel Moore is Assistant Professor in the Department of English at the University of North Carolina Wilmington, USA. Her interests include 20th-Century African American literature, gay/lesbian studies and southern culture. Her current research projects include an anthology about black southern queerness and a study of homoerotic spirituality in African American literary culture. She has published a number of journal articles.

Margaret Robinson, PhD, is a feminist scholar and bisexual activist based in Toronto. She holds a Doctoral Degree in Theology from the University of St. Michael's College. Her research interests include sexual ethics, religious prejudice, sexual identity development, and queer theologies. She is co-director of the Toronto Bisexuality Education Project.

Yehudis (Hudi) Schorr graduated from Towson University in 2008 with a Bachelor of Science in Womens Studies and a minor in LGBT Studies. A perpetual student, Hudi attributes her most poignant moments of learning to her 4-year-old daughter, Lizzy. Hudi sees herself as a child born from Gaia, attempting to navigate the vast orgy of existence without leaving too deep a footprint in her wake.

L. H. Stallings is a Durham, NC native who received her PhD in English from Michigan State University. She is the author of *Mutha is Half a Word!: Intersections of Folklore, Vernacular, Myth and Queerness in Black Female Culture* (Ohio State University Press, 2007), which critically engages folklore and vernacular theory, black cultural studies, and feminist and queer theory to examine the representation of sexual desire in fiction, poetry, stand-up comedy, neo-soul, and hip-hop created by black women. She is currently working on a monograph on Black print erotica, sexual rights and nation.

Starhawk is the author of many books (*The Spiral Dance, The Fifth Sacred Thing, The Pagan Book of Living and Dying, Dreaming The Dark, Truth or Dare,* etc.) celebrating the Goddess Movement and Earth-based, feminist spirituality. She is a peace, environmental and global justice activist and trainer, permaculture designer and teacher, Pagan, and Witch. Many of Starhawk's best political essays—credited with helping the global justice movement find and define itself—were collected into her book, *Webs of Power: Notes from the Global Uprising.* Her archives are maintained at the Graduate Theological Union Library in Berkeley, California and she is a panelist for the *Newsweek/Washington Post* website on religion, "On Faith."

Karen Yescavage, PhD, is Associate Professor of Psychology and Women's Studies at Colorado State University–Pueblo. She has worked over fifteen years as an educator, writer, and activist. She is currently working with Dr. Jonathan Alexander on a new book–*The Future of Sex.*

Foreword

Ibrahim Abdurrahman Farajajé

Last summer, I came into contact with the work of Osama Esid (osamaesid.com), a Damascus-born photographer now living in Minneapolis-St. Paul, Minnesota. I was particularly struck by what he said of his experience of black-and-white images in relation to "colored pictures." As a young person, he experienced black-and-white photographs as being locations of happiness lost; he undertook the process of hand-coloring the black-and-white images in order to give "happiness to those people who lived in that world that lost its colors…". He was haunted by the idea that there were people who lived in a world that had "lost its color." With the appearance of the Polaroid color camera in the late 1970s, Esid learned the origins of the colors. However, a new question arose for him: how did the colors get inside?

Many of us live in a world in which religions and sexualities are often perceived and portrayed as being in violently oppositional relationships. We are made to believe that there are also a limited number of societally-approved sexualities, genders, gender expressions and relational configurations. Things that contradict these ways of thinking are simply and actively trivialized, ridiculed, and erased. In other words, the colors get taken out.

The creative work of this anthology is to raise, amongst others, the following questions: How do we get the colors back inside? How might we imagine and experience the intersections between diverse sexualities, genders, gender expressions, relational configurations, religions and notions of the sacred? If all is not monochromatic and monodimensional, what are some of the ways in which these overlap and intersect?

An essential part of this anthology is subverting and problematizing the assumed oppositional relationship between sexualities and the sacred. For many individuals, at many moments, holding sexualities and spiritualities together seems to be contradictory. Some would say that this is impossible because, for them, spiritualities are by *definition* anti-sexual and sexualities are intrinsically and aggressively anti-spiritual.

A counter-dichotomous move that challenges this way of thinking is also inextricably connected to the opening up of the dazzling array of sexualities, genders, gender expressions and relational configurations that exist both within and beyond the borders of lesbian/gay and heterosexual. It resists the erasure of sexualities that do not fit easily into dichotomous thinking that has heterosexual on one side and lesbian/gay on the other. Even those categories contain within them such diversities of genders and gender expressions that it is difficult to speak of them with the assumption that one knows exactly what is meant by them.

Mixities and fluidities of modes of meaning and self-expression lead us beyond the confines of fictions of purity. This anthology then opens to us communities of discourse which include within them not only a broad spectrum of genders and gender expressions, but also of sexualities, religious traditions and spiritual practices that do not experience or express themselves oppositionally. In Frantz Fanon's analysis of the psychopathology of colonializm, colonization is defined as the forced imposition of a certain way of thinking and of being, accompanied by the systematic removal of all that it perceives as a threat to its hegemony. This work counters the dichotomous thinking that places sexualities and the sacred in radical opposition to each other while at the same time limiting genders to two and sexualities to either heterosexual or lesbian/gay. Much like the brilliant new volume, *Balancing on the Mechitza: Transgender in Jewish Community*, edited by Noach Dzmura (North Atlantic Books, 2010), this volume enages the reader in decolonizing acts of resistance that in turn become the sites of greater sustainability and justice, since it is precisely in working from these places of mixities and fluidities that it sustains and nurtures life, liberation and wholeness.

There arise at certain moments in time, events, individuals and spaces that engage in the work of interrupting and disrupting the assumptions of privilege, as well as committing the liberatory work of getting the colors inside. These are phenomena that bring to a stand-still (if even momentarily) ways of thinking and acting that are based on unexamined and largely unchallenged assumptions. One such moment is indeed the current volume, *Sexuality, Religion and the Sacred: Bisexual, Pansexual and Polysexual Perspectives*. The editors, Drs. Hutchins and Williams, both worked diligently with me in the preparation of their doctoral dissertations. Their interest in this area is longstanding; they are both deeply-committed to getting the colors inside, to thinking, living, and acting beyond the borders of apparent contradictions. Their work as scholars is grounded in post-dichotomous thinking about the relationships between religions, genders, gender expressions, relational configurations, sexualities, in all of their multiplicities, mixities and fluidities. The voices of the ancestors resound boldly through their words.

This work will make an important contribution to the area of Religious Studies. Many new scholars are helping shape language and thinking around the study of the relationships between the sacred and sexualities within the very context of Religious Studies. For those whose scholarly work strives to be counter-oppressive, multi-religious and committed to building just and sustainable communities, this current collection is a beginning.

This book is a starting place: may it inspire the sort of scholarship that will include an ever-growing diversity of religious traditions. What has not been included here will hopefully appear in future editions. May this book be an invitation to renewed commitment to getting the colors inside.

Our Hearts Still Hold These Intimate Connections: An Introduction

Loraine Hutchins
Towson University
H. Sharif Williams
Goddard College

EMBRACING OURSELVES/OTHERS IN LIMINALITY

We live at a time in postmodernity in which the themes of past eras have found their way back into our collective consciousness. Viral epidemics and pandemics such as HIV, swine flu, and bird flu have replaced bacterial plagues. Inverted totalitarianism[1] has replaced imperialism. Multi/transnational corporations have replaced empires. Wars on Islamic extremism have replaced the Crusades. The impact of these forces upon our collective consciousness is to force dichotomous, binary thinking. We are pressured to believe in right and wrong, good people and bad people. We are encouraged to be suspicious of nuance, complexity, ambiguity, and the diunital i.e., the union of opposites. Spirituality and religion, like sexuality, can be sites of contestation or compliance. They can broaden and expand our ability to embrace the liminal or embolden hostility toward liminality[2].

These may seem like lofty ideas, so theoretical as to be meaningless to the average person. Ask the bisexual-identified Muslim who wishes to enter the United States with a dildo about how theoretical these issues are. Ask the pansexual hotel worker who is using a prayer to the Orishas to remain healthy because s/he has no health care or job security if these issues are too removed from what is happening in everyday people's lives. Ask the machinist with two lovers, recently laid off and now dependent upon the food bank of the church, who is being told by a right wing media pundit that the Chinese or Mexicans are to blame for unemployment if these issues don't have tangible material consequences. Ask the bisexual academic, shuttling between assignments to several different classes at several different colleges trying to scrape together a living wage and still maintain her/his connection to grace as a part of the large pool of contingent faculty in higher education, if these issues are too academic. We live in a time when we are being pressured to contract inward upon ourselves and see queerness—sexual, spiritual, political, or social—as too radically inconvenient for the moment.

Even movements that intend to exact more freedoms have contributed to the denial of same. The way in which the gay liberation movement has engaged heterosexism has contributed to popular culture narratives of categorical sexualities with straight and gay as fixed, infallible, and totalizing forms of sexual identity. Same-sex marriage advocacy has been practiced in ways that are antagonistic to marriage equality. Authentic marriage equality would have to include polyamorous relationships between more than two partners and genderqueer relationships that embrace gender expressions beyond the binary of male and female.

We, therefore, have to take care to be critically self-reflective as we move in the world, particularly if we intend our actions to have socially just and ecologically sound consequences. How we frame our loves, sexual and sacred, can play an important part in critical self-reflexivity. We see this anthology on bisexualities and spiritualities as a contribution to that framing. In this Introduction, we offer you our summary of what's inside, the highlights and gaps, what we found interesting and what we still long to read about, areas where we feel the intersecting fields of bisexualities and spiritualities still have glaring present absences and absent presences. We chose to look at spirituality through a bi/pan/polysexual framework because of the opportunity this context offers in disrupting the dichotomous and foregrounding the liminal and diunital in matters of spirituality. We also wanted to see if there were spaces within theology and spirituality that had not been excavated, or could not be excavated, by a heterosexist or homosexual-centric framework.

This collection began as a special double issue of the *Journal of Bisexuality* (Vol. 10, No's. 1-2, Jan-June 2010). It began as the spiritchild of Loraine Hutchins. Loraine, one of the founders of the modern bisexual movement in the U.S., is known for instigating conversations about how bisexual-, pansexual-, and polysexual-identified persons experience, conceptualize, and practice spirituality and religiosity from the uniqueness of their lived erotic experiences. This interest stems from her previous work on the sacred and the sexual (Hutchins, 2007, 2002, 2001). In seeking a collection of work that was inclusive of various traditions and cultural contexts, she sought out writers who could contribute to the desired diversity of voices. H. Sharif Williams (also known as Herukhuti), a sex radical shaman of the Hip Hop generation, saw the original call for papers for the special issue and sought out Loraine. Through conversation, we discovered our common threads. Ibrahim Abdurrahman Farajajé served on both of our doctoral dissertation committees. We were colleagues of M. Paz Galupo—for Loraine as co-workers at Towson University and for Herukhuti as a contributor to a special issue of the *Journal of Bisexuality* guest edited by Paz (Williams, 2007). We also discovered how much we were each called to explore the sacred and the sexual.

We decided to partner on the special issue as guest co-editors. Our collaboration demonstrated a bridging across cities, generations, genders, ethnicities, and spiritual traditions. We hoped to be the nuance, complexity, ambiguity, and diunital that we want to see in the world. As we performed the editorial tasks associated with a journal issue such as drafting and distributing the call for papers, soliciting manuscript submissions, identifying peer reviewers, etc., we shared our work and her/histories with each other. We chose to make the relationship nuanced, complex, and deep. We learned about each other's loves, sexual and sacred. We rejected the option to have a disembodied and desacralized academic process. The space we created allowed us to engage in critical self-reflection and critical feedback with each other. After the special issue on Bisexualities and Spiritualities was released we approached the journal's publisher, Routledge and reached an agreement with them to re-release this collection as the book, *Sexuality, Religion and the Sacred*, you now hold in your hands. Since we had originally planned another journal issue on this topic and received two additional articles for it we obtained agreement from Routledge to include these last two pieces in the book. These two pieces address some of the gaps in the scope of the original issue. The original sequence of the table of contents has been re-organized to better feature the sum total of the whole collection.

We share these various aspects of our process with you to provide context for this collection, and to contribute to the project of dismantling the depersonalized, disembodied academic. To open the discussion of where we have come from and where we are going in these pages, we offer this prayer/invocation to our readers:

May you find joy
May you create love
May you experience grace
May you know peace
May you give birth
May you inspire desire
May you apply wisdom
May you offer honor
May you share ecstasy.

HISTORIES OF BI SPIRIT

How does one talk about a specific bi spirituality or even bi spiritualities? What makes any spiritual practice or philosophy distinctively bi-aware or bi-positive? Within the limitations of this space we cannot provide an adequate account of the history of bi/pan/polysexuality in spirituality and religion, or an account of the spirituality and religion in bi/pan/polysexualities of all peoples since the beginning of time. Simply allow us, instead, to highlight a few important and recent contributions to the literature within which the writings in this book are sourced.

Two decades ago—when Loraine Hutchins and Lani Ka'ahumanu were co-editing *Bi Any Other Name: Bisexual People Speak Out*—they concluded that peace-making and the integration of all parts of the self cannot be complete for some people without a recognition of bisexuality; that a blooming of bisexuality freely in society would be an integral part of the process of remaking the world. In *Bi Any Other Name* they wrote,

> Today there is a renewed sense that sex is spiritual without contradiction; that sex can be a sacred art, a spiritual discipline ... we dare to question the dichotomy between sacred and profane and claim all of life as sacred. We call the old tribal polymorphous ways back into being and assert that they are necessary (Hutchins & Ka'ahumanu, 1991, p. 92).

Since *Bi Any Other Name*'s 1991 release there has been an explosion of publishing on bisexual issues, but most of it on political and personal issues, not spiritual concerns. The organizing for the 1993 March on Washington for Lesbian, Gay and Bi Equal Rights and Liberation that swiftly followed *Bi Any Other Name's* release brought many

LGBT religious groups and leaders to Washington, DC.; including some out bi spiritual leaders and activists such as the bi eco-feminist leader, Starhawk, and Elias (now Ibrahim) Farajajé, a bi AIDS activist/theologian who taught at Howard University's divinity school at that time. Both Starhawk and Farajajé presided, as clergy, at the blessing ceremony for the opening of the Holocaust Museum held during the March on Washington weekend. Starhawk's keynote, "The Sacredness of Pleasure," (see pg. 182), was given at the National Conference Celebrating Bisexuality that same 1993 spring weekend in Washington, DC at American University. However it was not until April 2000 that Continuum Press released *Blessed Bi Spirit: Bisexual People of Faith*, an anthology edited by bi activist, and now Rabbi, Debra Kolodny. It featured 32 writers from a wide variety of religious traditions: Buddhist, Hindu, Pagan, Indigenous, Christian, and Jewish, who all addressed intersections of faith practice, sexual orientation and beliefs. Though there have continued to be articles in queer-friendly anthologies, zines, blogs and journals that reference bi-positive spiritualites, *Blessed Bi Spirit* remains the only anthology on bi spirituality we know of, to date.

Doing an anthology on sexuality and spirituality gives us this opportunity to take stock of where we've come and where we might next go. In taking stock of the voices and stories and ideas in this book one thing we noticed most was the disconnect between our dream of a bi-inclusive spirituality, versus the actual reality of a sex-negative world where love beyond gender or power imbalances is, at most, an afterthought, certainly not something we are encouraged to explore, create and cherish. As Serena Anderlini- D'Onofrio says in *Gaia and the New Politics of Love* (reviewed in this collection), bi people are often good at teaching the art of loving. She encourages us all to see people as renewable resources to be nurtured and mutually cared for in community rather than succumb to a one-way, alienated consumer (disposable relationships and things) mentality. Bisexuals, says Anderlini-D'Onofrio, are often really good at teaching people how to use gentle playful touch and utilize trust exercises to build community, when they feel comfortable and accepted as they fully are. But bi visibility comes in smaller, more baby steps first. Before we co-create the Gaia living earth vision we'll need more every-day garden-variety bi visibility first. We may visualize an eco-feminist, global, earth-honoring community that embraces all spiritualities and sexual diversities. But we won't get there without addressing the awkward questions about bi invisibility within religious communities first. This includes more people who have been afraid to come out, or who hesitate, deciding to come out as bi—not only in faith communities, but in intentional communities, educational communities, erotic communities, social networks, workplaces, local neighborhoods, and so on. It also includes understanding, being willing and able to teach and explore with others about all the ways these groups overlap and don't.

SEXUALITY, RELIGION AND THE SACRED

Christian and Unitarian Discourses

In this first category we commend to your attention Stephen Lingwood and Martha Daniels' pieces about the difficulties of serving as out bi clergy, even in progressive denominations such as the Unitarians and the Metropolitan Community Church

(MCC). Both pieces emphasis a hope and a fierce commitment to continuing dialogue within their respective religious traditions.

Lingwood questions the Church of England's admonition that bisexuals "follow the way of holiness" and choose heterosexual marriage, asserting that there is also nothing un-holy about other ways of being fully bisexual. Asking "what is the bisexual vocation within the greater task of queer liberation?" he replies that it is "to witness that liberation must not become another form of oppression," that humankind need not be divided in ways that prevent love. Lingwood ends by critiquing traditional interpretations of the Moses story; re-envisioning Moses' liberation quest in a more inclusive manner.

Bisexuals are "not even on the page" complains Martha Daniels, explaining that the same Methodist Church document that proscribes the behaviors of out lesbian/gay clergy doesn't even mention bisexuals. Daniels understands a different God. "God who created us as we are also loves men and women and those between. This God of the both and neither created and loves the both and the neither," she writes. "What might a Savior look like who partakes of a variety of genders," and "how would we sing of this God?" Wonderful questions indeed, and worth exploring in much greater depth. Daniels praises the transgender resources a handful of MCC congregations have created to help congregations understand transgender issues better, noticing that the same kind of effort on behalf of understanding bisexual people remains unfinished, both within MCC and within other denominations.

In fact, the only example we found of a religious education curriculum truly inclusive of bisexuality was a short set of lessons on bisexuality developed for adult religious education by the Unitarian Universalists' Welcoming Congregation Program in the U.S. This set of lesson plans is already serving as a model for other faith traditions looking to adapt material on bisexuality into their religious education plans. Co-editor Hutchins contextualizes her review of this curriculum within a general consideration of contemporary religious education resources on sexual orientation and sexualities. After reading it you may find yourself inspired to write curriculum and teach such lessons within the congregation you call home.

Certain Biblical texts are "inherently biased against the acceptance of bisexuality," and, sadly, gay and lesbian theologians perpetuate some of those biases as well, argues Phillip Bernhardt-House in his *Reenforcing Binaries* article. In it he explains how bisexual invisibility functions, and is even re-enforced, by a queer Christian theology that privileges monosexual ways of identifying and relating. Centering on the New Testament passage, Romans 1:26-27, he argues that current lesbian/gay exegesis of this text privileges exclusive same-sex desire at the expense of those who engage in it as a part of other identities and practices. He affirms that there are other, and better, ways to make Christian theology bi-inclusive, and that a monosexual bias can penalize anyone from loving more fully, regardless of their identification or affinities.

Indigenous and Decolonizing Spiritual Discourses

People of the Global South and people of color in the West have historically confronted the pressures to conform to heteronormative or homonormative standards imposed from European and European-American colonizers and self-proclaimed allies. Each of the authors in this section seeks to investigate those dynamics and reconstruct ways of being spiritual and sexual that affirm indigenous ways of being in the world.

Simultaneous to those efforts, the authors also interrogate from within the sacred places that have been marked taboo or unspeakable.

Adapted from her historic presentation at the 2006 Conference on Indigenous African Spiritual Traditions, Worldview, Family & Community Empowerment, Ritual, and Practice at Teachers College, Columbia University, Ifalade Ta'Shia Asanti's speech sets same-sex sexual practice among people of African descent in the context of a dual or twin spiritedness that leaves room for mixed-sex sexual practice as well. Asanti offers examples and concepts from African cultural history of sexuality and personhood that challenge prevailing arguments within Black nationalist and cultural-nationalist discourses, which have been antagonistic to or critical of homosexual or bisexual sexuality among Black people. Asanti's speech is grounded in the belief of the cultural unity of Africa and people of African descent. In doing so, she can be situated with Afrocentrists such as Molefi Kete Asante (Asante, 1988, pp. 57–58), and Clemora Hudson-Weems (Hudson-Weems, 2008, pp. 112–113). However, Asanti diverges from Asante, Hudson-Weems, and others in her claims that same-sex and bisexual practice among African people is indigenous and culturally consistent within the precolonial and neocolonial context of African cultural life. Although such claims are interesting, it is Asanti's engagement of bi/poly/pansexuality in the frame of two/twin/dual-spiritedness that makes the revised speech such an important contribution to our collection.

Co-editor H. Sharif Williams' "*Bodeme* in Harlem" article looks at the wisdom teachings, traditional ceremonies, and village life of the Dagara people of Africa, with particular attention to the shamanic gatekeeper (*bodeme*) roles played by those we, Westerners, might mistakenly perceive as merely "gay" or "bi." He reveals what it was like being part of the first group exclusively of United States–based people of African descent to work intensively with the popular African spiritual teacher from Burkina Faso, Malidoma Patrice Somé. Deftly blending queer theory explorations with cross-cultural understandings of spiritual and erotic community life, Williams allows us glimpses of his own process through autoethnography: "As we talked, I began to feel/sense that we had been brought together for the purpose of engaging in a spiritual work; my sexual desire shifted to an erotic desire in which a spiritual purpose had emerged." In such passages he reveals what he learns about the "inner knowings" of his attractions to others, and how this can be used to bring healing into whatever kinds of relationships we create.

In "Colonial Legacies, Decolonized Spirits," Father Kenneth Hamilton says, "The legacy of colonization has always historically meant the targeting of queer sexualities and spiritualities and the crushing of fluid sexual behavior in order to establish a heteronorm." Hamilton retells two horrific stories of crimes against queer people of previous centuries, showing how racism "came along with the suppression of queers of color, queers condemned by the 'heathen' 'darkness'." "He exposes the conflicted sexual desires of the White European explorers and conquerors of Latin America and Africa, emphasizing that reinterpreting the legacies of these colonizations also means "acknowledging the demonization of women and the effeminate" that has affected us all. Hamilton ends by examining traditional Christian views on sexuality in light of the contemporary AIDS epidemic in Africa and the rest of the world. He offers a new interpretation of what happened in Africa's colonial past, and now, bringing analogies of Uganda's current struggle with AIDS and alternative sexual expressions into the mix. Given recent controversies in the news over the way U.S. right-wing politicians and ex-gay evangelists fan the flames of hatred of gays in Uganda, this article could not be more current.

Humanities scholar, folklorist and erotica critic L. H. Stallings, critically engages Herukhuti's *Conjuring Black Funk: Notes on Culture, Sexuality, and Spirituality, Volume 1*. Stallings invites us to enjoy Dr. Herukhuti's humorous and passionate work through her own argument for the institution of a new field—one that will replace the old, tired realms of Queer Studies, even Black Queer Studies, with the fresh breath of Funk Studies. Stallings writes, "Rather than an axiologically oppositional framework of ranked binaries, Herukhuti, from the very beginning, insists on the alternative framework of funk, and if ever there were a sexual metaphor or symbolism of funk, bisexuality would be it." Check it out. You may find yourself humming Parliament Funkadelic lyrics from the 1970s and wanting to ask Herukhuti more about what he means when he talks about the study and practice of funk in the 21st century.

Feminist Spiritual Discourses

Several of our writers name Marcella Althaus-Reid, a queer bisexual theologian from Latin America, as one of the inspirations of their work. We are delighted that Margaret Robinson chose to focus on a reading of Althaus-Reid's writing in the specific context of developing a bi women's theology. Robinson's "Reading Althaus-Reid" piece shows how Althaus-Reid's contributions construct a particularly bisexual feminist theology, a philosophy rooted in postcolonial/liberation theologies that bridges North and South, gay and straight, female and male, monogamous and polyamorous, Christian and beyond Christian. Robinson uses her research among bi women in Toronto to illustrate Althaus-Reid's comment, "If people cannot honestly incorporate the sexual aspect of their lives into their experiences of the divine, then how can they possibly hope to live with integrity and in right relation with others?" —a beautiful statement for anyone concerned with a truly spiritual way of daily living. Many in this country, even in religious communities, are sadly unaware of Althaus-Reid's contributions. We commend Margaret Robinson for bringing her to our consideration.

Ten years ago Hutchins wrote an article juxtaposing historic versus current archetypes in feminist spirituality, "Bisexual Women as Emblematic Sexual Healers and the Problematics of the Embodied Sacred Whore." We chose to reprint this article from the *Journal of Bisexuality's* own archives because of its particular relevance to our themes. In the article Hutchins examines what happened after 1970s U.S. feminist researchers revived the ancient sacred prostitute archetype and brought the story of her serving her Goddess by offering people sexual healing into the popular imagination. This old image morphed, albeit with its own heterosexist and gendered baggage, into something currently different in the hands of those (many of them bi women and some men) who now identity as, and work as, sacred whores. "What does this phenomenon of women as erotic priestesses and sexual healers, particularly bi women as sexual healers, mean for all people in this culture?" asks Hutchins. Her article probes the many ways this archetype is being explored today—from festival celebrations to counseling groups, from medical consultations to sexual advice blogs, from New Age retreat center workshops to sacred prostitute services on internet escort websites.

Two pieces of literary criticism round out the feminist spirituality discourses. English Professor L.H. Stallings' "Bi bell" article positions black women's writing to, for, and about liberation as an "unacknowledged spiritual tradition, more sacred than secular." Stallings examines the work of bell hooks, as an example of this unacknowledged tradition, probing its bisexual, spiritual, and liberatory contents and implications—asking us to consider "the role of the black female bisexual intellectual in creating spiritual traditions for black women that examine numerous and varied sexualities practiced within, alongside, and in response to spiritualities." Through her reading of hooks' work, we see how it serves especially as intellectual resource and spiritual nourishment for black women, and, we would add, for many others as well. By acknowledging hooks' own disrobing of heterosexual privilege and bi-associating of herself, Stallings challenges readings of hooks' work that cast her as heterosexual, thereby queering a scholar already known for radical intellectual interventions. By spiritualizing hooks' work, particularly its erotic content, such as hooks' "pussy praise-songs," Stallings performs a radical intervention into spiritual discourse.

Alice Walker is one of feminist spiritualities' most influential contemporary thinkers. Her novels, essays, poetry and screen-plays explore gender, race, culture and spiritualities through a womanist lens. Marlon Moore's contribution, "Nonmonogamous Bisexuality as the Practice of Spiritual Freedom in *The Color Purple,*" offers us fresh insights into the bi and polyamorous themes of Walker's famous novel and the Spielberg film upon which it was based. Moore explains and connects the "group dynamic in which one woman moves among several men and women partners" as rooted in precolonial African tradition that is matriarchial. She then ties this to a discussion of "blueswoman evangelism" and argues that Walker's character, Shug, embodies an African-American expressive culture that "defies the simple sacred/profane binary." The examination of feminist spirituality and neo-pagan traditions meld in Moore's analysis of Walker's pagan interpretation of nature and the universe, saying that the teachings shared between Shug and Celie in *The Color Purple* create "a blueswoman's theology" that equates sexual and spiritual ecstasy.

Buddhist Discourses

Lisa Keele, a Buddhist practitioner, engages Buddhist sexual ethics in the article "The Third Precept" to foreground the ways Buddhist teachings can be used to reflect upon same-sex relationships and polyamory, i.e., the practice of maintaining multiple, simultaneous love relationships. In looking at Buddhist sacred and philosophical texts, Keele argues that "at least some interpretations of the third precept...can not only permit same-sex lovers and polyamorous relationships, but can actively guide a person through the ethical issues which may arise." Keele unravels and challenges sex-negative and sexually austere approaches to Buddhist sexual ethics to formulate "a non-discriminatory ethics of sexuality...which can guide anyone, regardless of sexual orientation or tendencies toward polyamory or monogamy, through the complexities which arise when sexuality is not repressed, but rather expressed, and can help one build a moral and fulfilling sex life, no matter one's personal orientation."

This book would not have been complete without at least some reflection on spirit-in-activism and the spirit of activism from an Eastern spiritual tradition. However, we were at a loss on how to fill this gap until Jonathan Alexander and Karen Yescavage offered a thoughtful and courageous exploration on how their political work has been sourced in and tempered by Buddhist values and practices. Their Bi Buddhist essay reflects personally on how LGBT rights activism can be nourished through the Buddhist understanding of mindfulness, particularly mindfulness about the suffering of self and other.

Neo/Pagan Discourses

No collection of articles surveying bi spiritualities would be complete without a nod to Starhawk, one of the most influential spiritual leaders of our time. She is a bisexual activist pagan priestess, a self-proclaimed Jewitch, author of many books on goddess/earth religions, and a co-founder of The Reclaiming Collective as well as a popular writer on the *Washington Post's* belief.net website. We therefore feature her stirring 1993 keynote speech, "The Sacredness of Pleasure." In re-reading its words we were struck anew with how courageous it is and how much more we need its vision now. "The Sacredness of Pleasure" sets the bar firmly in the camp of celebrating the erotic as sacred, without apology. As she says, just as fiercely now as she did 17 years ago in Washington, DC:

> To say that this earth is sacred is to take a very radical position for what is sacred cannot be defiled or exploited...when we hold the erotic as sacred, we say that our capacity for pleasure has a value in and of itself, that in fact it is one of the ways in which we connect with the deepest purposes of the universe.

She pleads that we "not abandon morality to the fundamentalists," arguing that "inherent in our own body's capacity for pleasure is our moral authority to determine just what sort of pleasure we want to take." Further, she asserts that we must define a new morality, as bisexuals, and that part of defending our moral authority to enjoy pleasure is defending everyone else's rights to pleasure too. Since its release, many people have used her speech as liturgy for ceremonies, private meditations and rituals. It has become a classic affirmation of the beauty, rightness and wholeness of loving beyond gender and loving all of life. We are pleased to make it available here for a new generation's savoring.

A comment researcher, Susan Harper often heard, when she was doing her research at Texas neo-pagan festivals and online pagan communities in the state was that "all cool women should be bisexual." Harper explores many aspects of the meanings of this phrase within the neo-pagan summer festival life in Texas, focusing on a particular group of bisexuals; women who attend these festivals and identify in some way as bi curious, bi certain and/or bi exploring, as an integral part of their spiritual identity and practice. Although she found evidence of persistent sexism and heterosexism amongst these women, and men, who define themselves as part of a woman-affirming and goddess- worshipping religion, she also found people engaged in self-reflection who make daily efforts to live their lives in a more female-honoring fashion. She concludes, "As women, and men, try to negotiate the different sexual and gender boundaries at work in the neo-pagan context, new power relations will likely result even as old power dynamics from the dominant culture need to be confronted."

Hudi Schorr, a recent graduate of Towson University who describes herself as a child of Gaia, writes a review of *Gaia and the New Politics of Love* by Serena Anderlini-D'Onofrio. Anderlini-D'Onofrio's new work resonates deeply and fully with so many of the themes in this anthology that it is impossible to list them all here. Like Starhawk, she has been warning us for years that Mother Earth (Gaia) is being abused at our own peril and that we must relinquish the trappings of useless consumerism in favor of understanding "the art of loving" as the truly "renewable resource" that will make us happy. Anderlini-D'Onofrio's eco-feminist vision of humans in cooperation with nature also echoes themes in Robinson's, Williams', and Hamilton's pieces. Each writes, as she does, about decolonizing our minds and bodies partly through learning to bring divergent fields of thought into productive dialogue with each other.

CONCLUDING THOUGHTS

With all the work that has been committed to this anthology, in fact because of it, we seek to know and learn more. In this work, we've heard from a number of Christian perspectives. They were the overwhelming majority of the submissions we received, though not the majority we selected. While we welcomed the opportunity to examine the various issues and questions raised by these articles, we want to have the same opportunities exploring bi/pan/polysexualities and Islam/Sufism, Judaism, Hinduism, Confucianism, Taoism, Bahaism, various Native American spiritual traditions, Santería, Vodou, Ifá, Wicca, and more.

We regret that our first attempt to create a more diverse view did not yield enough of these examples. Through our work soliciting articles for submission we have learned some of the challenges to our aims. While there are many bi/pan/polysexually-active laypersons, practitioners, adherents, and church members who could write beautifully moving accounts of their sexual and spiritual lives, there are few scholars working outside of heterosexuality and homosexuality who are writing about spirituality or religion. Among these scholars, there are few working outside of the Abrahamic traditions (Judaism, Christianity, and Islam). Therefore our pool of potential contributors is small.

At this time in human history, when we have so many challenges including ecological devastation, war, diseases, oppression, extreme economic hierarchies, why ask questions of sexuality and spirituality? This moment in human history precisely necessitates the questioning. We enter into the second decade of the 21st century of the Gregorian calendar with technological advances in communication, pharmaceuticals, and several other fields. We, collectively, may know more in these areas than any other humans to have lived previously on the planet. Yet, there are enormous challenges, in the Westernized world at least, to sexual and spiritual development. HIV and the fears associated with it have had a devastating effect on our access to each other. Religious fundamentalism and the fears associated with it have had a devastating effect on our access to each other. At the heart of our issues is the lack of access because it prevents, disturbs, and undermines connection. Without these connections, as Chinua Achebe (1994) cautioned, things fall apart. We need these intimate connections to stay alive.

As scholars, we seek practices and performances of bi/pan/polysexuality and spirituality that offer human beings opportunities to connect to each other and their world. Dare we suggest framings that challenge the distinctions between sacred and profane, spiritual and carnal, or otherworldly and mundane? Perhaps such challenges could provide us with the necessary ontologies and epistemologies to effectively address the problems the world currently faces.

Because we are educators, we not only witness the potential gestating within and among young and future scholars but we also are able to engage and encourage that gestation. What an incredible honor and blessing it is to have genderqueer, pansexual, queer, radical, and ally students who want to further diuntial, complex ways of living and being! We praise and give thanks for students of all ages who explore spiritualities and/or religions unencumbered by the dogma of fundamentalist thinking. We find great hope in them, and the students within ourselves, as we challenge each other to ground and balance our enthusiasms and curiosities with disciplined actions and critical self-reflections. We welcome the challenges each one's practice and performance offer us in how we conceptualize sexuality and spirituality and look to the next generation to give voice to the present absences and absent presences our hearts still hold.

NOTES

1. Wolin (2008) identifies inverted totalitarianism as the current state of political-economic organization of power. In totalitarianism, a political entity holds power over government, economics, and social life by means of violence, coercive power, and hegemony. In inverted totalitarianism, an economic power holds power over the government, economics, and social power by means of violence, coercive power, and hegemony.
2. Liminal or liminality means a state of openness, like at a threshold or borderland (Anzaldua, 1999). It's also described sometimes as a period of transition where normal limits to thought, self-understanding and behavior are not as present. Mixed-race people, hybrids, cyborgs and shapeshifters are also often put in this category. Some people even say sex is a liminal act.

REFERENCES

Achebe, C. (1994). *Things fall apart: a novel.* New York: Anchor.

Anzaldua, G. (1999). *Borderlands: La frontera–the new mestiza*, 2nd edition. San Francisco: Aunt Lute Books.

Asante, M. (1988). *Afrocentricity.* Trenton, NJ: African World Press.

Hudson-Weems, Clenora. (2008). Africana womanism & race & gender in the presidential candidacy of barack obama. Bloomington, IN, AuthorHouse.

Hutchins, L. and L. Kaahumanu (1991). *Bi Any Other Name: Bisexual People Speak Out.* New York. Alyson Publications.

Hutchins, L. (2001). Erotic rites: A cultural analysis of contemporary U.S. sacred sexuality traditions and trends. Doctoral Dissertation, Union Institute, Cincinnati, Ohio.

Hutchins, L. (2002). Bisexual women as emblematic sexual healers and the problematics of the embodied sacred whore, *Journal of Bisexuality,* 2(2/3): 205-226.

Hutchins, L. (2007). Playing With Sacred Fire: Building Erotic Communities in B. Firestein (ed.) *Becoming Visible: Counseling Bisexuals Across the Lifespan,* New York, Columbia University Press, p. 313-318.

Williams, H. (2007). A bisex-queer critique of same-sex marriage advocacy. *Journal of Bisexuality.* 7 (3/4).

Wolin, S. (2008). Democracy incorporated: Managed democracy and the specter of inverted totalitarianism. Princeton, NJ. Princeton University Press.

Not Even on the Page: Freeing God From Heterocentrism

REV. MARTHA DANIELS

Pastor, Metropolitan Community Church of Windsor, Windsor, Ontario, Canada

The author shares her journey from closeted United Methodist Church pastor-to-be through the assumptions of the United Methodist Church and the Universal Fellowship of Metropolitan Community Churches about homosexuality and bisexuality to an out bisexual pastor with the Universal Fellowship of Metropolitan Community Churches. She examines how the similar assumptions of modern Christians about God (male, White, heterosexual) distort images of God and the ways in which bisexual theologians, clergy and laity can offer other images and different ways to think about God, reflective of a more inclusive vision of God and of humankind.

TRIQUETRA

I have a tattoo. That's not exactly shocking or amazing these days, even for a member of the Christian clergy. Three interlocking circles in a Celtic knot pattern, it is called a "triquetra" and is often used to symbolize the Christian trinity of Creator, Redeemer and Sustainer (or God, Christ and Holy Spirit). Mine is in the colors of the rainbow. Taken together, the symbol, the colors and the placement (over my heart) represent my calling to Christian ministry and the diversity to which I am called and within which I serve. These three rings stand for integrity (which I define as consistency between action and belief), transparency (honesty, openness) and truth (the deeper truths of faith)—the standards by which I have come to live.

I first saw the rainbow triquetra and claimed it for my own while serving as a seminary intern in a United Methodist church just outside Washington, D.C. It took many years to be able to wear it permanently and proudly—I had a journey to begin first. At the time I found the triquetra, I was married (to a man), closeted, a mother, and a seminary student. I was also committed to diversity: supportive of the various groups on my seminary campus, working with the ethnic groups in our culturally diverse congregation and using inclusive language. I saw myself in the future continuing to work within the United Methodist Church (UMC) with culturally diverse congregations, with the HIV/AIDS ministry of the UMC, and supporting various groups working for human rights, all from the secure position of an assumed (by others) heterosexuality, confirmed by my marriage to a man. I recognized something of myself in that triquetra symbol seen on the cover of a now-forgotten book, but I could not fit it into the image of myself that I was presenting to the world: straight, pastor-to-be, wife and mother.

Several events changed that comfortable image. My father, with whom I had a difficult relationship, died in late 2000. In May of 2001, I visited Poland on a study trip, a pilgrimage to places of the Shoah (or the Holocaust, the murder of millions of Jews, gay men, Roma and others by the Nazis during World War II). In September, terror came very near when the World Trade Center fell, a plane flew into the Pentagon and Flight 93 crashed in Pennsylvania. By some cosmic confluence, I had friends and family involved in all three events—as almost losses or as witnesses. In January 2002, a member of the congregation I was serving, with whom I worked very closely, passed away suddenly. In February, I underwent a gruelling 3-day interview for probationary status prior to ordination, was narrowly approved and caught hints that I was thought a bit extreme in my views on inclusivity. In July, having graduated from seminary and been consecrated a probationary elder (a sort of pastor-elect), I began serving two small churches in rural Maryland, which were recovering from bitter conflict between them.

Taken together, these events brought me to the understanding that now is the time to be who I am; that there will always be those who view me as different and will not want my presence, my input or my gifts; and that the truth is what I am called to speak and to show, in spite of the (possible) consequences. In addition, I found I could not be effective as a pastor, as a leader, as a counselor as a model of a Christian in the community, unless I was authentic, honest and open. Most prominent among those things I needed to be open about was my sexual orientation. Integrity, transparency and truth all required me to be open, out and clear about my identity—a bisexual woman, who might be partnered with a man or with a woman; who was (nonetheless) called by God and a Christian.

I could not do that where I was at the time. The United Methodist Book of Discipline (the "rule book" for the denomination) states that "self-avowed homosexuals" will not be ordained.[1] I had not yet been ordained but consecrated as a probationary elder, a position I was meant to hold for 3 years before undergoing more interviews and final approval, at which time I could be ordained. Supportive friends pointed out that *bisexual* wasn't mentioned in the Book of Discipline; as a practicing bisexual, it didn't really apply to me—I could fight this and set a precedent. I saw the logic of this—bisexuals weren't even on the page, nor were transgendered individuals. I was not, am not, lesbian—I am bisexual. But I had seen the struggle of a transgendered pastor in my area to be appointed to a church and what it had done to her and to her family. My son was 14 at the time and already dealing with my imminent divorce from his father. I did not feel it was in my son's best interest to contest the Book of Discipline, with the inevitable publicity and furor. I put my mother's instincts above those of the activist and simply resigned my credentials in the UMC.

Where to go, then? I knew I had a call to minister—but within what framework, what denomination, what church? Although there were several options to choose from (at that time, these options included the Unity Church, Unitarian Universalist Church, or United Church of Christ, these being the only churches that ordained out gay, lesbian, bisexual or transgendered clergy), I had known of the Universal Fellowship of Metropolitan Community Churches (MCC) from seminary—many of my friends were preparing to serve in MCCs, and I knew there was a large one nearby.[2] Armed with an introduction from a close friend who was in the clergy formation process in the MCC, I contacted the pastor of that large church—and found myself welcomed, regardless of my orientation. So I began the transfer process to MCC—a church founded in and for the lesbian, gay, bisexual, and transgender (LGBT) community, which has more recently begun to actively reach beyond that community as well.

NOT EVEN ON THE PAGE

As I went through the training and approval process, however, I found that though there was no overt bi phobia, little undercurrents kept brushing my legs like minnows in a creek. A comment at a conference or a look in a worship service when I was preaching—the tone seemed to be, "OK, we accept that you identify as bi. We accept you. Now let's move on." Except that I couldn't, because it was too clear that some people felt I perhaps needed some counselling to "find my true identity." I also got a more general sense that I emphasized my bisexuality "too much," that I was constantly on a soapbox, had to bring in my sexuality at every turn. To the latter I can only say that my sexuality is as much a part of me as it is a part of my lesbian friends, my gay friends and my heterosexual friends—and if referring to males and females as attractive is dragging in my sexuality, if mentioning my male partners and my female partners is bringing it in at every turn—then so too does anyone who mentions a partner or an attraction at all. My mention draws their attention because it is not what they are used to, are familiar with or are expecting—and so it often makes them uncomfortable. In all fairness, however, I have to say that when the issue came up in a particularly difficult way for me, I had the unqualified support of my transition support team (the support group formed to guide and assist clergy transferring to MCC), the pastoral staff and the board of the teaching church, as well as leaders at the denominational level. Since that time the attitude of skepticism in MCC toward bisexuality has faded (though it is not quite gone), at least in my experience, and the church can hardly be faulted for individuals within it having the same assumptions that the society within which it exists does. If the church were not working to combat those assumptions, then it should be held to account. I have found that there are attempts to work against these assumptions, toward the full acceptance of bisexuality, although more could and should be done. Attitudes toward different-gender couples (of whatever orientation) need to become more accepting, and there should be no assumptions about relationships (two people coming to church together may or may not partnered—they may be friends or relatives, regardless of gender identity). Allowing self-disclosure as bisexual should be accepted at face value, without argument, as being lesbian, gay or transgendered is accepted. Finally, acceptance of polyamory as a part of a covenantal relationship must be a part of full acceptance of bisexual members. Although not all bisexual people participate in polyamory (or, indeed, are comfortable with it), it is nonetheless an aspect of bisexuality—and of homosexuality and heterosexuality. Polyamory is the (largely) unspoken taboo in the discussions around same-sex marriage. Supporters of same-sex marriage seem to feel compelled to assure opponents that they do not support polyamory, polygamy or polyandry. It's a delicate and complicated subject, and beyond the scope of this article. Nonetheless, it is true that polyamory is not practiced only by bisexual individuals but by same-gender loving individuals and heterosexual individuals as well. Bisexual activists are often reluctant to discuss the topic because it is such a source of controversy. However, if polyamory could be accepted as a potential part of everyone's sexual repertoire, we would see that full acceptance of one group (those who practice polyamory) potentially leads to acceptance of all (all sexual orientations) (King, n.d.).[3]

In my conversations with other individuals who identify as bisexual within MCC, certain topics have come up repeatedly, many of them mirrored in larger society and on college campuses (Rankin, 2003)—the need to change the church's bylaws to recognize multiple-partner relationships, the subtle pressures (as in any LGBT organization) to "choose" same-gender loving over different-gender loving, the reluctance on the part of many (clergy and laity) to identify as bisexual and the resulting lack of visibility ("how many of us are there really, if we were all out about our bisexuality?") and therefore support for others coming out as bisexual, and role models for youth and others; the assumption that if you are in a same-sex relationship then you are gay or lesbian (Rust, 2002)[4] and perhaps most painful from a clergy member's perspective, the assumption that if your partner is differently gendered, then you cannot serve a predominantly LGBT congregation as well as a clergy member who is in a same-gender relationship. We as bisexuals have not been fully integrated into MCC "culture," if you will. Transgendered individuals have not either, but great strides have been made in recent years to include the *T* in GLBT in MCCs. For example, the denomination has created resources to help nontransgendered people understand the issues transgendered people face and to help transgendered people feel welcome in worship and in the congregation. This has not happened for bisexual people; we are still barely acknowledged, and often simply another letter in the alphabet soup of inclusion.

The fact is our sexuality makes people uncomfortable, because we represent ambiguity. Most people don't like ambiguity, they want a yes or no, right or wrong, up or down answer. They are very uncomfortable with "both," or "neither," or "maybe." The Catholic Church says of many things "It is a great mystery." I cannot agree with the Roman Catholic church in most things, but in this I think there is truth. We cannot explain, pin down or make clear everything—and why would we want to? This is part of the awe of the Divine—that which cannot be clearly defined, but simply is.

We bisexual people upset the binary—the either/or of sexuality—homosexual or heterosexual. Ironically, some of our gay and lesbian brothers and sisters want us to do what they are told to do by homophobic people—choose a more "correct" sexuality. In the case of the homophobes, gay men, lesbians, and bisexual people are all expected to choose different-gender partners, to "choose" heterosexuality. In the case of our biphobic gay brothers and lesbian sisters, bisexuals are expected to "choose" only same-gender partners, to have credibility within the LGBT community. Neither the homophobic straight people nor the biphobic lesbians and gay men can understand or accept someone who does not choose one gender over another, but who follows her or his instinct and attraction to another person. It is unsettling and disturbing to them to be unable to "slot" us as either straight or same-gender-loving, much less straight and same-gender-loving. However, in the service of integrity, transparency, and truth, we must continue to speak our truth, to maintain our place as the bridge, the both/and of the LGBT community, that which speaks to, mediates between, same-gender-loving and different-gender-loving people and groups (Kolodny, 2000).

And speaking personally, I have found that my own attraction to women who cross-dress, cut their hair short, act in ways that are read as "masculine" and who are often read as men (i.e., the stereotypical "butch" or "stud") tends to disturb some individuals in the gay and lesbian community. It is as if others can accept two self-identified lesbians taking on traditional "butch-femme" roles, but when I, a feminine-appearing bisexual woman, partner with a butch, I am seen as "lapsing" back into heterosexuality. The assumption seems to be that I am attracted to such women because they read as masculine and therefore may be seen as "substitute" males. It is the old canard about bisexual people—having our cake and eating it too—as if I were with a man and a woman at the same time when I am with a butch. This is their projection, however, and certainly not my understanding of my attraction.

TRANSPARENCY, TRUTH AND INTEGRITY

When I applied to the church I now serve I made my sexual orientation clear—I spoke of my bisexuality in the sermon I preached as a candidate, well before the congregational vote that resulted in my being called here. Again—transparency, truth and integrity—I spoke my truth, knowing it had to be told and better that it be in the beginning. It has not been an issue in the church. It has been a factor in dating, however; many ads on the Internet dating sites specify "no bisexual women" and when I have practiced integrity and am transparent in the first conversations, identifying as bisexual, I have been told more than once that the other person is no longer interested in pursuing a relationship, because of my identification. That said, it was not an issue in my last intimate relationship, and in fact, I have been told more than once that my willingness to speak my truth, to identify openly as bisexual, not only in church and community settings but in the media, has allowed others in the community to speak their truth as bisexual women and men. It's always easier to stand up if you know you're part of a group, if there's someone at your back. One reason I was intentional about my identity as a bisexual woman was that the relationships I have been in most recently have been with women—and therefore it is assumed by many that I am lesbian, a misapprehension I had to correct, in the interest of integrity and transparency.

So much for personal experience. What has it shown me about North American Christian theology in the early 21st century?[5]

HOW WOULD WE SING OF THIS GOD?

We who are Christians, in spite of many years of work and sincere attempts to get away from it, are still tied to a heterocentric, White, male God. Even though many of us are working against this bias, it is firmly rooted in our culture, our church music, our art, our dogma and even in our prayers. God is still seen as a White male patriarch, who, if he were married, would be married to one woman.

I am not trying to make any arguments here about God's potential sexuality or gender identity—such a discussion would, I think, be pointless—but about the assumptions humans make about God. God is imaged in ways that are familiar, known, and nonthreatening to the one fashioning the image. Thus, often we find God to be in the image of the imager . . . and until very recently, that meant a White heterosexual male in a rigid hierarchical structure. It is inconceivable to many Christians (theologians and laypersons alike) that God might be any other way—female, non-White, nonheterosexual.[6] At best, God may be seen to "take on" these other characteristics for a time, but only to "sanctify" them, not as a permanent part of who God is.

And yet I would argue that because God is in each of us (we being made in God's image), God partakes of who each of us is—all our genders, all our races, all our orientations and all our places in society. In Genesis we read that God made us in God's image—and if we are varied and diverse, then God too, must be varied and diverse.

The special gift of the bisexual individual is to bring that sensibility of the margin into the center. As we are both and neither, so too is God. With our understanding of both sides of the bridge between the outside and the center, surely we can bring to our spirituality that sense of both and neither, of being a connection between and among God and God's people.

In all the Gospels, Jesus works from the margins toward the center. He spends his time with people generally considered to be outcasts, or at least suspect. These were the tax collectors, who collaborated with the occupying Romans; the sex workers or prostitutes; the country people who could not hope to fulfill all the laws given in the purity codes of Moses, and were thus called "sinners"; and the hated Romans themselves, in at least one case (Jennings, 2003; Kolodny, 2000).

If we can image a truly inclusive God, who partakes of every race and nation and orientation, surely that image can be understood, at least partly, in terms of bisexuality. I love women and men, as God who created us does. I can appreciate the beauty, the attraction, of the entire gender spectrum. The turn of a hip, the warmth of gentle eyes of love, the electricity of an erotic touch, the clean curve of a cheekbone, the power of a kiss on my forehead—these are, for me, a part of a person, not a gender. God who created us as we are also loves men and women and those between. This God of the both and neither created and loves the both and the neither.

What might our theology, our worship, our relationship with God look like if the Christian church was able to image God as both and neither male or female? How would it change our Christology and soteriology?[7] What might a saviour look like who partook of a variety of genders? How would we sing of this God? How would this understanding affect our relationships with each other? What would it do to our understanding of the role of clergy? How would it change our Christian education? Our outreach and community support? Such an understanding would cascade through all that we do and say and believe.

In my dreams and fantasies, I see a worship service in which not only does gender not dictate who presides, but in fact has no role for a "presider." The people gathered to worship would all participate in creating worship, each contributing through voice or action or thought, no one person having precedence or power or ranking above another because nothing puts one person above another—not gender or education or race or age or sexual orientation or anything else.

I hear songs in which God is celebrated as male and female, as light and joy and hope, as no gender and all genders, as Crone and Grandfather, as Mother and Father, as dark skinned, light skinned—in short, a God who reflects the humanity created by that God.

I imagine a theology in which there is no question of whether God is nurturing, whether God is powerful, whether God is tender or loving, strong or awe inspiring—of course God is, God is all these things and more.

I experience a relationship with God in which I can image God as multigendered, multiraced, as many faceted as a gem, and in which I am accepted and loved in all my many facets.

My theological claim, then, is that in the absence of a binary, either/or structure, God may be imaged in any way that is consistent with God's essential being, as much as we humans are able to know what God is and is not: thus God is not evil, God does not hate, God does not condemn us for what our parents did or were, nor for who we are, and so on. However, any other image of God is legitimate that is consistent with that essential being—the fecund Mother, the wise Grandfather/Crone, the loving Father, the all-knowing Spirit, even Shiva the destroyer (who is also Brahma the creator and Vishnu the preserver). The way opens to image God in ways that are constructive and lead us to a better understanding of God rather then setting up barriers of fear, judgment, disgust, or anger between us and God. Indeed, in many Christian theologies, an understanding of God as judgemental or angry is sinful, because it creates a barrier, a distance, between us and God.[8]

It is a clichéd truism in the LGBT community that one must "come out" many times—the first coming out to oneself, then to family and friends, to God, to co-workers, to prospective employers, to doctors and so on, an experience that is repeated often throughout the rest of our lives (new doctors, new neighbors, new employment, etc.). The day I received my tattoo, I knew I had truly come out—a bold, rainbow knot, swirling and vibrant, showed all the world who I was and am. I had carried that image with me for many years, and now I had etched it on my heart, in spite of fear and threat of disapproval or expulsion. The dancing circles of rainbow love, of integrity, truth and transparency cannot be denied or hidden away.

Like the God I celebrate, my tattoo displays truth, diversity, courage, strength, honesty, integrity and transparency. When we image God as neither male nor female, of all genders, of all sexualities, God is freed to be who

God will be—an explosion of diversity, a bridge, an endless circle—a trio of circles, in fact.

I have, in reality, just begun this journey of understanding God in all God's diversity, ambiguity and mystery. I will never come to the end, because there is always more to learn, a never-ending circle of exploration. No human can begin to understand all that God is. But all of us can begin with an image of God that is free of our own constraints and definitions, an image of God that allows God to be God in all God's circling rainbow diversity.

NOTES

1. The Book of Discipline states, "While persons set apart by the Church for ordained ministry are subject to all the frailties of the human condition and the pressures of human society, they are required to maintain the highest standards of holy living in the world. The practice of homosexuality is incompatible with Christian teaching. Therefore, self-avowed practicing homosexuals are not to be certified as candidates, ordained as ministers, or appointed to serve in the United Methodist Church" ¶304, 3, (The United Methodist Church, 2008). Notice the assumption is that the "practice of homosexuality" is incompatible with "holy living." Nor is bisexuality even considered as a possibility—I am not even on this page.

2. Universal Fellowship of Metropolitan Community Churches (commonly known as MCC) was founded in Los Angeles in 1968 by Rev. Troy Perry. Most congregations and clergy are LGBT, but in recent years we have begun to reach beyond the LGBT community.

3. "Injustice anywhere is a threat to justice everywhere" (King, 1963).

4. Rust provides an excellent description and capsule summary of "monosexism," the structures and beliefs of society that only heterosexuality and homosexuality are valid forms of sexual expression.

5. By this, I mean that I speak from this place: a White Christian female of privilege living in North America. Others with a different vantage point will have different stories and different theologies.

6. Young's wildly popular book *The Shack* (2007) images God as an African American woman and the Holy Spirit as an Asian woman. These images seem to be a large part of the power of the book for LGBT laypersons—the freeing imagery of God as other than a White male.

7. Soteriology: the doctrine of salvation (McKim, 1996).

8. See, for example, David R. Blumenthal and Rita Nakashima Brock's *Facing the Abusing God: A Theology of Protest* (1993, Westminster John Knox Press), which examines the image of a wrathful deity in the Hebrew Bible (Old Testament), and the implications this carries for survivors of child sexual abuse and the Holocaust.

REFERENCES

Blumenthal, D. R., & Brock, R. N. (1993). *Facing the abusing God: A theology of protest*. Louisville, KY: Westminster John Knox Press.

Jennings, T. J. (2003). *The man Jesus loved: Homoerotic narratives from the New Testament*. Cleveland, OH: Pilgrim.

King, M. L. (n.d.). *Letter from a Birmingham jail, April 16, 1963*. Retrieved May 25, 2009, from www.historyisaweapon.com/defcon1/kingjail.html

Kolodny, D. R. (Ed.). (2000). *Blessed bi spirit: Bisexual people of faith*. New York: Continuum.

McKim, D. (1996). *Westminster dictonary of theological terms*. Louisville, KY: Westminster John Knox.

Rankin, S. R. (2003). *Campus climate for gay, lesbian, bisexual, and transgendered people: A national perspective.* New York: The National Gay and Lesbian Task Force Policy Insititute. Available at: http://thetaskforce.org/reports_and_research/campus_climate

Rust, P. C. (2002). *Bisexuality: The State of the Union.* Retrieved May 25, 2009, from FindArticle.com: http://findarticles.com/p/articles/mi_qa3778/is_200201/ai_n9069533/pg_18/

The United Methodist Church. (2008). *The Book of Discipline of the United Methodist Church.* Nashville, TN: United Methodist Publishing House.

Young, W. P. (2007). *The Shack.* Los Angeles, CA: Windblown Media.

Reenforcing Binaries, Downgrading Passions: Bisexual Invisibility in Mainstream Queer Christian Theology

REV. PHILLIP A. BERNHARDT-HOUSE
University of Michigan, Ann Arbor, Michigan, USA

The focus of this article is the text of Romans 1:26–27, and its exegesis by various (mostly gay) historians and theologians is explored. The tendency in its interpretation within queer-affirming Christianity is to read modern homosexuality as an inborn condition, whereas what Paul's epistle critiques is those who go against their "natural" sexual orientation—thus, heterosexuals who act homosexually are said to be sinful, and thus by implication homosexuals who act heterosexually would likewise be sinful. However, this construction remains dualistic and excludes bisexuals, tacitly reinforcing a binary between homosexuality and heterosexuality, with no other sexual possibilities allowable.

The move toward a more inclusive, lesbian, gay, bisexual, transgender and queer (LGBTQ)-affirming stance in many religions and denominations of Christianity in the early 21st century is a phenomenon that can only be greeted with praise and appreciation, especially in the face of some religious groups that continue to demonize all actual or perceived homoerotic or gender-atypical acts and identities. Despite this more inclusive overall trend, the question does have to be asked: Are there some religious texts and approaches that are inherently hostile toward LGBTQ people, and particularly in light of the present journal's topic, are there some religious texts and approaches that may implicitly or explicitly exclude bisexuals due to interpretive or even structural theological points?

This article argues that Christianity—though some denominations have moved toward a wider acceptance of homosexuality, and have included "B" (and occasionally "T") in their inclusivity statement acronyms—contains certain texts relating to sexual ethics that are inherently biased against the acceptance of bisexuality, and particularly insidiously, some of the most blatant examples of this occur in the "queer theologies" of a number of gay-affirming theologians and scholars.[1]

It is no secret that biphobia is still alive and well in a great deal of the wider queer community, and misperceptions and flawed understandings of bisexuality are quite common. (The idea, e.g., that bisexuality is a convenient identification for those who have not fully accepted their homosexuality—"Bi-Town is just a stop on the way to Gay-Town.") Religious communities having some of these same prejudices would, therefore, not be surprising. It is also quite obvious that there are, always have been and very likely always will be, bisexual people (whether they were descriptively bisexual, or would be actually and actively identifying as bisexual) among the various flocks of practicing and faithful Christians in every denomination.[2] Arguments can and have been made for why Christianity should fully embrace people of any possible sexual orientation, and yet the fundamental structure of certain Christian exegeses of their scriptures—especially Romans 1:26–27—may in fact preclude the acceptance of bisexuality, even though it may be interpreted to embrace and allow for homosexuality.

Before treating this passage and its interpretation at length, a word should be said on the issue of "essentialism versus social constructionism," a vital debate to the understanding and study of homoeroticism and sexual orientation in wider historical contexts. Although a position between these two extremes is probably closer to reality for most theorists and scholars working in these areas, it would be useful to understand the basic aspects and the potential pitfalls of each position. Essentialists would assume the position of homosexuality (or, at very least, homoeroticism) being an inborn, transhistorical behavior and even identity, distinguishable from what is found more commonly, that is, a heterosexual or even heteronormative style of romantic and sexual relations.[3] Social constructionism (a theoretical stance spearheaded by French philosopher Michel Foucault) takes the position that any label or definition of *sexual orientation* is, by nature, bounded by the historical and social factors during the temporal period that gave rise to it; thus, the terms *homosexuality*, *bisexuality* and even *heterosexuality* can only be discussed meaningfully as they apply to the time periods after these words were coined (i.e., circa the last century and a half). The social constructionist viewpoint has been favored by most queer theorists and historians of sexuality; however, the more essentialist viewpoint has been (and continues to be) favored by a number of gay theologians. The often implicit critique of the social constructionist viewpoint (and not only among gay Christian theologians and activists—e.g., Harry Hay's idea in the Radical

Faeries that queer people are "a separate people whose time has come") is that if there is not a transhistorical, transcultural unity among homoerotic desires across great spans of time, geography and cultural shifting, and if the tendency toward homoeroticism is not in some sense inborn and "essential" to one's being, and beyond the capacity for individual choice, then it is not a hard-wired necessity for those so inclined, and can therefore be changed, or at very least repressed. The obvious critique of essentialism by social constructionists is that the perceived "gayness" of certain historical characters and social institutions, from Athenian pederasty, Alexander the Great, and the Roman Emperor Hadrian, all the way down to the (postemergence-of-homosexuality-as-discrete-category) iconic figure of Oscar Wilde, were not "exclusively homosexual" in their behaviors most certainly, and not even "exclusively homosexual" in what can be known of their emotional attachments. Exclusive homosexuality has been a phenomenon that would have been rare, if not impossible, in many premodern societies for a variety of reasons, including general social pressures toward marriage and reproduction as a necessity for the continuation of the human species; and in the modern and postmodern periods, exclusive homosexuality remains quite rare. Further, the differences perceived in gender presentation and sexual activities, rather than biological sex, were often the determining factors in what sexual relationships were possible for a person: thus, a Roman male citizen could penetrate women or other males, as long as those males were inferior in social status (e.g., slaves, conquered foreigners, youths), and not be considered anything other than a complete and virile male citizen, whereas a Roman male who allowed himself to be penetrated anally or—even worse—orally would be considered effeminate and pathetic (Parker, 1997).

In subsequent discussion of the Pauline text, therefore, it should be noted that the term *homosexuality* will be used in relation to the passage only when another author refers to it in his or her writings. This author will make every attempt to use *homoeroticism* (which, though still biased toward a modern and essentialist understanding of sexual orientation being determined by comparison of the desirer's gender to that of his or her desired erotic object, at least makes it possible that homoerotic feelings can be exhibited by anyone regardless of any perceived or actual gender identity in that person's given culture's understanding) in the discussion which follows as a more accurate understanding of the activities (rather than identities) involved.

Romans 1:26–27 is the only place in the entire Christian canon of scripture (including the Hebrew Bible and some of its accepted apocrypha) that specifically mentions female homoeroticism,[4] and it is also one of few, if not the only, unambiguous passages in the New Testament that speaks about homoeroticism directly. The passage occurs in relation to Paul's discussion of gentile idolatry and ignorance about God (as creator of the world) leading to condemnation and sinful practices.

> For this reason God gave them up to degrading passions. Their women exchanged natural intercourse for unnatural, and in the same way also the men, giving up natural intercourse with women, were consumed with passion for one another. Men committed shameless acts with men and received in their own persons the due penalty for their error. (Romans 1: 26–27)[5]

Because of the injunctions toward procreation in the Hebrew Bible (the "original commandment," to be fruitful and multiply, in Genesis 1:28), Paul saw sexual relations between males and females to be divinely ordained. Thus, homoeroticism was interpreted as a result of the sin of idolatry (explained in Romans 1:21–25). The "due penalty for their error" in the latter part of the above passage is not—as some conservative, evangelical, fundamentalist and dominionist Christians would have it—AIDS/HIV (Goss, 1993, p. 24). Rather, it is the "unnatural" sexual activity itself; in other words, homoeroticism is not the sin, it is only the symptom of the more grave sin of unfaithfulness and idolatry (Hays, 1986, pp. 190, 192; Scroggs, 1983, pp. 115–116).[6] Although this is still quite far from being in any sense an "affirmative" passage, and indeed it impugns the entirety of the non-Christian (and non-Jewish) population and their religious ideas, this much can be agreed upon, at very least, about the message and meaning of these verses.

A moment should be spent considering this passage's lines about the "due penalty for their error," and the way that this phrase has been interpreted as Paul playing the role of Christian soothsayer in his prediction of the rise of AIDS/HIV, the "gay plague." Particularly detrimental in this construction is the perception that the spread of the disease from the "strictly gay" population (for whom it was "meant") to the straight population has been laid at the feet of bisexual men. This scapegoating is, in essence, a reversal of the most basic Christian message (Daly, 1973, p. 76), and a lack of acceptance of responsibility on the part of heterosexuals who transfer blame in this fashion. Lack of information and education on the part of everyone in the early stages of the disease's spread is as much to blame as anything, and in many places (including conservative religious schools where misinformation on all matters of sexuality is still pervasive[7]) is still to blame now. In the post-AIDS-awareness era, the only responsible persons are individuals, who must be vigilant in safer sex practices for their own health, as well as out of concern for their partners' well-being.

Idolatry is a further issue of importance to discuss in relation to this text. The idea of idolatry as "attachment to particulars" colors gay Anglican theologian Michael Vasey's (1995) remarks on this passage who opines that the new creation and the "kingdom" envisioned by Paul will be one in which all tyrannous desire, social disintegration and regulating institutions around sex will pass away, thus one should not be attached to anything too heavily (p. 134). Richard Hays (1986) argued that homosexual behavior as portrayed here by Paul is a sacramentalization through sex of idolatrous approaches to the Divine (p. 191). If Paul was speaking about the excesses of idolization of one's beloved in a homoerotic relationship—which, although possible, he was most likely not—then heterosexuals are often no less guilty of this phenomenon as those who are homoerotically inclined. Paul's further remarks in Romans 2:1 indict everyone and reinforce the teaching that in judging others one condemns oneself (Hays, p. 195). However, when this point is interpreted by some modern fundamentalists, it becomes a reductionistic viewpoint that perceives all nonheterosexuals as only interested in sex. Again, the same can often be said about some of those whose sexual impulses are (purportedly) "natural," that is, heterosexuals.

Perhaps the most detrimental aspect of Romans 1's interpretation for bisexuals, and most to the point of the present discussion, is the exegesis of the passage that has been given by many gay and gay-affirming scholars and theologians. Catholic priest John J. McNeill's (1976) landmark work *The Church and the Homosexual* states the following: "there is ample evidence that in most instances where Scripture deals with homosexuality the author probably had in mind what today we would call perversion, namely, the indulgence in homosexual activity on the part of those who were by nature heterosexually inclined" (pp. 41–42). McNeill's work, which had a profound effect on gay Catholic medievalist John Boswell (Kuefler, 2006, p. 4), is echoed in Boswell's (1980) own influential study *Christianity, Social Tolerance, and Homosexuality*:

> What is even more important, the persons Paul condemns are manifestly not homosexual: what he derogates are homosexual acts committed by apparently heterosexual persons. . . . Although the idea that homosexuality represented a congenital physical characteristic was widespread in the Hellenistic world . . . it is not clear that Paul distinguished in his thoughts or writings between gay persons (in the sense of permanent sexual preference) and heterosexuals who simply engaged in periodic homosexual behavior. (p. 109)

Later biblical scholarship by Martti Nissinen (1998) followed this same interpretive pattern: "The text speaks of people who deliberately turn their natural sexual orientation upside down and take an adversary role in it. To use modern terms, Paul refers to heterosexual people who knowingly and voluntarily make themselves homosexuals" (p. 109). The idea of "exchange" in Paul's passage does seem to point toward an interpretation along these lines.[8]

One of the effects of this interpretation is that not only does it exonerate "true homosexuals" of any possible suggestion that their orientation is sinful, but it further makes what is "natural" for them (i.e., their own homoerotically inclined orientation) divinely ordained and unchangeable. In other words, the forcing of gay men and lesbians into "reparative therapy" by oppressive Christian denominations would thus be interpreted as a contravention of natural law, and a sinful and disordered practice. Although this viewpoint is fair enough, and indeed the existence of programs like Exodus International and other such "cures" for homosexuality (usually through forced heterosexuality) are appalling and deplorable, a structural bias yet remains that is most unnerving for a bisexual position.

New Testament scholars Robin Scroggs (1983, pp. 145–147) and Richard B. Hays (the latter in a pejorative manner, using the term *switch-hitting*; 1986, p. 200) noted that most homoerotic sexual behavior around the turn of the era was not, strictly speaking, exclusively homosexual, but instead bisexual. Those who are "heterosexual by nature" but engage in homosexual relations from time to time are also, at least by descriptive definition (even if not by self-conscious identification), bisexual. The bias in such statements is thus obvious: there are only two ways to be sexual in Christianity, homo- and hetero-. Following this, and the respect for and repetition of these viewpoints in gay theological discourse, comes the subsequent silence about bisexuality in anything but the inclusive acronyms often attached to particular affirming movements or congregations, or statements of inclusivity.

If the heterosexist notion of total sexual dualism is necessary to uphold the possibility of homosexual inclusion and acceptance despite (or even due to) Paul's words, then this leaves bisexuals—who from a heterosexual or a homosexual viewpoint might be perceived as "switching" between the two orientations, and perhaps even "exchanging" their natural homo- or heterosexuality for an unnatural hetero- or homosexuality—entirely out in the cold as far as visibility and acceptance are concerned. These interpretations perpetuate the erroneous idea that (despite some exegetical treatments to the contrary; Hays, 1986, p. 209) nonheterosexuals have a "choice" in their orientation, and bisexuals in particular have a greater ability to make that choice. Bisexuals (unlike other nonheterosexuals) can be attracted to either sex, thus they should make the "right" choice (which most ecclesiastical authorities would say is for opposite-sexed attractions, and which most so-called queer theologians would say is for same-sexed attractions), which would be the one that is "natural" for them according to the dictates of whichever philosophy happens to be operative in the exegete or theologian's mind. However, if only one choice is deigned "right," then the choice has been made already; and yet, no matter what, the underlying reality of bisexuality as a discrete phenomenon is still not fully respected in any of these options.

If bisexuality is one among many possible options along the spectrum of sexual orientation (and all scientific studies of it seem to indicate this is the case, not only among humans but among many animals as well[9]), then it would have to be concluded that it is just as "natural" for some people to be attracted to any biological sex or expression of gender as it is for some people to be attracted to only one (whichever one it might happen to be).

If this were the case, then no expression of bisexual sexual desire or sexual activity would then, therefore, be outside of the norm and "unnatural" for that orientation. This seems quite obvious for most bisexually behaving people, and for those who self-identify as bisexual, and indeed it should be a fact that is respected and accepted by everyone (most especially those who are homoerotically inclined), at least in an ideal world. However, the existence and recognition of the validity of bisexuality can also problematize homoeroticism as such, because then religious viewpoints that are not sympathetic to homosexuality could potentially use bisexuality's existence to suggest that those who are exclusively homoerotic in their orientations simply have not given heterosexuality a chance, and in a reversal of the common cliché mentioned above, "Bi-Town" might be used as a stop on the forced relocation to "Straight-Town" for the willing citizens of "Gay-Town."

Of course, the situation need not be this dire at all, and the existence of bisexuality does not have to be a disruptive force for the status quo of either homosexual acceptance or of heterosexuality. However, given the dualistic structural emphasis of a great deal of Christian theology, the perceived dualism of sexual orientation and its interplay with Christian scripture makes full acceptance of bisexuality a remote possibility, not to mention throwing a proverbial monkey wrench into this particular Pauline passage. One of Jesus' most popular sayings, occurring in similar versions in at least three different gospels (the canonical Matthew 6:24 and Luke 16:13, as well as the apocryphal Gospel of Thomas logion 47) is "No one can serve two masters; for a slave will either hate the one and love the other, or be devoted to the one and despise the other." In a religion with such a strong dualistic bias, it is no wonder that the perceived liminal, transgressive stance of bisexuality can too often only be understood as disloyalty to one of two masters, whichever one the interpreter happens to believe is the "true master."

Although the treatment of bisexuals by mainstream Christianity is certainly not a model of inclusivity, bisexual Christians must also not be blind to the plight of other sexual minorities. It is a tragedy that dualistic approaches to questions of nature have forced otherwise well-meaning gay and lesbian Christians to condemn their bisexual co-religionists without even naming them; but, with conscious efforts, even these obstacles can be overcome. Furthermore, trans folk of all stripes are often demonized even more within Christian circles, because they are perceived to be attempting to "play God" in terms of their choice to change their gender identity and undergoing surgery to make their bodies more in line with their chosen gender expressions. The interpretation of the "natural" as inborn genetic fact exhibited in biological sex, and the further gloss of this "naturalness" as the "will of God," and its willful alteration by trans people being categorized as a sin even more grave than the idolatry imputed to those who "exchange natural for unnatural" in the passage from Romans, is a tragic fact for many trans folk who have been subjected to a harsh Christian upbringing. One wonders what the theological implications of an all-powerful, but also all-loving deity who implants diverse desires and variant gender expressions in people, but then deems acting on any of these to be sinful and deserving of eternal damnation, might end up being: either the deity concerned is not all-loving (and thus probably not deserving of regard), or perhaps that deity as interpreted by the religious groups in question does not exist at all.

Strangely enough, and despite the specific death penalty prescribed for committing homoerotic acts in the scriptures of the religions concerned, Judaism and Islam may be more friendly to the possibility of behavioral bisexuality than Christianity, if the above examination is accurate.[10] As long as the procreative norms are observed in Judaism and Islam, and a "marriage of convenience" is in effect, then the quiet and confidential sexual acts that might happen between people of the same sex are not as problematic as they are in terms of Christian scriptural interpretations. It should be viewed as a supreme irony, as well as a stern rebuke, to the Christian tradition that a repressive, closeted situation like that which often prevails for homoerotically inclined people in many countries dominated by conservative Islamic governments can be considered more affirming of bisexual existence through silence than so-called queer Christianity's best attempts at queer-positive biblical readings have been.[11]

Still, there are other possibilities. Marcella Althaus-Reid (2003) argued that the importance of a bisexual theological viewpoint is indeed essential to addressing many of the problems of sexual, social, colonial and economic injustice in the modern world, even within the Christian tradition (pp. 14–17). This is an exemplary position for the inclusiveness which many attempts at Pauline exegesis in favor of homosexual inclusion have failed to produce. The Christian tradition, however, cannot be reduced to the content and implications of only one scriptural passage, this particular Pauline passage nor any other from the New Testament and Hebrew Bible.

Certainly, there are many other religious viewpoints outside of the Christian tradition presenting themselves as viable options for bisexuals who wish to be fully visible and self-affirming in their practice of their sexual orientation. In all of these, however, the ability of bisexuality to destabilize dualisms and binaries of all sorts, which more often than not are employed in manners that denigrate one option to the benefit of the other, is something which should not only be taken very seriously but should be employed thoroughly and consciously by individual theologians, ethicists and bisexual spiritual practitioners themselves, in all religious traditions, in as many aspects of their religious practices and theological constructions as possible.

NOTES

1. Much of the argument in this article derives from the author's unpublished master's thesis (Bernhardt-House, 2000), particularly chapter 3, "Bisexual Exegesis." The author states for the record that

though raised ostensibly Christian (particularly, but not exclusively, Roman Catholic), the author does not identify as Christian of any sort, other than being post-Christian—which is to say, the author is in full recognition of the influence of Christianity upon the author's life, the wider society, and on the definitions and conceptions of religion generally for Western people, though not having any investment in the beliefs of Christian denominations, nor any practice with or membership in any of the Christian communities.

2. Some of these will be discussed further later; but for the moment, it is useful to examine some of the contributions in the anthology edited by Kolodny (2000).

3. However, see the fascinating work of Lochrie (2005), on the nonexistence of heteronormativity in the premodern period.

4. For a dissenting view, which suggests that the reference in Romans is to non-procreative female sexual acts, e.g. anal or oral intercourse, see Miller (1995).

5. All biblical quotations in this article refer to the New Revised Standard Version, unless otherwise noted.

6. A dissenting view on this comes from Cantarella (1992, pp. 191–210), which takes this passage as a blanket condemnation of homosexuality as a sin. Despite this book's title, not much greater insight into bisexuality as a phenomenon unto itself is discussed nor given in this book's overall argument.

7. For a particularly vivid account of such a situation, see Adams (1998).

8. The author has seen these same arguments, worded slightly differently, in the informational literature handed out by a number of LGBTQ-affirming Christian churches, at Gay Pride marches, festivals and on bulletin boards.

9. See, for example, Bagemihl (1999).

10. Even considering the Levitical and Deuteronomic proscriptions against (male) homoeroticism in the Hebrew Bible, modern Judaism as a whole is far more accepting of homoeroticism generally than any of the other major creedal monotheistic faiths. See, for example, Shneer and Aviv (2002).

11. This is a large topic, and one that should probably be explored in a study of its own, but it seems appropriate to mention it at this stage for comparative purposes.

REFERENCES

Adams, M. (1998). *The preacher's son*. Seattle, WA: Window Books.

Althaus-Reid, M. (2003). *The queer God*. London and New York: Routledge.

Bagemihl, B. (1999). *Biological exuberance: Animal homosexuality and natural diversity*. New York: St. Martin's Press.

Bernhardt-House, P. A. (2000). *Serving two masters: Bisexual theological foundations*. Unpublished master's thesis, Gonzaga University, Spokane, WA.

Boswell, J. (1980). *Christianity, social tolerance, and homosexuality: Gay people in Western Europe from the beginning of the Christian era to the fourteenth century*. Chicago, IL: University of Chicago Press.

Cantarella, E. (1992). *Bisexuality in the ancient world* (trans. C. Ó Cuilleanáin). New Haven, CT, and London: Yale University Press.

Daly, M. (1973). *Beyond God the father*. Boston, MA: Beacon Press.

Goss, R. (1993). *Jesus acted up: A gay and lesbian manifesto*. San Francisco, CA: HarperCollins.

Hays, R. B. (1986). Relations natural and unnatural: A response to John Boswell's exegesis of Romans 1. *Journal of Religious Ethics*, *14*, 184–215.

Kolodny, D. R. (2000). *Blessed bi spirit: Bisexual people of faith*. New York and London: Continuum.

Kuefler, M. (2006). The Boswell thesis. In M. Kuefler (Ed.), *The Boswell thesis: Essays on Christianity, social tolerance, and homosexuality* (pp. 1–31). Chicago, IL: University of Chicago Press.

Lochrie, K. (2005). *Heterosyncrasies: Female sexuality when normal wasn't*. Minneapolis, MN: University of Minnesota Press.

McNeill, J. J. (1976). *The church and the homosexual*. Boston, MA: Beacon Press.

Miller, J. E. (1995). The practices of Romans 1:26: Homosexual or heterosexual? *Novum Testamentum: An International Quarterly for New Testament and Related Studies*, *37*, 1–11.

Nissinen, M. (1998). *Homoeroticism in the biblical world* (trans. K. Stjerna). Minneapolis, MN: Fortress Press.

Parker, H. N. (1997). The teratogenic grid. In J. P. Hallett & M. B. Skinner (Eds.), *Roman sexualities* (pp. 47–65). Princeton, NJ: Princeton University Press.

Shneer, D., & Aviv, C. (Eds.). (2002). *Queer Jews*. New York and London: Routledge.

Scroggs, R. (1983). *The New Testament and homosexuality: Contextual background for contemporary debate*. Philadelphia, PA: Fortress Press.

Vasey, M. (1995). *Strangers and friends: A new exploration of homosexuality and the Bible*. London: Hodder & Stoughton Ltd.

Bi Christian Unitarian: A Theology of Transgression

STEPHEN LINGWOOD
Bank Street Unitarian Chapel, Bolton, Greater Manchester, UK

Many bisexuals draw their spiritual guidance from more than one religious tradition; in this case from Christianity and Unitarianism. Yet many Christian denominations still judge bisexual people even more negatively than they do homosexuals. The Church of England, for instance, advises bisexuals to "follow the way of holiness" and choose heterosexual marriage, rather than stay in their "ambiguous" sexuality. This kind of official church view shows a fundamental misunderstanding of bisexuals, for whom gender is not a barrier in sexual relations. With views such as this it is not surprising that very little explicit bisexual theology has developed within Christianity. Yet there are deep and profound messages for bisexuals within Christianity if one is able to see them. Bisexual love can be seen as paralleling the love of God, which is not limited by boundaries of faith, particularly from a Unitarian perspective. The story of Moses offers a parable for bisexual liberation theology, suggesting that bisexual people are called out of the closet to join in the work of liberation of all people; and that liberation itself cannot involve excluding or "ethnically cleansing" any group of people.

INTRODUCTION

There is very little explicit bisexual theology in the world. I wish here to begin an exploratory conversation about what it means to be religious and bisexual, specifically writing as a bisexual Unitarian Christian. I begin by discussing some issues related to the nature and definition of bisexuality, then survey some Christian church documents and theologians writing about bisexuality, and then begin, tentatively, to construct a bisexual theology. Some of my reflections will be inevitably personal and draw upon my own life and experience as a British bisexual man who is also a Unitarian.

In constructing my bisexual theology I draw upon the theme of transgressing boundaries. Bisexual lives often transgress the boundaries of gender, faith and oppressor/oppressed. This transgressing offers a way of understanding and illuminating the love of God as understood in the Christian tradition.

DEFINING BISEXUAL

Definitions are difficult things, and that is certainly true when discussing sexuality in general and bisexuality in particular (Mondimore, 1996, p. 179). When I identify as a bisexual man there may be all kinds of questions and issues this raises for some people. As many bisexuals know, the concept of bisexuality challenges many. Identifying as gay is much simpler, conceptually: *gay* simply reverses the gender of the person of sexual interest, but it does not automatically call into question the stability of the dominant understanding of gender. However, bisexuality is much more challenging, because in some ways bisexuality queers the whole system of male/female, homo/hetero. In one sense, to the bisexual, gender does not matter. In saying this I am not suggesting that in all ways bisexuals are "gender blind." Purely in terms of sexual attraction some bisexuals may not "see" or regard gender, whereas other bisexuals definitely do. Neither does this mean that bisexuals are immune from sexism. What it does mean is that, in terms of sexual attraction or activity, bisexuals effortlessly cross gender lines therefore calling into question the impenetrability and ontology of those lines. To live a life where gender (in some sense) does not matter is threatening to a world that has built its thinking on the premise that it does. Bisexuality threatens to transcend or transgress a rigid understanding of two mutually exclusive genders and sexual orientations (Klein, 1993, pp. 5–12; Nagle, 1995, pp. 305–306).

To neutralize the threat of bisexuality two responses are often offered: either no one is bisexual, or everyone is bisexual. Both of these responses steal the identity of the bisexual person. Some people believe that bisexuals are fence-sitters who are "really" either gay or straight. Many gay people think bisexuals have only taken one step out of the closet. It is true that many people say that they are bisexual as part of the process of coming out as homosexual (Mondimore, 1996, pp. 181–182). Nevertheless many people remain bisexual all their lives.

The claim that everyone is bisexual comes from the acknowledgment that sexuality is something more complex than two discrete categories of heterosexual and homosexual, which is certainly true (see LeVay, 1996, pp. 46–52). Many otherwise heterosexual people, especially during or before puberty, may engage in some homosexual activity; many people will have had some kind of sexual experience, feelings or dreams with more than one gender. Sexual experience is vast and diverse, as has been proved since the studies of Alfred Kinsey (see Mondimore, 1996, pp. 78–89). However, I would not consider such experiences as constituting a bisexual identity in and of themselves.

To speak personally, I identify as bisexual because identifying as either gay or straight would feel dishonest; it would be denying part of myself that I judge to be significant, and would feel like being in the closet. If a person identifies as bisexual it means that his or her homosexuality and heterosexuality are significant enough for that person to consider himself or herself bisexual. A bisexual person does not need to act on those sexual feelings for both sexes to be happy (or to be bisexual).

To deal with these issues my definition of a bisexual is someone for whom gender is not a barrier to sexual relations. This avoids the dualism of "men and women" or "homosexual and heterosexual" in the definition, which also can suggest an inevitable polyamorous (nonmonogamous) lifestyle. For me, personally, bisexuality means that I could marry and be monogamous with someone of any gender.

THE STATE OF BISEXUAL THEOLOGY

"Them" Theology

I begin this brief survey of the state of bisexual theology today by discussing the "them" theological conversation. By *them* theology, I mean Christian theology and ethics carried out about bisexual people, but not by bisexual people. In this kind of theological reflection bisexuality is often a problem, an issue to be dealt with by theologians and church officials at high levels of ecclesiastical power.

This will not take long. Recent sexual ethics reports from the Evangelical Alliance, the United Reform Church, and the Roman Catholic Church have not mentioned bisexuality at all (Church of England, 2003, pp. 214–215). Yet where bisexuality is discussed there are huge misunderstandings about the nature of bisexual people and their lives. This paragraph from the Church of England's *Some Issues in Human Sexuality* (2003) is worth reproducing in full:

> We recognize that there are those whose sexual orientation is *ambiguous*, and who can find themselves attracted to partners of either sex. Nevertheless it is clear that *bisexual activity* must *always be wrong* for this reason, if for no other, that it *inevitably involves being unfaithful*. The Church's guidance to bisexual Christians is that if they are capable of heterophile relationships and of satisfaction within them, they should

> follow the way of holiness in either celibacy or abstinence or heterosexual marriage. In the situation of the bisexual it can be that counseling will help the person concerned to *discover the truth of their personality* and to achieve a degree of *inner healing*. (p. 215, emphasis added)

Let's examine what this document is saying about bisexuality in detail: First that bisexuality is ambiguous. This is based on the assumption of a dualistic heterosexual/homosexual system in which one has to fall into one category or another. To be bisexual is to be confused, ambiguous, undecided about what identity one is going to drop into. Bisexuality is not seen as a sexual orientation, but rather the absence of a sexual orientation. There is something dehumanizing about this. To be a person is to have a sexual orientation, to have a sexual orientation is to be either straight or gay, so if one refuses to be either straight or gay, one has no sexual orientation, therefore no real personhood: one is ambiguous.

This logic is further expanded with the advice given to bisexuals to get counseling to discover the truth about themselves. The assumption being that bisexuality is not a truth about themselves, but a lie, a delusion, a confusion. To be bisexual is to live a lie, and it is an unhealthy lie, as suggested by the statement that counseling will give the bisexual healing by giving them a "truer" identity, rather than this bisexual confusion.

Now let us turn to the central criticism in the document, "bisexual activity must always be wrong … [because] it inevitably involves being unfaithful" (Church of England, 2003, p. 215). That bisexual activity inevitably involves being unfaithful seems like a true statement, but it is in fact deeply misleading. A subtle but deeply important shift has happened with language. The first sentence understands bisexuality as a sexual orientation (or the lack of one) and an identity, then this statement about infidelity speaks about sexual activity, then the rest of the paragraph slips back into bisexual orientation and identity.

What is bisexual activity? Perhaps the document has in mind a woman or man who is in a heterosexual marriage who goes outside that marriage occasionally for same-sex genital sexual activity. But that is surely only one way in which a person could be said to have had bisexual activity across a lifetime. For example, a bisexual man could have had a relationship with another man at a young age, which involved kissing but not genital sexual activity, then could have met a woman later in life who he married and spent the rest of his life with monogamously. That man could continue to openly identify as bisexual, could openly admit same-sex attraction, but remain in a healthy heterosexual relationship.

This would be perfectly within the Church of England's teaching on marriage and sexuality, would it not? Yet it would also be bisexual activity. Here we see bisexual activity across a lifetime not inevitably leading to infidelity. And of course it must be affirmed in no uncertain terms that having a bisexual identity does not inevitably lead to infidelity. Indeed this is a biphobic stereotype that is very damaging and hurtful to bisexual people.

It is my experience that bisexual people are as capable of monogamy as anybody else. Being bisexual means one thinks more deeply about monogamy or alternatives to monogamy, but it does not inevitably lead to nonmonogamy. This is a fundamental misunderstanding about bisexual people. Bisexual people do not have to have sex with both genders; it is simply that they acknowledge the possibility of being with either (or any) gender.

Even sympathetic treatments of bisexual people assume that being bisexual means having sex with more than one person in the same period of time. Adrian Thatcher (Church of England, 2003) wrote, "Perhaps marriage is unsuitable for bisexual people? It is difficult to see how marriage can withstand the strain of one partner also in a homosexual relationship outside the marriage, but such marriages exist, inside and outside the Church, and some of them appear strong fortresses of acceptance and love" (pp. 216–217).

His statement may be true. But the point is two separate issues are being treated as one issue: one is bisexuality, the other is polyamory, or responsible nonmonogamy. The fact is that the word *heterosexual* could easily replace the word *homosexual* in Thatcher's sentence above and the meaning would not change—maintaining a heterosexual relationship in addition to (heterosexual) marriage could cause strain. Heterosexual people can (and do) have heterosexual activity outside of a heterosexual marriage/relationship; homosexual people can (and do) have homosexual activity outside of a homosexual marriage/relationship. This issue is not unique to bisexuals. Bisexuals can be happy in monogamous heterosexual or monogamous homosexual relationships. Or they can be in some way polyamorous. Many are, but many are not, and it is offensive to suggest that bisexuals are incapable of choosing monogamy. Bisexuality and polyamory are two distinct issues.

Finally to the "Church's guidance to bisexual Christians"—that they should be celibate or heterosexual. There is something very disturbing about this statement—namely that love does not figure in the equation. Surely the foundation of marriage is love. If a bisexual man falls in love with a woman, fine, but if he falls in love with a man, then that love is to be denied according to this guidance. The "way of holiness" seems to override the issue of with whom one happens to fall in love. The "way of holiness" is in fact an insistence to erect a boundary to love where the bisexual sees no such boundary. It introduces an additional factor into the decision to get married. In addition to the normal healthy reasons to get married there is the fact that heterosexuality is favored. In this scenario if a bisexual man has to choose who to marry between a man with whom he has a genuine love, and a woman with whom he has only some shallow affection then the "way of holiness" suggests he should choose the woman. I would argue that this is not a good way to build lasting lifelong unions. The person one has sex with and marries should depend on to whom one is attracted, and with whom one falls in love. That rule should apply to everyone: heterosexuals, homosexuals, and bisexuals.

On the issue of bisexuals (as well as homosexuals and transgender people), it is important for the people being talked about and legislated against to be consulted and allowed to find their own voices. It is to this that we now turn.

"Us" Theology—Telling Our Stories

"Us" bisexual theology is theology carried out about bisexuality and faith, by bisexuals. It is very difficult to find such theology. Perhaps we should not be too surprised by this; there has always been very little research into bisexuality, compared to homosexuality (Klein, 1993, p. 3). It was only in the 1990s that bisexuals began to organize politically (Rust, 1995, pp. 1–2; Uddis-Kessler, 1995, p. 18), the landmark probably being the publication of Hutchins' and Ka'ahumanu's (1991) *Bi Any Other Name: Bisexual People Speak Out*. This book allowed bisexuals to tell their stories to each other. Such storytelling will always help a group to build identity and solidarity. The sharing of stories is always the first step in meaning making, community forming and discernment. As MacIntyre (1984) pointed out, "I can only answer the question 'What am I to do?' if I can answer the prior question 'Of what story or stories do I find myself a part'" (p. 216).

Similarly bisexuals have also told stories about their spirituality and faith. Debra R. Kolodny's (2000) *Blessed Bi Spirit: Bisexual People of Faith* is a major anthology of bisexual faith stories (see also Andrew, 2000, for an example of a bisexual spiritual autobiography). This is the vital first step for creating bisexual theology—to have a pool of stories that can be used as the foundation for building our theology, our politics, and our vision.

The bisexual community has built on this foundation of stories to begin to do theology as a community. Bisexual conferences have included workshops on bisexual theology (North American Conference on Bisexuality, Gender and Sexual Diversity, 2001), but little of this has been published.

Within the academy, the only theologian I am aware of who is doing anything that could be called bisexual theology is Marcella Althaus-Reid (2003), though it seems more appropriate to call her theology queer rather than bisexual. However, her writing has a degree of impenetrability that would make it difficult for many bisexual people of faith to use her theology to help them weave the stories of their lives with the stories of faith, something that I take to be one of the major tasks of theology.

Also worth noting is the queer theologian Carter Heyward who in one book (1984) spoke about her attraction to men and women but then wrote,

> The problem with bisexuality in my life (and I can speak only for myself) is that it has been grounded too much in my utopian fantasy of the way

> things ought to be and too little in the more modest recognition of myself as a participant in *this* society at *this* time in *this* world, in which I have both a concrete desire for personal intimacy with someone else and a responsibility to participate in, and witness to, the destruction of unjust social structures—specifically, the heterosexual box . . .
>
> It has been my experience that to live now as bisexual is to live somewhat abstractly in anticipation of a future that has not arrived. That is why, for several years, I have been coming out of bisexuality, coming out of a utopian vision in order to focus my sight on the urgency and immediacy of the concrete present. (p. 80)

This eschatological projection of bisexuality is in fact quite common. Many thinkers have posited bisexuality in the future or the past but denied it a reality in the present (see Angelides, 2001, p. 17). Although Carter Heyward (1984) had the freedom to identify as lesbian in her own life, it is worth exploring what she is saying here.

First, there is an assertion that bisexuality is not practical, that destroying unjust social structures is better achieved through lesbianism than bisexuality. I would argue against this. As I have said above, I believe bisexuality transgresses the boundaries that maintain the system of male/female/hetero/homo, which highlights the injustice of this system of thought (see Nagle, 1995, pp. 305–306).

Second, Heyward (1984) considered bisexuality abstract and utopian. This is a puzzling assertion. Bisexuality *is* about "concrete desire for personal intimacy"; it is a name given to the concrete realities of people's lives: their relationships, sexualities, thoughts and feelings. There is nothing abstract about this. And there is nothing utopian about bisexuals demanding freedom from oppression in the here and now. Why should bisexuals wait until some eschatological future to live out the truth of their lives? "Justice too long delayed is justice denied" (King, 1963). The time to act is always now.

CONSTRUCTING A BISEXUAL THEOLOGY

What Would Bisexual Theology Look Like?

Having surveyed the current state of bisexual theology I wish now to turn to the task of constructing a tentative bisexual theology. Such bisexual theology, and all future bisexual theology, should be theology from an explicit bisexual perspective—written by bisexual people reflecting on what it means to be a bisexual person of faith. Bisexual theology is the process of bisexual people finding their voices. Bisexual theology challenges monosexual theology for its biphobic bias. Bisexual theology honors the diversity of bisexual people's lives in homosexual and heterosexual unions, monogamous people and polyamorous people, and all cultures, religions and gender diversities. Within this diversity, I want to plough my own furrow in constructing a bisexual theology within my own Unitarian tradition. However, I believe that this approach will share much with other bisexual theologies.

Love Beyond Boundaries: Bisexual Universalism

> As a bisexual, I choose both/and instead of either/or. I find it natural to honor all the wisdom traditions of the world, and I find it unnatural to think that anyone has a monopoly on truth. I find Unitarian Universalism suits this both/and perspective. (Schranz, 2001, p. 119)

Above, I defined a bisexual person as someone for whom gender is not a barrier to sexual relations. The sexual lives of bisexual people transgress and trespass across boundaries considered deeply important by many people: male/female; homo/hetero. Entering into the realm of faith, perhaps it should not surprise us that many bisexual people also transgress boundaries of faith:

> When I am confronted about my religious identity I tell people I am a Zen Catholic Pagan. Some folks have no problem with this, but they are few. To most, the phrase itself is an incongruity, as much of a contradiction as the concept of being bisexual and married. (Rosefire, 2000, p. 73)

In postmodern Western society many people (and bisexual people more than most in my experience) are embracing multiple religious participation (see Berthrong, 1999), as described above by Rosefire (2000). Multiple religious participation involves a personal faith that draws from more than one faith tradition. Although this approach is certainly not limited to Unitarianism it has been a part of Unitarian religious life for more than 100 years (see Marshall, 2007, pp. 69–74). It is an expression of what might be called a universalist faith that sees truth in all major religious traditions.

The issue of multiple religious participation and universalism brings up many theologically issues, and there is not space here to delve into these in any depth. Nevertheless I think it is worth considering how the notion of transgressing boundaries can and does play out in the faith lives of bisexual people.

Marcella Althaus-Reid (2003) wrote, "Theology is the art of critical bisexual action and reflection on God and humanity . . . it is only bisexuality which displaces and causes tension to the established heterosexual dyad implicit in the theologian's identity and task" (p. 15). What I think Althaus-Reid is saying is that living bisexually causes old systems and boundaries to begin to crumble. Bisexuality forces me "to closely examine each step along the way" (Rosefire, 2000, p. 73) and that close examination begins to see the problems of the boundaries and systems we have set up between gay and straight, between man and woman, between A and B. This is the "heterosexual dyad" that bisexual people refute with their boundary-crossing lives.

This is when theology truly becomes queer: when the systems set up, even between different religions are no longer seen as capable of containing the reality of people's bisexual lives.

The bisexual person witnesses to the possibility of sexual love transgressing gender boundaries. When the bisexual person brings this perspective to faith there is a greater sensitivity to seeing the possibility of divine love transgressing boundaries. It is arguable that the dominant story in the Judeo-Christian tradition is the slow evolution from particularism to universalism. First, God's concern is understood to be only for one ethnic group, then God's concern is seen as extending to a new nonethnic group in the followers of Christ, and then (for the Unitarian, at least) God's concern is seen as extending to the whole of humanity, whatever religion, race or ethnicity.

The bisexual person, whose sexual love is not limited by gender boundaries, is more open to an understanding that God's love is not limited to any one particular group. Indeed, to the extent that God's love extends to men and women, God can be called bisexual. Not only in gender, but in all ways God's love is not limited by the human boundaries that so concern humanity. God's love flows freely over our systems of limitation. This is why bisexual theology will tend toward some kind of universalism.

The Bisexual Vocation in Queer Liberation: Moses' Heterosexual Privilege

Nevertheless a liberal universalism that simply declares "all people are equal" does not take seriously enough the need to deconstruct systems of oppression. So our bisexual theology needs also to concern itself with the task of liberation. What is the bisexual vocation within the greater task of queer liberation? How can the oppression of bisexual people (biphobia) offer insights into the nature of that queer oppression and liberation?

Bisexual people are an invisible minority. If I have a girlfriend I am assumed to be straight, if I have a boyfriend I am assumed to be gay. It is very difficult to implicitly tell people that one is bisexual; the bisexual person usually has to say the words explicitly. Which is a difficult thing to do, and many bisexual people will not say those words, letting people make their own assumptions.

For bisexual people it is especially tempting to assume a straight identity, to live in the heterosexual world, denying their own identity. This can lead to the criticism from the gay community that bisexuals enjoy heterosexual privilege in their straight relationships (Highleyman, 1995, p. 82), which to some extent is true. However, the relevant question in constructing a bisexual liberation theology is: what should bisexual people do about this privilege?

To answer this question I want to approach a formative liberation story in the Judeo-Christian tradition from a bisexual perspective. In the archetypal story of liberation in the Bible Moses enjoyed privilege, and we can draw a parallel between this privilege and the privilege of a bisexual person passing as heterosexual (this parallel, without the bisexual component, is drawn by Cleaver, 1995, p. 30). Moses was adopted as an Egyptian (Exodus 2:5–10), and lived as an Egyptian in a place of privilege. How much was he aware of his Hebrew identity? His own mother nursed him (Exodus 2:9) and presumably made him aware of whom he truly was. Yet wouldn't it have been easier to live as an Egyptian and a prince? Wouldn't it have been easier to ignore or suppress his "Hebrew side"? He was Egyptian, or at least passing as one, which is as good as, and could have continued passing as Egyptian all of his life, without rocking the boat.

But he didn't. Why? Because he saw the oppression (Exodus 2:11). He witnessed the oppression for himself; right in front of him he saw forced labor and violence against Hebrews. Part of him knew that this was oppression against his own people, however much he was successfully passing as an Egyptian.

The bisexual person passing as straight also sees oppression. It is in the moment of observing gay bashing, discrimination, and hatred that the bisexual person has to make a decision. Will the bisexual person see that this is discrimination against their own people and do something about it?

Standing up against oppression is risky. Moses "outed" himself by standing up against the oppression of the Hebrews. He could not stand up against the oppression of the Hebrews without people realizing he himself was Hebrew too. So the bisexual person risks being outed as queer despite his or her passing as heterosexual. The privilege is revoked. Someone thought to be "one of us" was in fact "one of them" all the time. The danger can be serious. Moses fled in terror (Exodus 2:15).

Moses fled to Midian (Exodus 2:15). He left the oppression behind. In this new environment Moses once again passed as an Egyptian (Exodus 2:19), as a bisexual in a new environment might once again pass as straight. But the story does not end there, because of God.

Moses was happy enough as a shepherd in Midian, away from the oppression of the Hebrews, but God was aware of their oppression (Exodus 2:24) and called out to Moses. God appeared to Moses in the burning bush and announced his identity, "I am the God of your father, the God of Abraham, the God of Isaac, the God of Jacob" (Exodus 3:6 NRSV translation). God was not simply announcing God's own identity here, more so God was announcing Moses' identity "I am the God of *your* father . . . Abraham"—"your father is Abraham, you are Hebrew!" Moses was terrified and hid his face (Exodus 3:6). I would suggest this was not because of the majesty or greatness of God, but because of the fact that God reveals truth, and for Moses the truth about himself, that he was Hebrew, was what he had been running away from all his life. It was this that was terrifying: the truth about his identity. He was afraid to look at God because God acts as a mirror. As the

Sufi Farid ud-din Attar (1984) wrote in the conclusion to *The Conference of the Birds*,

> Silently their shinning Lord replies:
> "I am a mirror set before your eyes,
> And all who come before my splendour see
> Themselves, their own unique reality. . .
> Though you have struggled, wandered, travelled far,
> It is yourselves you see and what you are." (p. 219)

God shows you yourself, and what you are. God outs the faithful person because God is a revealer of truth, God is a Light that will shine on every part of the self. Self-knowledge is a proven fruit of the life of faith (Rosefire, 2000, p. 65).

This has been the experience in my own life. I was once praying in the Church of Reconciliation in the Taizé community in France toward the end of my stay there when I was 17 years old. I had been praying all evening in the church, and it was approaching midnight. I was in the presence of God. A young man walked past, and for a fleeting moment I was attracted to this man. Usually I would have suppressed such a thought and tried not to think about it, but because I was in a prayerful place within myself I was forced to acknowledge this thought, this truth, and look it straight in the face for the first time in my life. In that moment, in that church, I came out as bisexual to myself and to God. Or rather God came out to me by revealing this truth to me. God announced to me by God's presence in my attraction to a man, "I am the God of your people, the God of the gays, the God of the lesbians, the God of the bisexuals, the God of the transgender people." A great burden was lifted from me that night. I was no longer burdened with the guilt and repression of a life in the closet, but I was out as bisexual. But God does not out people for only their own well-being, God outs people so that they can fight oppression and work in solidarity with the oppressed. Moses still had a great deal before him, and so do bisexuals.

But what is the bisexual vocation in liberation? Like Moses bisexual people may live in the world of the oppressor and the oppressed. A bisexual person knows the difference between walking through the park holding hands with a man and doing the same with a woman. A bisexual person knows exactly what oppression is because a bisexual person knows exactly what the difference is. At the same time, being an out bisexual person may lead to oppression and exclusion in gay and straight communities. Bisexual people are a bridge between different communities and a minority within a minority. This gives bisexual people a unique perspective on the nature of oppression and also the nature of liberation. The first step needed in our bisexual liberation theology is coming out. Bisexual people need to be out of the closet in straight and gay communities.

The Hebrews did of course gain their liberation with Moses as their leader. But when they reached the Promised Land they set about ethnically cleansing the area, killing indiscriminately (Joshua 6:21). Is that what queer liberation looks like? When gay men set up a space for their own people (the gay nightclub) will bisexual men be welcome? Will women be welcome? Are bisexual women welcome in lesbian space? Are trans people welcome anywhere? How much do we set up our Promised Lands by ethnically cleansing those who are not pure descendents of our gay/lesbian forefather/foremothers? Does monosexual gay liberation look like a slaughtered Jericho? (Joshua 6:21).

Yet purity cannot last. Ruth, a Moabite (Ruth 1:4) became the ancestor of King David and subsequently Jesus of Nazareth (Matthew 1:5–6). Jesus was descended from an impure line. This is a metaphor for the love of God that is not contained within boundaries or ethnicity. Jesus witnessed to a God whose love is not limited to one group of people. In his preaching of the Kingdom of God Jesus showed an understanding of liberation that is not monosexual, monovisioned, monoconcerned, only concerned with the liberation of one group over another, but rather bisexual, or even polysexual, polyvisioned, polyconcerned. The kingdom of God suggests that that liberation can only come when all people are liberated. In this liberation we are called to love our enemies and persecutors (Matthew 5:43–48). This is a difficult vision but a necessary one if liberation is ultimately going to dissolve the "one of us" and "one of them" mentality that is the source of much biphobic oppression. A bisexual theology of liberation witnesses that the oppressed must not become the oppressor in the new land, rather liberation involves the removal of oppression, distrust and hatred for all people.

CONCLUSION

When bisexuals do theology for themselves the "problem" is not located in bisexuality itself, but rather in the boundaries that bisexuality ignores and transgresses. Bisexuality, rather than presenting a problem for Christianity, in fact displays a strong parallel with a major theme in the Judeo-Christian story: namely love that transgresses boundaries. The bisexual vocation within queer liberation is to witness that liberation must not become another form of oppression, and that, ultimately boundaries must not divide humankind in a way that prevents love.

REFERENCES

Althaus-Reid, M. (2003). *The queer God.* New York: Routledge.

Andrew, E. J. (2000). *Swinging on the garden gate: A spiritual memoir.* Boston, MA: Skinner House Books.

Angelides, S. (2001). *A history of bisexuality*. Chicago, IL: University of Chicago Press.

Attar, F. (1984). *The conference of the birds* (A. Darbandi & D. Davis, Trans.). London: Penguin Books.

Berthrong, J. H. (1999). *The divine deli: Religious identity in the North American cultural mosaic*. Maryknoll, NY: Orbis Books.

Bible: New revised standard version (Anglicized edition). (1995). Oxford, UK: Oxford University Press.

Church of England. (2003). *Some issues in human sexuality: A guide to the debate: A discussion document from the House of Bishop's Group on Issues in Human Sexuality*. London: Church House Publishing.

Cleaver, R. (1995). *Know my name: A gay liberation theology*. Louisville, KY: Westminster John Knox Press.

Heyward, C. (1984). *Our passion for justice*. New York: Pilgrim Press.

Highleyman, L. A. (1995). Identity and ideas: Strategies for bisexuals. In N. Tucker (Ed.), *Bisexual politics: Theories, queries, & visions* (pp. 73–92). Binghamton, NY: Haworth Press.

Hutchins, L., & Ka'ahumanu, L. (Eds.). (1991). *Bi any other name: Bisexual people speak out*. Los Angeles, CA: Alyson Books.

King, M. L. (1963). *A letter from Birmingham jail*. Retrieved October 10, 2009, from http://www.africa.upenn.edu/Articles_Gen/Letter_Birmingham.html

Klein, F. (1993). *The bisexual option* (2nd ed.). Binghamton, NY: Haworth Press.

Kolodny, D. R. (2000). *Blessed bi spirit: Bisexual people of faith*. New York: Continuum.

LeVay, S. (1996). *Queer science*. Cambridge, MA: MIT Press.

MacIntyre, A. (1984). *After virtue* (2nd ed.). Notre Dame, IN: University of Notre Dame Press.

Marshall, V. (2007). *The larger view: Unitarians and world religions*. London: Lindsey Press.

Mondimore, F. (1996). *A natural history of homosexuality*. Baltimore, MD: John Hopkins University Press.

Nagle, J. (1995). Framing radical bisexuality: Toward a gender agenda. In N. Tucker (Ed.), *Bisexual politics: Theories, queries, & visions* (pp. 305–314). Binghamton, NY: Haworth Press.

North American Conference on Bisexuality, Gender and Sexual Diversity. (2001). *Bisexual spiritualities find voice at NACB 2001*. Retrieved October 10, 2009, from http://binetbc.bi.org/2001/pressrelease.html

Rosefire. (2000). Is it too much to ask? In D. R. Kolodny (Ed.), *Blessed bi spirit: Bisexual people of faith* (pp. 65–77). New York: Continuum.

Rust, P. C. (1995). *Bisexuality and the challenge to lesbian politics: Sex, loyalty, and revolution*. New York: New York University Press.

Schranz, A. (2000). From orientation to orienteering. In D. R. Kolodny (Ed.), *Blessed bi spirit: Bisexual people of faith* (pp. 118–123). New York: Continuum.

Udis-Kessler, A. (1995). Identity/politics: A history of the bisexual movement. In N. Tucker (Ed.), *Bisexual politics: Theories, queries, & visions* (pp. 17–30). Binghamton, NY: Haworth Press.

Developing a Bisexual Adult Religious Education Curriculum

LORAINE HUTCHINS
Towson University, Towson, Maryland, USA

In 2007 the Unitarian Universalists of America developed the first, and, it appears, only adult religious education curriculum on bisexuality available in the U.S. today. This review discusses the history behind and elements of the Bisexuality Curriculum. The curriculum is discussed in terms of where it fits in the larger context of religious education on sexuality in general, as well as a brief evaluation of how it has been used by specific congregations in the three years since its release.

INTRODUCTION: TALKING ABOUT SEX IN CHURCH?

When I was a young adult, coming of age at Brightwood Park Methodist Church in Washington, D.C., in the mid-1960s, Sunday School lessons were peppered with lively discussions of parallels between the Civil Rights Movement and Biblical times. But there was never an understanding that the rights of sexual minorities are also part of a true and whole vision of civil rights, nor was there any permission to examine the concepts of sexual orientation and gender identity within a positive religious and moral context. It was just assumed that all good Christians were straight and gender conforming, or at least should try to be. Sexual pleasure and erotic intimacy were simply not proper topics of religious instruction or exploration, God forbid!

I do remember some early stirrings of change back then; an issue of a church-affiliated magazine called *Motive* that was dubbed particularly "controversial" because the editor published a cluster of articles on homosexual rights. The church cut the magazine's funding after that issue. Nineteen hundred and sixty-six, the year I graduated high school, was the same year *Time* magazine's cover story declared "God Is Dead." Having lost hope in seeing the church discuss either sexuality or spirituality in a rational, heartful way I turned to alternative cultures and venues for my spiritual and erotic quests instead.

However, in the interval since then a lavish feast of theological, political, cultural and literary/historic reinterrogations of sex and gender in religion have occurred; albeit more in academia than in mainstream popular arenas. The impact of many of these discussions still hasn't permeated the average Sunday School class or religious education course yet. Most major religious denominations still don't devote much time to teaching about sexuality (unless it's admonishments about not having any deep and intimate erotic relations outside of marriage).

There's not even much advice on sex and loving available for married couples within the church, or in any faith's educational efforts. Though this has begun to change a bit in some isolated examples,[1] they are not very well supported within mainstream religious institutions yet. How would our lives be different if people learned about sexuality, and acceptance of sexual diversities, not only in school, in community, at home, but also in religious education classes of all kinds? Not reactionary moral judgments or admonishments or prescriptions, I mean real scientific facts, with no shaming or embarrassment, real teachings about the range of possible loving relationships, identities and the various amazing wondrous ways human intimacies manifest and unfold?

What if these sexuality education lessons even actually included bisexuality—not as something stigmatized, misunderstood, ignored or an afterthought—all of which is usually the case?

What if these religious school sexuality lessons were not only inclusive of same-sex loving (which a small, but increasingly respected portion of them are), but also included a rightful place for teaching about bisexuality and other sexual diversities in a spirited, spiritfull, way?

Well, over the past few years lesbian, gay, bisexual, transgender (LGBT) people in the Unitarian Church have helped develop that denomination's first Bisexuality Curriculum adult religious education model. This curriculum didn't directly grow out of the Unitarian Universalists' (UU) general and beloved all-ages religious education curriculum on sexuality, "Our Whole Lives," or OWL,[2] but it was most likely fertilized in the receptive ground of OWL's enthusiastic support in at least a critical mass of U.S. UU congregations.

This review features an examination of the Bisexuality Curriculum[3] the Unitarians recently developed for use in adult religious education classes. The discussion of the curriculum is wrapped around a discussion of what's available across the range of U.S. religious education on sexuality in general.[4] I felt it was important to examine this curriculum not just alone, but in context: to see how it compares to what else is out there, and to ask—what might be the next steps to integrate such models into various curricula for all people of all faiths.

WHAT'S AVAILABLE, IN GENERAL, ON RELIGIOUS EDUCATION AND SEXUAL MINORITIES?

What's available now in general? Alas, still not much. Of course there are some few church publications featuring sexual communication within marriage that emphasize the intimacy building as well as the procreative value, of marriage, but by and large no major religious denomination tackles the sexuality of everybody, married and not, gay and straight, as a topic of study in religious education in its own right.

The major exception to this has been church documents on religious tolerance of gay people.[5] However, simply urging tolerance is a long way from allowing or instilling age-appropriate sexuality and intimacy education modules for every age group of the religious community. There has been some progress, primarily through the vehicle of "welcoming," "affirming," "reconciling," (i.e., LGBT-friendly) movements in progressive congregations within denominations and localities/regions, that is, church-wide educational efforts to help straight people better understand and support gays. But, as I have said, not much is institutionalized or protected, expected, understood, welcomed, yet.

INSPIRATIONAL OWL(S)—A TWO DENOMINATIONAL COLLABORATION STORY

Although it is not that well known beyond Unitarian and United Church of Christ circles, the OWL (Our Whole Lives) religious education curriculum is quite popular among progressive religious educators. It certainly is a key part of the inspirational ground from which the Unitarians' Bi Curriculum seems to have sprouted. So what is this OWL?

Originally developed as a joint effort by the Unitarian Universalists of America (UUA) and the United Church of Christ,[6] OWL is a series of sexuality education curricula for six age groups: Grades K–3, Grades 4–6, Grades 7–9, Grades 10–12, young adults (ages 18–35), and older adults. OWL, in all its versions, has been part of Unitarian and United Church of Christ congregational resources on the national level for over a decade now.

The OWL curriculum helps participants make informed and responsible decisions about their sexual health and behavior and equips them with age-appropriate information on sexuality, delivered in the context of a caring spiritual community. Although I could not find other denominations with an analogous curriculum on such a national scale, I have heard that some individual religious education teachers from various denominations use and adapt OWL lessons for their own classes and in individual workshop settings for conferences and other congregational events.

The Bisexuality Curriculum

The 20-page Bisexuality Curriculum is a mix of didactic and constructivist pedagogies. It is didactic in that there are some obviously correct (right vs. wrong) answers expected regarding definitions of bisexual identity and so on, but it is also constructivist in the sense that the exercises leave a lot of room for participants to come to develop their own meanings and come to their own conclusions. It is divided into four sections. It includes a glossary and resource list, and three handouts: the Klein Grid,[7] a series of Relationship Trading Cards, and a script on sexual orientation identities. It also includes brief instructions and supplies/prep lists that make replicating the sessions in your own community easy.

The last handout mentioned above, the GSO (Guess the Sexual Orientation) Script contains short bios of five different people (contestants) whose sexual orientation the participants are supposed to "guess" on the basis of behavioral/experiential descriptions of their lives. It is designed to show how variable people's self-labels are, regardless of their life stories.

The team of educators, clergy and laypeople (see endnote 3) who developed the bicurriculum submitted a grant request to an independent UU-focused funding program. Their inspiration to do this came from their work in the Unitarian church's Welcoming Congregations program, which is the LGBT-friendly organization that works within the denomination to create more welcoming local efforts for queer peoples. People in the Welcoming Congregations program felt that it needed to be more sensitive and informative in the area of bisexuality and thus wrote the grant proposal asking for support to make this happen.

The team developed the curriculum and released it in 2007. Its stated goals were to familiarize people with basic definitions related to bisexuality, to give them knowledge and language to counterassumptions and stereotypes they may hear, to place bisexuality in a context that examines its relation to other orientations, gender identity questions and to multiple adult relationship forms (polyamory, polyfidelity). Additional goals were to show the links between oppressions; make it easier for bisexuals to be out, accepted and understood; empower participants to help make their communities, organizations and congregations more just and welcoming; and to create safe and friendly spaces where people can get to know each other better.

As they say in the curriculum's introduction: "Most likely, there are members and friends of your congregation who are bisexual. Most likely, they are seen as either straight or gay/lesbians. Most likely, a big part of their identity is missing from the public eye."

They go on to say that the UUA's *Welcoming Congregation* curriculum has helped begin to bring the issues of bisexuals and bisexuality to the forefront. Historically the Unitarian Universalists Association of Congregations General Assembly first passed a resolution concerning equal rights for persons of nonstraight sexual orientation more than 40 years ago.

As the writers say:

> Bisexuality is a sensitive subject for many people, and it is necessary for the session leaders to have more than a cursory understanding of bisexuality. Leaders should also understand oppression of historically marginalized groups and linked identities. Leaders must have good people skills to be able to deal with controversies and questions and to keep the exercises and activities moving along. (p. 4)

The writers designed the four sample sessions for any size group. Segments can run between 2 and $2\frac{1}{2}$ hours each. A group can also divide the sessions into two parts and make it an eight-session series. They emphasize that this curriculum, and the Welcoming Congregation one, should be offered on a regular basis (once is not enough).

This has certainly been my experience in this kind of work over the years. Repetition helps people reach deeper levels of understanding, get past their blocks and thoroughly learn to embrace people of all sexualities and identities and get real with each other.

- Session One: the first session is designed to introduce the curriculum as a whole and to challenge the concept of dualities. It is designed with three activities, time for discussion and a homework assignment (filling out the Klein Sexual Orientation Grid).
- Session Two: the second session is designed to help us understand our sexual and affectional relationships, to consider the impact of invisibility on bisexuals, and to begin to define bisexuality. The session begins with a discussion of the homework from last session and then moves into a 20-minute exercise on relationships where people brainstorm the attributes of their ideal partner, apart from sex and gender, but including it. This is followed by the "Guess the Sexual Orientation" exercise and discussion, as well as a homework assignment about closets and coming out.
- Session Three: the third section is about the impact of being in the closet and how coming out deepens our relationships in community. This session includes a discussion about polyamory, how it does, and doesn't, relate to bisexual identities. It includes plans for a panel presentation[8] of individuals with different relationship modes who share about their lives. It is followed by a visioning exercise about healthy relationships and a homework assignment about noticing representations about gender and relationships in popular culture.

- Session Four: the fourth session, called "Moving Forward," has the most ambitious agenda: to understand how oppression felt by historically marginalized groups is similar and to create a plan for being more welcoming to bisexuals and other historically marginalized groups in your congregation.

Although I feared the leader guidelines for this session were a little too abstract, I loved the "What Will We Do Now?" questions for the closing minutes, such as do your worship leaders need to be more inclusive during sermons, readings and other elements of worship; would you like your minister to reach out specifically; does your community need a support/drop-in center for BGLT people; does your congregational leadership need to be more diverse?

Participants in this last session are challenged to create a plan to bring to their congregational leadership and have everyone in the group make a commitment to do something concrete about the plan within the next several months. Participants write down their tasks, and the leaders mail them back to them to remind them after an interval. The last closing circle ends, fittingly, with a reading by the famous bisexual anthropologist, Margaret Mead.

Some Facts About the Curriculum in Its First Years of Use

The team announced its release in June 2007 and made it available for Web download that October. They also asked people using it for feedback and reports on how they were using it. Most noted an affiliation with a UU congregation, and about 50 of those congregations were Welcoming. Geographically, curriculum users are from all over the United States as well as from Canada, Mexico, New Zealand, Germany and India. One of its author/developers, Dana Dwinell-Yardley, told me that the survey was first sent out to curriculum users in Fall 2008 and that out of the 83 people who'd requested the curriculum at that time, 26 responded. Of these, 20% had used the curriculum in their congregations during the past year. From the survey results it also appears that people are using it in a variety of ways: to supplement other lessons, only using part of it, adapting it for seminary class or campus queer group, pulling some of the info into a workshop on polyamory, and so on.

CONCLUSION: WHAT'S NEXT, NOW THAT THIS SEED IS PLANTED?

The moment I heard about this curriculum from one of its co-authors—UUA minister Rev. Ann Schranz, Monte Visa UU Congregation in Mountclair,

California—I wanted to obtain it and read it: for its own sake and to be able to understand it as a contribution to the larger body of religious documents on sexuality education available in the United States today. I looked diligently to see if I could find any examples of specific sex ed curriculums in Jewish, Catholic, Muslim, Hindu, Buddhist or other denominations too, for contrast and comparison. I was not able to come up with much other than perhaps the Bi Curriculum's great spiritual grandmother, OWL.

However there are some embryonic buds in other traditions I'm keeping my eye on. For example, there is a group of Episcopal and Anglican bishops, clergy and laypeople called The Chicago Consultation, which supports the full inclusion of GLBT Christians in the Episcopal Church and the worldwide Anglican Communion. They believe that, as they say on their Website, "our baptismal covenant requires this." They have just released a study guide for Episcopalians, *Christian Holiness and Human Sexuality: A Study Guide*. I looked at it. A good manifesto, perhaps a discussion guide. Not a curriculum.

Melany Burrill's 2009 publication, *All God's Children: Teaching Children About Sexual Orientation and Gender Diversity*, which was given to me by one of my old Sunday School teachers, Arlene Kiely, of Dumbarton Methodist Church in Washington, D.C., is a beautiful document that can supplement the reading list of someone developing bi curriculum resources. And it stands alone as a fine and useful document in its own right. *All God's Children* is a fertile compendium of ideas, stories, resource lists and great questions and answers about how to teach some sexuality issues. Kudos to this 20-page pamphlet for being so trans and bi inclusive!

Another hopeful sign is some of the work of Rev. Debra W. Haffner and her colleagues/associates at the Religious Institute on Sexual Morality, Justice, and Healing. They've produced *A Time to Seek: Study Guide on Sexual Diversity* (2009). *A Time to Seek* is not really a study guide, but it is definitely a useful concept paper, an open statement that lays out definitions, discussion guide pointers, FAQ-type info rundowns on LGBT sexuality stats, and, on p. 32, an interesting summary of Denominational Perspectives listing what is known about various denominations and institutions that "support full inclusion of LGBT persons, including ordination and marriage for same-sex couples." It includes the Central Conference of American Rabbis/Union for Reform Judaism and the Reconstructionist Rabbinical Association/Jewish Reconstructionist Federation and the Unity Fellowship Churches and MCC, as well as the UUs and the United Church of Christ. There is also a list of denominations that allow their clergy to "perform marriage or union ceremonies for same-sex couples." It goes on to include a list of "denominations that ordain openly lesbian and gay clergy members."

Are we to conclude that no denominations ordain openly bi clergy members (since none is mentioned), and none that ordain trans clergy members?

I'm certain some of them do, knowingly or unknowingly, but that not many of them will, openly, until there is more safe welcoming space created in our places and communities of worship, space most likely to be created by the cheerful welcoming spirit of simple tools and contributions like the UUA/Welcoming Congregation/Interweave's "Bisexuality Curriculum" and its grandparent family of sex/spirit ed curriculum for all ages, OWL. Haffner used to direct the Sex Information and Education Center of the United States (SIECUS), the best archives of sex ed curriculums around the country and a resource and advocacy center in its own right. However, she moved on to found the Religious Institute a number of years ago. The Religious Institute maintains the best Website I found on keeping up to date on what a variety of faith communities are doing, and can do, to provide a progressive values narrative and context to sexuality, with an eclectic, inclusive human rights and responsible social values perspective as well.

And to conclude in this list of interdenominational, interfaith examples of sex-positive, bi-inclusive religious education/sex education modules let me mention one constant absent presence, the kind, caring influence and keen guidance of bi theologian, activist, priest, teacher, healer Ibrahim Abdurrahman Farajajé: professor, provost and faculty leader for many years at Starr-King School for the Ministry, the Unitarian theological school in Berkeley California affiliated with the Bay Area's Graduate Theological Union (http://www.sksm.edu/faculty).

Farajajé mentored at least one clergy member who developed the Bi Curriculum, Rev. Anne Schranz, of the Monte Vista UUC in Montclair, California. He is famous for developing classes with tongue-in-check titles such as "The Sociopathology of Heteropatriarchy." He is a practicing Sufi, who founded a department of Islamic Studies at Starr-King and has innovated many uniquely queer feminist theology courses during his tenure at the school. He currently directs a branch of the school in Istanbul, spending part of his time in both places.

Unfortunately the fascinating discussions on sexuality, the body, spirituality, across a range of world religious traditions and erotic narratives that take place in his classrooms have not yet been recorded into a reference book or anthology. It would be a worthy project to undertake, one that would increase what is available in the way of sex-positive literature and teaching materials tremendously. Documentation of his sex-positive teachings could be gathered with some similar examples from other colleagues in different faith traditions and centers of learning and put together in a way that frames each contribution as part of a representative whole.

We need each other's light to shine upon us or we will not find our ways home. It is not only important to me that this little bi curriculum exists as a seed sprout, but also that it have the fertile soil of like-minded users and thinkers and participants to multiply its impact, way beyond any one 20-page format or single use. As the old ones say, may many flowers bloom.

NOTES

1. Anecdotal reports of sacred sex and sex counseling/intimacy tips workshops for adult church members in certain evangelical megachurches, as well as similar events planned and delivered at smaller progressive congregations in a handful of different Christian and Jewish denominations, have been reported to me, but I would have to do a bit more research to find the exact materials and lesson plans they use and how many, what kinds of adult students, couples only or not, are involved, and so on.

2. OWL (Our Whole Lives) is really a many-faceted program, not just a series of booklets by age group. There are regular teacher-training workshops in various regions and a whole set of related publications available at the UUA Bookstore on the web with titles such as *The Advocacy Manual for Sexuality Education, Health and Justice: Resources for Communities of Faith; Come Out and Win; Confessions of the Other Mother: Non-Biological Lesbian Moms Tell All; Gay Marriage, Real Life: Ten Stories of Love and Family; Out Law: What LGBT Youth Should Know About Their Legal Rights; Unitarian Universalism: A Religious Home for Bisexual, Gay, Lesbian and Transgender People,* and much more. See the main UUA website, publications area. Readers must go to http://www.uua.org/leaders/idbm/bglt/index.shtml/ and follow instructions to request Bisexuality Curriculum there.

3. The Bisexuality Curriculum is downloadable as a pdf file from the Unitarian Universalists of America via the uua.org Website. It was conceived, written and designed by the Curriculum Team: Rev. Jane Dwinell, Dana Dwinell-Yardley, Allyson Diane Hamm, Scott McNeill, the Rev. Amy Zucker Morganstern, and The Rev. Ann Schranz.

4. I did not do a formal survey of all religious education in the United States in this regard. I did do a quick and dirty informal survey, as evidenced by the information and resources listed here.

5. See the excellent listings on Debra Haffner's site, (http://www.religiousinstitute.org), in this regard.

6. Apologies for not pursuing the United Church of Christ (UCC) side of this story more fully. I would love to hear more from those who know its history.

7. The Klein grid, as developed by Dr. Fritz Klein in his 1993 book, *The Bisexual Option*, and often reprinted in sexuality education classes. The grid is available at the American Institute of Bisexuality's Website, http://www.bisexual.org/kleingrid.html.

8. Note: of course the limitations of recommending this sort of panel presentation means expecting the local group to have access to a variety of individuals with different relationship styles and identities whom they can draw upon to come speak to the class. Not every community has this variety of resources readily at hand.

REFERENCES

Burrill, M. (2009). *All God's children: Teaching children about sexual orientation and gender diversity*. Fort Wayne, IN: Life Quest, Christian Community, Inc.

Interweave Continental: Unitarian Universalists for Bisexual, Gay, Lesbian and Transgender Concerns. (n.d.). Available at: http://www.interweavecontinental.org

Klein, F., & Reinhardt, R. (1993). *The bisexual option*. New York: Haworth.

Office of Bisexual, Gay, Lesbian and Transgender Concerns of the UUA. (n.d.). Available at: http://www.uua.org/obgltc

Palmer, T., & Haffner, D. W. (2009). *A time to seek: Study guide on sexual and gender diversity*. Norwalk, CT: Religious Institute for Sexual Morality, Justice and Healing.

Welcoming Congregation Program. (n.d.). Available at: http://www.uua.org/members/justicediversity/bisexualgay/index.shtml

Living with Dual Spirits: Spirituality, Sexuality and Healing in the African Diaspora

IFALADE TA'SHIA ASANTI

"Living with Dual Spirits" is adapted from the author's historic presentation at the 2006 Conference on Indigenous African Spiritual Traditions, Worldview, Family & Community Empowerment, Ritual, and Practice at Teachers College, Columbia University, in 2006. It sets same-gender sexual relationships and practices among people of African descent in a context of a dual or twin spiritedness that leaves room for heterosexual relationships/practices as well. The examples and concepts cited from African history challenge prevailing arguments within Black Nationalist and cultural-Nationalist discourses, arguments which have been antagonistic to or critical of homosexual or bisexual sexuality among Black people in the past. The author diverges from many of her peers and predecessors to assert that same-sex and bisexual practices among African people are integral to the cultures and histories discussed, not outwardly imposed or imported.

INTRODUCTION

As a result of the sexually repressive climate in Africa, caused to a great degree by the rape, enslavement and colonization of African people, sexuality, in the context of the indigenous African experience, is a rarely explored topic. Subsequently, as a result of the spiritual and religious colonization of the descendents of Africa living in America, we find a great deal of shame, guilt, secrecy and repression among Black Americans in the area of sexual expression.

Today we explore sexuality in the context of indigenous life, culture and spirituality in Africa in a nonoppressed and precolonized environment. We also explore briefly, the challenges experienced while embracing one's sexual identity as a person of African descent through the lens of mainstream (White) gay and lesbian culture in America.

Finally, "Living with Dual Spirits" explores the cultural, spiritual and ritual experiences of those who identify as Black and same-gender loving bisexual transgender (SGLBT) in the context of life in America and in indigenous (ancient) Africa and how the healing and affirming of SGLBT people of African descent is a vital part of the healing and empowerment of African people as a whole. I loosely define SGLBT identity as, "One who has a male or female gender at birth but whose life expression may overshadow or even dominate the gender identity assigned to them by Western society and/or one who is born with a natural ability to mate and share love/healing with the opposite gender and those of the same gender."

Not Gay, Not Lesbian

We begin in America surveying the social and cultural values of the mainstream lesbian and gay community. Institutionally, we also evaluate the capacity of the mainstream gay and lesbian community to support, empower and affirm people of African descent who are moving through what is commonly called the 'coming out' phase, that is, the period when one begins to recognize and embrace their sexual/gender identity.

As the descendents of Africa living in America and Africa move through the challenges of embracing their sexual and gender identity, support from the community at-large, from religious and cultural institutions, and community-based organizations becomes imperative in how well they navigate this often bumpy terrain. The cultural relevance of services and support are what I speak of here, and the understanding that White gays and lesbians do not, as a majority, face the same levels or brand of oppression economically, politically or socially as SGLBT people of color and African descent.

Presently, for most Black/African SGLBT individuals, there is a cultural disconnect that occurs as they are forced to matriculate into a class and community that does not understand the cultural challenges they face. Add to this the fact that gay Whites have an automatic chance at a certain quality of life based on their ability to obtain advanced education and/or to move through various levels of professional development, unlike their SGLBT African American, Native Indigenous and Latino counterparts whose quality of life is deeply affected by racism and White supremacy.

Embracing 'gayness' supports the illusion of acceptance, affirmation and success into what has become its own mainstream society of predominantly White men and women who again, for the most part, have access to a lifestyle not automatically given to Blacks/Africans. Although some Blacks adopt the gay label and culture as part of their identity, it does not erase their identity or their plight as people of African descent. Nor does it prepare them to navigate through a culture (gay and nongay) that oppresses them on multiple levels because of their sexual or gender identity and the color of their skin.

It is imperative that those who provide services and support to SGLBT communities receive cultural competency training to effectively serve culturally diverse SGLBT communities. It is equally important that international SGLBT organizations understand the cultural and religious implications of the gay and lesbian identity in indigenous African culture and the impact of religious colonization in Africa on diverse expressions of sexuality.

It is also critical—and I explain more later—that individuals and organizations understand the impact slavery had on the sexual development and sexual affirmation of Africans and their descendents living in America in regards to providing culturally relevant services to SGLBT people of African descent.

Africa's Sexual Liberation and Reclamation

Prior the advent of 'gay' culture and the religious colonization of Africa and other indigenous nations, there was no segregated movement made of up 'lesbians and gay' people. Although homophobia arrived on America's shores with 18th and 19th-century slave owners and missionaries, divisions between heterosexual and SGLBT people in early Black American families and communities did not exist. To survive the constructs of slavery, there was an unspoken solidarity among Blacks. Unfortunately, as slavery was abolished, so was racial solidarity based on ethnic identity and cultural struggles.

As the context of slavery changed, prejudice and discrimination among Blacks was introduced. It began with external dividers such as skin color, hair texture and facial features, and later, plantation status, education, economics, religion and sexual identity became factors in the socioeconomic divisions among people of African descent.

On the other side of the table, we have concrete evidence of the cherishing of diversity in indigenous African societies. Historical research documents reveal ritual, spiritual and cultural names that were systematically assigned to individuals who self-identified as SGLBT. Names were based on human characteristics, personality effects and physical attributes as is common in indigenous societies (Murray & Roscoe, 1998, pp. 279–282).

In addition, indigenous Africans clearly recognized the spiritual role of a man born with feminine energy and a woman born with male energy. Thus, sometimes, the names for same-gender loving, bisexual and transgender Africans were distinguished 'titles' based often on a particular spiritual gift or power that a person was imbued with because of their dual spirited nature.

In *Boy Wives and Female Husbands: Studies of African Homosexualities,* scholars Stephen Murray and Will Roscoe referred to hundreds of African tribes with names and titles for same-gender loving, bisexual and transgender people that were documented through a decade of their research. Here are a few examples. The Ambo-Quambo call bisexual people *kimbanda*, which means, "two-spirited diviners with sacred spiritual knowledge." The Amhara called female African homosexuals *wande-wande*, which means "woman with masculine energy." The Dahomey Fon (Republic of Benin) from Niger/Congo called SGLBT individuals *gaglgo*, that is, person with soul that has two genders. In Mombasa, the Bantus gave bisexual men and women the title *mwaami*, which means "sacred two-spirited prophet.' And among the Zulu, same-gender loving women are called *inkosi-ygbatfazi*, which means "chief of the women." In Nigeria, among the Yoruba, there is the revered Goddess deity *Olokun* (pronounced Oh-low-koon) who is often identified as a hermaphrodite (Conner & Sparks, 2004, p. 73).

Although many would assert that African culture has no place for such people, these ancient names and esteemed titles were formerly and historically assigned to same-gender loving, bisexual and transgender people. This truth is documented throughout history, in language and culture. This is not the history or language of yesterday, but of thousands, perhaps millions of years ago. We find, too, that in African American blended families and in indigenous African societies, SGLBT people have dual spiritual purposes and reasons for being. The journey to embracing a life of expressing love from dual spiritual positions is as diverse as it is unique.

Some become same-gender loving, bisexual, or transgender, as a result of traumatic experiences, natural curiosity and opportunity. Others are born with a nature that demands they acknowledge their inherent SGLBT self, as not to acknowledge this sacred self would be to commit psychological and spiritual suicide. This crisis is revealed in the suicide rates of African and African American same-gender loving individuals who force themselves to fit into colonized ideas and images of family introduced during and after the Maafa (slavery).[1] There are a myriad of ways in which same-gender loving; bisexual and transgender people function in African communal and ritual settings. In indigenous Africa, a man with several wives could have two wives who form a bond on emotional, spiritual and even sexual levels (Murray & Roscoe, 1998, p. 234).

What we find interesting here is that in a culture without Western influences and pressures stemming from religious and social oppression, even when communal living includes sexual or romantic relationships between two women or two men, wives and husbands retain the importance of sustaining and supporting the collective family. In other words, families who define themselves for themselves stay together. It seems that this is the foundation of what we know as a new, growing trend of 'blended families' in American culture. We also see that in indigenous culture, when such a bond is recognized as human nature, there is no need to label it, or for that person to leave, that is, 'come out' to embrace who they are. They simply merge their being with the essence of their soul. One would have to assume that the shaming and condemnation of individuals who embrace their sexual identity is learned behavior, as the oppression of nature—nature expressed as sexual identity—is not a part of indigenous African culture. Consequently, the roots of sexual oppression are traced back to Western Christianity as tactics to maintain social, religious and gender control.

The Path to Healing

As we survey the social and psychological crisis among Africans living in America, we find a critical gap in our healing and unification. We as Africans in America have not created enough safe spaces for SGLBT Africans to heal and be healed and have thus pushed them to seek healing from communities who are often ill equipped to respond to their cultural, psychological and spiritual needs.

We must explore the perceptions of SGLBT people of African descent that derive from Western influences on the accepted constructs of what defines Black/African, 'family' life. Given the fact that SGLBT people of African descent are our sons and daughters, sisters and brothers, mothers and fathers, grandmothers and grandfathers, they, like us, occupy sacred and spiritual roles in the African family and global society. To abandon, vilify and reject them is to abandon, vilify and reject ourselves.

In fulfilling this exploration, we absolutely must also explore gender roles impressed upon African people by Westernized societies. In uncolonized African and other indigenous societies, assigned gender roles are interchangeable and in some regions, were nonexistent.[2] In many African indigenous societies, particularly ancient African and other indigenous societies, two men can dance together, wear female-identified facial and body decorations for ritual purposes, dress in female gender-identified clothing and share intimate and sometimes sexual interactions with members of the same sex. Women often took on the role of the patriarch, leading large sectors of male communities.

However, again, in ancient indigenous societies, there was an inherent understanding of the importance of sustaining the family. Thus, SGLBT men and women would often procreate and/or become primary providers and caretakers for their family, as they do in American society every day. In indigenous Africa, if men or women were not set to procreate (due to biological limitations), they almost always found a sacred role within the community to fulfill their spiritual directives. Males and females could become a healer, initiator, medicine maker, midwife, first wife, village caretaker, gatekeeper and other communal roles. These roles may or may not include sexual interaction based on the needs and values of the matriarch or patriarch heading that clan or family.

Debunking the Myths

There is a social myth that SGLBT people are non-African by nature, that their very presence is a threat to the African communal structure and the Black family. Although we ignore the real threats—threats such as religious oppression, domestic violence, sexual abuse (rape, incest), HIV/AIDS, cancer, diabetes and heart disease, illiteracy, poverty, gang violence—the Black community, as well as indigenous African communities continue to be divided and victimized. Our communities remain paralyzed, incapable of authentic restoration, redemption and healing.

In actuality, millions of SGLBT people of African descent are biological parents. Many times it is they who are the primary and/or independent caretakers of their own children, and often other people's children, including children who have been abandoned by heterosexual parents. However, we don't want to talk about that. SGLBT people of African descent are also often the caretakers of the elders and are major benefactors in sustaining the Black community/family as a whole. There is a great spiritual debt owed to SGLBT Blacks, many of whom have sacrificed their entire lives to the movement for Black empowerment only to be ostracized and abandoned because of their spiritual incarnation as SGLBT.

Where do SGLBT people of African descent fit into the spiritual scheme of things, culturally speaking? Some well-meaning Nationalists and Pan Afrikanists say nowhere. Consciously or unconsciously, influenced by falsely interpreted teachings of Christianity or Islam, some Black activists commit acts of psychological and spiritual violence against SGLBT individuals in the name of Black power. Most are blind to the source of their inherent disdain for individuals who have been sustainers in the movement for Black healing and African unity for eons.

We must come to know and understand our brothers and sisters whose spirit and being was and is acknowledged as uniquely sacred by our ancestors. We must make amends to those we have harmed by our ignorance. Our inherent sexual sacredness as Africans, our ancient spiritual perspectives—though tainted by colonization—is something we must reembrace if we are to facilitate our greater healing spiritually and otherwise.

Our Spiritual Revival

First and foremost, to heal our sexual selves, to revive and revitalize the movement for Black/African empowerment through our spirituality, we must acknowledge and embrace several powerful truths and take action on these truths as if our lives depend on it.

1. We must commit ourselves to the unification of our global African family by any means necessary, leaving no African out of the equation.
2. We must view every African as important to the healing of our nation and not allow our differences to divide us and dilute the power of our movement.
3. We must prioritize the issues we spend our time addressing based on each issue's level of destructiveness to our community.
4. We must recognize the spiritual and ritual roles of SGLBT Africans in ancient Africa as they manifest in SGLBT people of African descent in modern society.
5. We must access our potential for global healing using history, ritual and spiritual duality as an indispensable piece of our foundation.
6. We must facilitate regular, healthy, civil dialogues between SGLBT and heterosexual people of African descent.
7. We must foster and sustain a movement for healing and reconciliation among people of African descent and their allies.

Through knowledge and education, through tapping into the wisdom of our ancestors, we can establish bridges that will allow us to work with and among communities where traditionally, SGLBT people of African descent are rejected based on Western ideals and notions. We must address issues such as "preserving the sanctity of marriage" and the belief that homosexuality is 'immoral' or that it interferes with the sustaining of the Black family. On the contrary, African people loving African people has always sustained the African family; why would it change because the genders of the players change?

Finally, we must gather our sisters and brothers and talk candidly about this so-called immoral sexual behavior that "destroys the Black family." In fact, we need to talk about all immoral behavior, sexual and otherwise, that destroys the Black family including infidelity, incest, sexual abuse, rape, alcoholism and domestic violence according to each issue's level of destructiveness.

Christian doctrine outlines immoral sexual behavior primarily as sex outside of the institution of marriage, having sex outside of the goal to procreate, sex that involves oral copulation, sex that forces marriages to end due to infidelity. I submit: are these so-called immoral acts restricted to SGLBT relationships and communities? We're getting honest here. We must admit the truth if we are to heal. Heterosexually identified individuals participate in these behaviors on a mass scale, yet they are an accepted part of Christian, African, Pan African and Nationalist movements.

If we are to base our rejection of African SGLBT people on these ideals, we must go beneath their surface to the overall goal of the promoters. As painful as it might be, we must explore the constructs of Christianity as the predominant religion and the early missives of gender control and domination behind this movement.

We must too, explore the role that the Christian faith played in spiritually and physically enslaving indigenous nations. Africans were systematically taught by Christian missionaries to relinquish the honor, recognition, belief and faith in Gods of African descent and to end any ritual practices that connected one to their indigenous African heritage. Is this the spiritual basis upon which we condemn our SGLBT African brothers and sisters?

I reference the writing of scholar and cultural healer, Malidoma Somé, a heterosexual Dagara man who is currently completing a book called *The Gift of the Gatekeepers*, which chronicles the presence of SGLBT people in African culture and their sacred role in African societies. I had the honor and privilege of interviewing Dr. Somé, whose teachings as a Dagara man echo the sentiments in this essay. As Dr. Somé writes about indigenous African life among the Dagara, he speaks of a people who were considered some of the most sacred human beings on earth. In the Dagara tribe these people were known as the 'gatekeepers,' the ones selected by God to spiritually protect the community through ritual magic given to them by the ancestors as a result of their dual-spirited human manifestation. Not only were the gatekeepers venerated and celebrated as an important part of the African cultural and spiritual landscape, they were viewed as vital to the well-being of the entire community.

Our history as African people—our true history—is one of the most intelligent and powerful weapons we have at our disposal. Our sexuality, our inherent sexual power, is deeply connected to our spirituality through the essence of our being. Indigenous leaders understood this and subsequently honored the natural manifestation of spirit beyond the visual and mental constructs of societal limitations of human life. If we are to truly understand the spiritual power of who and what we have been born as, and into in this life, we must move beyond what we see visually to what exists spiritually within each human being, the Ori—our inherent spiritual and sexual identity given at birth.

A New Spirituality

I once heard someone say that religion is about the day we die and whether we will go to heaven or hell, and that spirituality is about what we do with our time now, the days in front of us. As an initiated Orisa/Ifa priestess, as a sacred embodiment of our ancestor's legacy, history and traditions, I have been called to do the work of reeducating, restoring, healing and empowering the African community. I am called to do this work in the body and in the spirit of a Black/African, mother, grandmother, daughter, teacher, seer and two-spirited woman who loves and heals African men, and also has the power to heal and love African women (and other conscious people).

I have come to learn over the years that my work is and must be bigger than my sexuality, my gender or my race. My vision is, and must be, larger than any connection to sex or sexuality. Neither my body, my ethnicity nor my birth gender can limit my span of healing. And so I say again that we must come to know our sexuality for what it is—a sacred part of us that expresses a part of the divine spiritual force inside of us. We must come to see our spirituality and our sexuality as a tool to heal and empower ourselves and others.

This work is about reclaiming our stolen history and spiritual legacy. This work is also about our looking at the religious beliefs and spiritual values that we may have become attached to simply because they were all that was there, because it is what our parents or loved ones believed and taught us to believe. There are many who thirst for spiritual authenticity. But there are many of us who are too wounded and attached to what was passed down to us to receive a message and medicine that might authentically liberate us.

If we allow each other to find the individual paths that lead to our collective empowerment we will be able to effectively do our work from a unified front. This healing may take a lifetime. May this presentation be a start. We must remain open to experience love, reconciliation, understanding and healing on deeper and deeper levels as African people. This healing is in fact, the essence of African spirituality. *Ase. Ase. Ase-o!*

NOTES

1. http://www.youtube.com/watch?v=c4t2ZIICSQ0, http://www.youtube.com/watch?v=Tn252Y22Zq0, and http://www.youtube.com/watch?v=LM8wlEyZeKA
2. Stereotyping Women in Ancient African and Roman Society http://www2.ulg.ac.be/vinitor/rida/2000/vanniekerk.pdf

REFERENCES

Conner, R. P., & Sparks, D. (2004). *Queering Creole spiritual traditions: Lesbian, gay, bisexual and transgender participation in African inspired traditions in the Americas*. Binghamton, NY: Haworth Press.

Murray, S., & Roscoe, W. (1998). *Boy wives and female husbands: Studies in African homosexualities*. New York: Palgrave MacMillan.

Bodeme in Harlem: An African Diasporic Autoethnography

H. SHARIF WILLIAMS

Black Funk: The Center for Culture, Sexuality, and Spirituality, Brooklyn, New York, USA

This autoethnography describes the author's experience in a learning community of people of the African diaspora[1] *in New York City engaged in studying the cosmology, cosmogony, ritual, talismanic magic, oracle divination and principles of ecological well-being of the Dagara people under the tutelage of Dr. Malidoma Patrice Somé. The author uses the chronicle of the experience to critically examine the discourses on* bodeme *or gatekeeper, a Dagara concept that has implications for understanding bisexuality, polyamory and genderqueer embodiment from an African perspective.*

"Can you talk to us about the role of *gatekeepers* in Dagara society?" The man—seated in a chair at the center of the opening of a horseshoe-shaped gathering of rectangular tables and benches in the cafeteria of a public elementary school—paused to inhale before making his response to my question. We, approximately 80 members of the African diaspora, filled those benches listening with great interest. Those of us who read his comments and those of his ex-wife on the topic of gatekeepers also inhaled—hoping that his answer would allow us to exhale lifetimes of questions, confusion and/or marginalization.

I had been waiting the several months of organizing the training sessions to ask Malidoma the question. During those months, I spoke to Malidoma once. One of his students, a Jewish White man, had been helping us to make the training a reality. He called Malidoma during one of the steering committee meetings so that we who had volunteered to work on the committee could speak to the man that we would bring to Harlem, USA (also known as Harlem, New York) and, finally, to Black people, Dr. Malidoma Patrice Somé—Malidoma as those of us who have worked with him call him.

For decades, Malidoma has worked with people in Europe and the United States to share the wisdom tradition of the Dagara people of West Africa. He has facilitated workshops, trainings and other events in which people learn Dagara cosmology, cosmogony, ritual, talismanic magic, oracle divination and principles of ecological well-being. He has authored several books including an autobiography that details the story of his abduction and abuse at the hands of European missionaries when he was a child. The men's movement in the United States, largely White, middle class and male, embraced Malidoma early in his career as an indigenous knowledge teacher, oftentimes booking him with Robert Bly and Michael Meade at the same event. Sobonfu Somé, Malidoma's former wife, has worked similarly and presented ideas consistent with an Africana womanist perspective in which the lives of all members of the community, including women, are forefront in the discussion of community health (Hudson-Weems, 2004).

After a couple of years of attempts to contact Malidoma personally, I had the opportunity not just to train with him but to co-organize the first series of training sessions for Malidoma with a group comprising exclusively people of the African diaspora. In my previous attempts, I would make contact with someone, with one exception always White, who had worked with Malidoma and who charged themselves with vetting me before they would help me in any way to contact him. They acted as station agents who would not permit me passage unless I proved my credentials. Eventually, I gave up my attempts to make contact with Malidoma. When the opportunity to help organize the training sessions appeared, I saw it as an example of the prerogative of spirit trumping the prerogatives of petty people.

The night of the first training session, as we sat around Malidoma, I decided to ask the question, "Can you talk to us about the role of *gatekeepers* in Dagara society?" I had read everything I could find about the concept of gatekeepers. Malidoma and Sobonfu had made statements about people who they referred to as gatekeepers in Dagara culture.

> The whole notion of "gay" does not exist in the indigenous world. That does not mean that there are not people there who feel the way that certain people feel in this culture, that has led to them being referred to as "gay."
> The reason why I'm saying there are no such people is because the gay person is very well integrated into the community, with the functions that delete this whole sexual differentiation of him or her. The gay person is looked at primarily as a "gatekeeper." The Earth is looked at, from my tribal perspective, as a very, very delicate machine or consciousness, with high vibrational points, which certain people must be guardians of

> in order for the tribe to keep its continuity with the gods and with the spirits that dwell there. Spirits of this world and spirits of the other worlds. Any person who is at this link between this world and the other world experiences a state of vibrational consciousness which is far higher, and far different, from the one that a normal person would experience. (M. Somé in Hoff, 1993, n.p.)

> There are many gates that link a village to other worlds. The only people who have access to all these gates are the gatekeepers.
> They are not only in contact with the elemental gates, but also with many others. They have one foot in all the other worlds and the other foot here. This is why the vibration of their body is totally different from others. They also have access to other-dimensional beings such as the *kontombile*, small beings who are very magical and knowledgeable.
> Gatekeepers are encouraged to fulfill the role they're born to, to use their gifts in the interests of the community. (Somé, 2003, n.p.)

I wanted to learn more about them for a couple of reasons. I was in the midst of my doctoral studies and had intended to explore the concept in some way for my dissertation. I also felt personally drawn to the concept based upon my spiritual, sexual and cultural experiences. One of my main reasons for wanting to participate in the training was the opportunity to have a discussion with either Malidoma or Sobonfu on the topic. I finally had the opportunity so I took it with some awareness of the potential impact this would have in the context of the particular group assembled—people of the African diaspora. "Can you talk to us about the role of gatekeepers in Dagara society?" But I was not and could not be fully aware of the ramifications of having this conversation in this context. Malidoma was also not aware, having not worked with a group of people of the African diaspora previously.

The academic literature on attitudes of Black people toward same-sex sexual practice and homosexuality provides some context for predicting the impact of the question and its answer (Lemelle, 2004; Lewis, 2003; Negy, 2005; Schulte, 2004; Stokes & Peterson, 1998; Waldner, Sikka, & Baig, 1999). In a recent study, 228 people identified as African American lesbian, gay, bisexual, transgender (LGBT) folks (4% of whom indicated they immigrated to the United States) were surveyed about their experiences (Human Rights Campaign Foundation [HRCF], 2009). Sixty-two percent of those surveyed indicated that they had experienced having their sexuality or gender expression condemned as sinful a lot or to some lesser degree within their cultural community. Fifty-three percent indicated that they had experienced discrimination based upon their sexuality or gender expression a lot or to some lesser degree in their cultural community. Those statistics are complicated by the 66% of the survey respondents who also indicated that they experienced being treated like any other member of their cultural community a lot or some of the time.

Because I grew up and lived in them all my life, I, probably more than Malidoma who had lived among Europeans and Whites for most of his life, was aware of the presence and role of homophobia/hatred, heterosexism, and sexism in Black communities in the United States. However, in my positionality[2] in the group as one of the members of the steering committee, a doctoral student working in the area of sexuality and spirituality, and my previous training as a traditional African spiritualist/shaman, I wasn't concerned about any potential heterosexist backlash. I wanted to have the conversation and have it in a way that contextualized the work we would be doing in Dagara indigenous knowledge and wisdom tradition.

"Can you talk to us about the role of gatekeepers in Dagara society?" Malidoma began to respond to the question in the way he responded to it in the published material on the topic (see the above quote). As he spoke, I took in the room. Some heads unflinchingly remained steady with eyes focused on him and away from the other listeners in the space. Others attempted subtle surveillance of the room—eyes seeking to connect with the knowing eyes of another for mutual acknowledgement of the significance of Malidoma's words. The topic wasn't on the agenda for our training; but there it was, appearing in the moment for our collective consideration.

In his answer, he used the Dagara word—*bodeme*—in addition to the English word *gatekeepers*, which he had been using previously. But then he did something that he purported he had not done in any of his previous trainings—he called those of us who identified with the concept to stand up, literally. He stated that because we had begun the training with the discussion it made sense for us to take our rightful place in the rituals and spiritual work of the group. People began to look at each other. "What is he talking about?" "Who is he talking about?" A few folks began to stand up—to claim *bodeme* identity. I was one of the early risers. I looked around the room to see who else had stood or might stand.

Until that point, I hadn't cruised[3] the room as I would in a LGBT- or queer-identified space. In those spaces, I usually looked around to see who I found attractive, who may have found me attractive, or who I might have shared a mutual attraction. I had been socialized to take an erotic environmental scan of such spaces. However, in Black community spaces, I had been socialized to show up in a different way. In Black community, I had learned to be useful, making myself available to the community for whatever I could provide or offer. I hadn't been in a Black community space in which LGBT or queer themes were a part of the discussion.

Consequently, I was surprised when I saw a number of the men and women in the room stand as I had. In a room of approximately 80 people, roughly 10 men and 2 women stood up to claim *bodeme* identity including one of the other co-organizers and one of Malidoma's assistants, an African Canadian woman. Malidoma indicated that *bodeme* play special roles during Dagara ritual, and we, those of us who stood up, would fulfill those roles during the training sessions. But he also said that he could not tell us everything about what it meant to be *bodeme* because he was not *bodeme* and *bodeme* were notoriously secretive in Dagaraland; only *bodeme* knew the inner workings of the *bodeme* society. He agreed to tell us what he knew about *bodeme* and encouraged us to look within our individual and collective selves for further answers.

We would have to discover and create what it meant to be *bodeme* in the diaspora—relying upon Malidoma's sharing and our own intuitions. The training sessions would become a great context for that process. I would have the opportunity to learn, in a very intimate way, the challenges and benefits of adopting—from within the Pan-African world—a cultural resource outside of its specific ecological and cultural context and using it in a different ecological and cultural context.

As a training group, we would work together for a year—meeting in New York City or Upstate New York on weekends to learn about and then engage in Dagara rituals associated with each of the five elements of the Dagara medicine wheel: water, fire, earth, mineral and nature. Friday evenings would usually be the gathering time. Malidoma would share information we needed in preparation for the ritual or talismanic work the next day. Saturdays would be the day of the ritual or talismanic work. Sundays would be debriefing time.

We would learn and practice talismanic medicine, that is, the use of a combination of organic material, spiritual energy and incantation to produce effects on the spiritual and material realms. We would learn and practice the ancestralization of the deceased, that is, the rituals involved in helping a deceased member of one's earth community to become a member of the ancestor community. We would become a ritualizing, learning community.

Ritual space has physical boundaries and topographies. In reflecting upon ritual, Somé (1993) stated:

> We call spirits into a circle of people in order to help achieve goals that cannot be achieved in any other way. This calling needs to remain in safe containment, the way a baby remains hidden prior to being born. Safe containment means keeping the space away from any impurities, any unwanted intrusions. (p. 38)

One of the easily identifiable roles of the *bodeme* were during ritual—creating the boundaries of ritual space and protecting, opening and closing the gates of ritual space. In effect, *bodeme* were responsible for creating the container for ritual to take place.[4] With each ritual process—preparing for ritual, creating the ritual space, performing ritual and practicing ritual after-care—the *bodeme* became more confident and assertive in meeting their responsibilities.

One of the main challenges to and benefits of our adoption of the *bodeme* concept was that the concept was rooted in an ontological and axiological framework with which we had become unaccustomed. Rather immediately we began to apply our ontological and axiological frames—cultivated in the diasporic experience—to the concept of *bodeme*, a cultural resource cultivated in a continental African experience among the Dagara people. We were engaged in learning and reformulating. As we learned and tried on the new clothes of the concept within the training sessions as well as out in the world, we were necessarily reformulating what *bodeme* meant by being *bodeme* in a world and context that was radically different than its origins.

The *bodeme* concept was not the only thing that was unfamiliar to us. We were also dealing with the lack of familiarity among us as a group. We were not a village community that had shared generations of daily connection and relationship. Although a number of us had known each other previously through other organizations, events or processes, for the most part, we were strangers to each other before coming to the training. We were members of a learning community with a very recent history. Therefore, we did not have the history of shared intimacy and familiarity to help us work out at the interpersonal level the challenges we were all facing on the level of deep culture in integrating the *bodeme* concept into our worldview as learning community of diasporic Africans.

The participants in the training group who did not identify with the *bodeme* identity began to perceive the establishment of a dichotomous hierarchy within the group, *bodeme* and non *bodeme*. "Who are these folks and why are they taking over?" "There sure are a lot of gays and lesbians in this process." No one would ask about bisexuals because, in my experience, in Black community in the United States if you engage in any form of same-sex sexuality you are homosexual—it's our sexual equivalent of the one-drop rule for racial identity in the United States.[5] Tensions developed. The association of a spiritual concept with any form of sexuality, but particularly same-sex sexual practice, was a first for many members of the group. The concept was in direct conflict with the internalized heterosexism that many members of the group experienced. Simultaneously, it provided other members of the group—those who experienced same-sex desire—with a sense of belonging, purpose, and an identity consistent with an African axiology.

hooks (1994) said, "I came to theory desperate, wanting to comprehend—to grasp what was happening around and within me. I saw in theory then a location for healing" (p. 59). For theory to have the healing possibilities that hooks articulates we must have conceptual clarity when engaging, applying and performing theory. In articulating the *bodeme* concept, previous authors have contributed to a reading of the concept that positions the sexuality of *bodeme* as homosexual. Yet a closer reading of the description of *bodeme* sexuality yields a different understanding—a bisexual formation of sexual relations in which *bodeme* have heterosexual family relations and homosexual spiritual relations.

Hoff (1993) began the misreading by failing to use an African ontological and axiological framework in titling his publication *Gays: Guardians at the Gates*—opting instead for the Eurocentric term *gay* given his primary audience—White men. In choosing this title, he contradicted a significant part of the content of his interview with Malidoma—ignoring Malidoma's statement, "The whole notion of 'gay' does not exist in the indigenous world." Malidoma helped Hoff (and the rest of us) in the misreading by his use of the terms *gay* and *homosexual* in the interview. Sobonfu also aided the misreading in titling a section of her book in which she discusses *bodeme*, *Homosexuality: The Gatekeepers* (2003). The title created a compelling frame for reading the section even though she opened the section with, "The words 'gay' and 'lesbian' do not exist in the village."

I believe Malidoma's and Sonbonfu's contribution to the misinterpretation of *bodeme* sexuality in the West is a consequence of the exuberance of compassionate teachers who want to share with a spiritually starving Western world the spirit food of their nation and the structural pitfalls of attempting to take a cultural product outside of its ecosystem to use in a different ecosystem—indigenous meanings get lost in translation. I am mindful that the term *gatekeeper* in certain cultural contexts in the United States is a pejorative word for people who stand in the way of someone's access or progress like the Whites who initially prevented me from meeting Malidoma. Their gatekeeping was very different, in intention and quality, than the gatekeeping Malidoma and Sobonfu discuss as the *bodeme* spiritual function in community. However, the use of the word *gatekeeper* can draw forth in an audience meanings intended and unintended by the speaker.

Of course, the English words *gay* and *lesbian* do not exist in Dagara villages in which the local language or the language of the colonizers, French, is spoken. Equally conceivable yet contested is the idea that the sexual identity categories *gay* and *lesbian* have not existed in Dagara villages, at least not prior to the modern era. I agree with Altman (2001), "The ideas of 'gay/lesbian' as a sociological category is only about one hundred years old, and its [existence and] survival even in Western developed countries cannot be taken for granted" (p. 22).

Likewise, the existence of the concept and sexual identity category *bisexuality* in Dagara villages should not be taken for granted either. Bisexuality, as it is often articulated in the West, is similarly problematic as a frame for understanding non-Western sexual cultural practices because of its ontological and axiological roots in European or Eurocentric worldviews. However, if we carefully read the existing literature on *bodeme*, we see dynamics that are far closer to what could be called—in the West—a bisexual formation of sexual relations in which *bodeme* have heterosexual family relations and homosexual spiritual relations.

In Hoff (1993), Malidoma spoke about the heterosexual family relations and same-sex desire of *bodeme*:

> How I got to know that they were gay was because on arriving in this country and seeing the serious issues surrounding gay people, I began to wonder it does not exist in my own country. When I asked one of them, who tad (sic) taken me to the threshold of the Otherworld, whether he feels sexual attraction towards another man, he jumped back and said, "How do you know that?!" He said, "This is *our* business as gatekeepers." And, yet he had a wife and children—no problem, you see. (n.p.)

We, in the United States, would be quick to label this configuration of sexuality *down low* or with the, more clinical, public health terminology *BMSMW* (black men who have sex with men and women). However, we would be wrong for doing so. We would be making the mistake of applying our cultural frame of reference to a cultural product that does not fit within that framework. In Somé (2003), Sobonfu cautioned Westerners about misreading the nature of being *bodeme*:

> They need to understand that in the village, a person doesn't become a gatekeeper because they desire power, or even because of a sense of sexual orientation. No. Gatekeeping is part of one's life purpose, announced before birth and developed through rigorous training to ensure that its power is not misused. A gatekeeper is responsible for a whole village, a whole tribe. It is no game. (n.p.)

In our learning community in Harlem, we collectively struggled with the meaning of and purpose for *bodeme*. In his attempt to translate the concept in his sharing it with us, Malidoma used Western concepts with which he was familiar. He pulled from his understanding of our conceptual universe and spoke about gays and lesbians in his discussion of *bodeme*—even though his own description of *bodeme* has not coincided with gay and lesbian identity in the West.

For the most part in the West, people who identify as gay and lesbian have homosexual relationships in the context of a heterosocial society (i.e., a society in which the genders and sexes share social space more often than they are separated). In Dagara society, *bodeme* form heterosexual family relations through marriage and engage in homosexual sexual-spiritual practices in the context of a homosocial society (i.e., a society in which the genders and sexes more often do not share social space and are separate from each other). In Dagara culture, wives and husbands may not share the same sleeping quarters—sleeping instead with the children and other family members of their gender (Somé, 1995).

This difference in the configuration and organization of intimate social space is a significant difference between Western societies and certain non-Western societies including the Dagara. It challenges our Westernized understanding of what it means to live, love and have sex in the Dagara village. How would it feel to be a woman with a husband or man with a wife who you shared intimate time and space in the Dagara form? How would it feel to have homosocial intimate life in the way the Dagara have structured their world? Add to those considerations homosexual-spiritual practices of the *bodeme* and the complexity of what the *bodeme* concept becomes more evident. The theoretical and conceptual contributions of Africana womanism are equally, if not more, useful to understanding this phenomenology as the work of Eve Sedgwick (1985) who theorized the effect of homosocial desire on Western cultural thought and action. Africana womanism urges us to ground our understanding gender, sexuality and other human relations in the ontological and axiological frames of the African continent/diaspora and her peoples (Hudson-Weems, 2004). It is through such grounding that concepts such as *bodeme* become more understandable even as they remain unfamiliar and challenging to our Westernized sensibilities.

But what happens when our Westernized sensibilities fail us as African diasporians? One of our great challenges in conceptually assimilating *bodeme* consciousness and embodiment in the learning community was our Westernized sensibilities. Most of us, across sexualities, had internalized the discourses of the sexual cultures of the contemporary United States. We had come to understand sexuality through the binary of homosexuality and heterosexuality. We had come to attach meanings to nonheterosexuality that were cultural products of mainstream sexual discourse. Consequently, Malidoma's association of *bodeme* with gay and lesbian identity had the simultaneous effect of challenging internalized heterosexism and emboldening gay/lesbian identity in the learning community. Although the former effect could be considered a constructive form of decolonization, the latter effect, it could be argued, Africanized a Westernized form of sexual identity politics and discourse—thereby reinscribing a colonizing paradigm.

With few exceptions, our (Harlem) *bodeme* did not engage in heterosexual courtship or family relations that mirrored the heterosexual family relations of Dagara *bodeme*. The Harlem *bodeme*, again with few exceptions like me, continued to perform and practice the same homosexual sexual culture as Black gay and lesbian folks in New York City did. This is not surprising because there was no call to do anything differently in that regard. Our community roles and responsibilities were relegated to the performance of ritual—which were pretty significant and purposeful in and of themselves.

During the year, we—Harlem *bodeme*—met several times to talk about our experiences in taking on this new identity in the context of the learning community and the other communities in which we inhabited. We were a majority male group, and our communications were punctuated by the communication style of Black same-sex-attracted male pop culture: humor, *shade*, meaningful/less flirtation, skepticism, mutual suspicion and communal longing. *Shade* is a form of subtle communication developed in Black same-sex attracted male communities. Delany (1996) described *shade* thusly:

> It gives relief from the sun. And when one queen casts it at another—or at a straight heckler—it raises eyebrows and makes the corners of the lips twitch. You might say shade's a subtler form of dishing, a mode of repartee with a black accent whose connotations are more ironic and notably more nuanced than what's usually meant by the largely straight term "dis (as in the verb 'disrespect')." (p. xvii)

Our relationships with each other were complex and complicated. We carried the baggage of our previous learning of how to be with each other into our learning of how to be with each other in the context of the Dagara wisdom training. We strove to find new ways of engaging each other rooted in this new paradigm. We relied upon old ways of being when aspects of the relationship challenged us. This led to a number of experiences. Some of us, as they say in Harlem, fucked each other. Some of us, as we say in Black community, fucked each other over. We battled for position in leading group process or taking responsibility for working with the two leggeds or four leggeds during ritual. We also worked together to produce beautifully moving and profoundly meaningful ritual among our group and within the larger learning community. The following narrative is an example:

> One night, one of the Harlem *bodeme* and I were walking from Prospect Park in Brooklyn, N.Y., to my home at that time in Clinton Hill, Brooklyn, N.Y.. He was a member of the earth clan; me, a member of the fire clan. As we walked along DeKalb Avenue, I spotted a short Latino guy, roughly 25 years in age, looking at us. Initially, I wasn't sure if he was casually looking at us or cruising. I told my earth clan brother to slow down and stop by a nearby tree with me to see what would happen.
>
> Sure enough, the man crossed the street and approached us. We began talking. We exchanged names. As we talked, I began to feel/sense that we had been brought together for the purpose of engaging in a spiritual work; my sexual desire shifted to an erotic desire in which a spiritual purpose had emerged. I had had similar senses previously. It was because of those earlier experiences that I learned to be aware of what my inner knowing told me about the reason for my attraction to someone (Herukhuti, 2007). There was work to be done with this man—a healing—that would be for all of our benefits.
>
> He asked us where we were headed. We told him back to my place. He asked if he could come with us. In the supraconscious state that I had achieved during the conversation, I asked him what he wanted to happen between the three of us. He indicated he assumed we would have sex. I told him, "We could fuck, yes. But there's more to what this situation has to offer you than fucking. You can choose to see the two of

> us as two dudes who you can get with and that's it. Or you can choose to see the two of us as healers who have the ability to help you open up a space of healing for you. It's your choice but before we leave this tree you have to make a choice. You have to decide how you will see us from the moment we leave this spot." He chose healing.
> The three of us walked back to my place. I instructed my earth clan brother to wash the man—a regular wash with soap and water and a spiritual bath with sage smoke, what Native Americans call smudging, and a mixture of frankincense, myrrh, and sandalwood oils. While they were bathing, I prepared the space with sage smoke, lavender flower smoke, florida water, and ash that had been produced through the fires we used in ritual. Ash is very important to Dagara spirit medicine. We performed ritual for hours that night into the morning.

The young man and I kept in contact for a long time after that night. He was battling an addiction to drugs, homelessness, and his dependence on commercial sex for income. He participated in several more rituals with me, lived with me for short periods of time, and slept in my bed with me when he spent the night. We never had sex, even when he offered it as payment for my work with and treatment of him. We were intimate—spooning together as we slept or my caressing him and showing him affection. Eventually, I ended the relationship when I determined he was not ready to fully engage the healing process and free himself from the shackles that bound him to dependencies. There was nothing more I could do with him at that period in his life. I ended the relationship believing that all the seeds had been sown and he would harvest what he needed at some point in his life if it were the destiny of his present life incarnation. We each have our own journey to walk and can't do the walking for another.

My life during that period was full of growth and learning. I was involved in the learning community while also completing my doctoral dissertation. That first night with Malidoma I was living with a woman with whom I had been in a relationship for nearly 10 years, co-parenting two children she had from a previous relationship. A mere 3 months later, I ended the relationship and moved into my own apartment. Numerous forces converged to make it apparent to me that I needed to step outside of the nuclear family structure that she and I had achieved to claim a different way of being in the world. This different way of being wasn't primarily sexual. I had been bisexually active and polyamorous in the context of the relationship—that is, having sex with my primary partner and periodically having sex with others. The different way of being was in my spiritual and social practice. I needed my own (physical and psychic) space to be able to have the kinds of experiences I described above.

It was painful leaving behind two children, aged 13 and 16 at the time. Although I wanted to maintain the relationship with the children, their mother, and by extension the children, did not. I sacrificed my relationship with children I loved for my spiritual and sexual life in ways that I might not have had to do as a *bodeme* in a Dagara village—a homosocial community.

In my own place, I began to form intimate, spiritual relationships with men, women and trans folks inside and outside of the learning community. Some of those relationships were sexual, others were not. One such relationship was cultivated through working closely together on the logistics of the learning community. She and I were clan members. She teased me about my stuffy, "stank" attitude and gave me orders to complete this or that task. Initially, I was not fully aware of my attraction to her. I was being a *good brother* as I had learned how to be in Black community. This meant that I called her "sister" and did as she requested. In addition to several years older than I was, she was my sister and therefore deserved my respect. At this point in my development, I had not realized how my affinity for matriarchal social organization and being sexually dominated by women—as in the practice of bondage/discipline, domination/submission and sadism/masochism—complemented and fed each other.

Consequently there were a number of blinders to my perception that prevented me from acknowledging or at least being aware of the sexual attraction between us. Once I became aware of the mutual attraction, I had questions. Did I want to add a new variable—a sexual relationship with a member of the learning community—to the already complex, complicated and conflicted environment of the learning community? Did I want to start what I knew would be an intense emotional-spiritual-psychic-sexual relationship with a woman after just ending a 10-year emotionally intense relationship with a woman and regaining my capacity to be emotionally available to men? Could I achieve and maintain an erection with a woman again?

I pulled myself into a heterosexual dynamic as I attempted to make sense of my feelings in the relationship. Although I had counterhegemonic sensibilities, I could not completely escape the socialization of gender dynamics and politics between men and women that I had received as a member of a Black community in the United States. I began to place expectations upon myself as a man in the relationship that weren't necessary or consistent with my counterhegemonic sensibilities. I worked to resist this internalized script and to show up authentically in the relationship.

The fact that there were two other people from the learning community that were attracted to the two of us complicated the dynamic. We were not just working out the dynamics of heterosexual, homosexual and bisexual sexual practice but we were also working out the dynamics of polyamorous practice. Polyamory, the practice of experiencing erotic love with/among multiple people, has been ignored in the *bodeme*-focused discourse. If *bodeme*—among the Dagara—have heterosexual conjugal relationships and engage in sexual-spiritual practices with each other, polyamory might be an appropriate and useful frame to employ in discussing *bodeme*. To what degree is the absence of polyamory in the discussion a consequence of the hegemony that monogamy enjoys in heterosexual and homosexual discourses in the United States?

Another absence in *bodeme* discourses in the United States is the lack of critical engagement of the way in which the embodiment of *bodeme* can transgress, transverse and/or transform gender norms. Somé (2003) wrote:

> The gatekeepers stand on the threshold of the gender line. They are mediators between the two genders. They make sure that there is peace and balance between women and men. If the two genders are in conflict and the whole village is caught in it, the gatekeepers are the ones to bring peace. Gatekeepers do not take sides. They simply play the role of "the sword of truth and integrity." (n.p.)

In the West, we have used the terms *transgenderism* and *genderqueer* to label similar relationships with gender. Although there have been debates between the nuances and differences between transgender and genderqueer embodiment, I want to highlight the potential in them to transgress, transverse and/or transform gender norms. What does it mean to "stand at the threshold of the gender line" in the contemporary United States? Perhaps it means being transgender or genderqueer. We did not have anyone in the learning community who identified with these forms of embodiment until my godson-daughter joined us in several rituals.

He joined us, initially, for a water ritual that a group of us from the learning community gathered to perform at Indian Ladders Falls in the Delaware River Gap. I wanted to bring my work with him into a spiritual community context and expose him to the Dagara wisdom tradition. Our work together started as a result of my helping him develop a healthy relationship with the spirits that moved through and in him (Herukhuti, 2007). This was the first time he and I had conducted any spiritual work together in a communal setting. His ability to embody the energy of a female spirit was a potent and essential component to what happened during the water ritual. It was that ability which contributed to the locating of a water gate, a physical gateway to the wisdom of water, and our collective ability to open that gate for the purpose of the ritual.

In this context, an Indigenous conceptualization of what is in the West called transgender or genderqueer moves beyond just transgressing, transversing and/or transforming gender norms into a spiritual understanding. In Herukhuti (2007), I asserted:

> In fact, many indigenous peoples have creation stories in which original humankind was androgynous, i.e., both male and female. In these stories, the original or primordial humans were direct and complete representations of the Divine, an androgynous entity. As early human beings became more disconnected from their divine origins, androgyny represented a divine ideal that was out of the relative grasp of the average

> human being. Certain people are, however, touched by this spirit of our ancient past and blessed with the gift of androgyny or transgender. These members of our families carry important energies for our communities. They carry a form of energy from our primordial past and offer us a glimpse into a different kind of reality. (pp. 186–187)

In the water ritual, we were able to access, experience and see the work of that energy from our primordial past as it provided us access to the water gate and its wisdom.

As a result of the relationships and experiences I had in the learning community, I began to ask of and answer for myself a more important question than the one I posed to Malidoma that night in Harlem: "What is the role of *bodeme* in New York City society?" I continue to ask and answer that question each day as I live, love and learn in Black community as a *bodeme*. That work involves my effort to understand what *bodeme* means to the Dagara as well as my effort to bring meaning to the concept from my location in the African diaspora. I am equally committed to a fidelity toward much of what *bodeme* mean to the Dagara and the applicability of what being *bodeme* can mean for me here in the United States. To do that work, I am constantly translating and transporting between the wisdom of several worlds, seeing what is clearly important for healing and the hidden sources of healing, performing my role as healer in the context of community, and carefully considering the ways in which my sexual practices as a *bodeme* have tangible, material consequences for the healing of the world.

NOTES

1. By *African diaspora*, I am referring to people of African ancestry living outside of Africa.
2. By *positionality*, I mean my social location and the social currency I enjoy as a result of my social identities, privileges and challenges.
3. Cruising is the concept used to delineate the choreography of determining and expressing mutual attraction in a public place between same-sex attracted people.
4. It is for this reason that I have not shared the details of the rituals in this article. Ritual magic relies upon the nondisclosure of the details of ritual. This belief, though personal, is consistent with African and other indigenous approaches to ritual. For an example of the African approach, see Somé (1998).
5. The one-drop rule was a classification code developed in the United States to designate someone to be of the black race—a person needed to have only one drop of black blood inherited from an ancestor to be considered black. For more information, see Daniel (2007).

REFERENCES

Altman, D. (2001). Rupture or continuity? The internationalization of gay identity. In J. C. Hawley (Ed.), *Post-colonial queer: Theoretical intersections* (pp. 19–42). New York: State University of New York Press.

Daniel, G. R. (2007). *Race and multiraciality in Brazil and the United States: Converging paths?* University Park, PA: Pennsylvania State University Press.

Delany, S. (1996). Introduction. In B. Murrow & C. H. Rowell (Eds.), *Shade: An anthology of fiction by gay men of African descent* (pp. xvii–xx). New York: Avon Books.

Herukhuti. (2007). *Conjuring black funk: Notes on culture, sexuality, and spirituality, volume one*. New York: Vintage Entity Press.

Hoff, B. (1993). *Gays: Guardians at the gates—An interview with Malidoma Somé.* Retrieved September 29, 2009, from http://www.menweb.org/somegay.htm

hooks, b. (1994). *Teaching to transgress: Education as the practice of freedom*. New York: Routledge.

Hudson-Weems, C. (2004). *Africana womanism: Reclaiming ourselves* (4th ed.). Troy, MI: Bedford Publishers.

Human Rights Campaign Foundation. (2009). *At the intersection: Race, sexuality, and gender*. Washington, DC: Author.

Lemelle, A. J. (2004). Black masculinity matters in attitudes toward gay males. *Journal of Homosexuality, 47*(1), 39–51.

Lewis, G. B. (2003). Black-white differences in attitudes toward homosexuality and gay rights. *Public Opinion Quarterly, 67*(1), 59–78.

Negy, C. (2005). A comparison of African American and White college students' affective and attitudinal reactions to lesbian, gay, and bisexual individuals: An exploratory study. *Journal of Sex Research, 42*(4), 291–298.

Schulte, L. J. (2004). The relative importance of ethnicity and religion in predicting attitudes towards gays and lesbians. *Journal of Homosexuality, 47*(2), 127–142.

Sedgwick, E. (1985). *Between men: English literature and male homosocial desire*. New York: Columbia University.

Somé, M. (1993). *Ritual: Power, healing, and community*. New York: Penguin Compass.

Somé, M. (1995). *Of water and the spirit: Ritual, magic, and initiation in the life of an African shaman*. New York: Penguin Compass.

Somé, M. (1998). *The healing wisdom of Africa: Finding life purpose through nature, ritual, and community*. New York: Jeremy P. Tarcher/Putnam.

Somé, S. (2003). *Homosexuality: The gatekeepers*. Retrieved September 29, 2009, from http://w3.ime.net/~bmhc/soulvp03.htm

Stokes, J. P., & Peterson, J. L. (1998). Homophobia, self-esteem, and risk for HIV among African American men who have sex with men. *AIDS Education and Prevention, 10*(3), 278–292.

Waldner, L. K., Sikka, A., & Baig, S. (1999). Ethnicity and sex differences in university students' knowledge of AIDS, fear of AIDS, and homophobia. *Journal of Homosexuality, 37*(3), 117–133.

Colonial Legacies, Decolonized Spirits: Balboa, Ugandan Martyrs and AIDS Solidarity Today

KENNETH HAMILTON

Notre Dame de Namur University and Graduate Theological Union, Belmont, California, USA

The longing and journey toward "decolonization," of body, mind and community, is a key element in queer/bi spirituality. "Colonization" is that complex notion that refers to external acts of conquest; it also involves the inner colonization or alienation of the minds and souls of the colonized. Two poignant examples from queer history illustrate how the "heteronorm" was/is established over queer bodies and spirits: one, Balboa's murder of "sodomites" (Panama, 1513) and, in 1886 (B)Uganda, the demonization of the African queer/bi ruler, Mwanga. For contemporary Western queer/bi persons, political-spiritual solidarity with historic and present-day demonized sexualities, such as in the AIDS pandemic, is a generous, life-giving response.

INTRODUCTION: DECOLONIZATION AS A QUEER SPIRITUAL PARADIGM

In the following pages I offer the notion of "decolonization" as useful in trying to understand and form an authentic queer "spirituality." "Colonization," first of all, is that complex notion that refers to external and internal processes over time and cultures. It refers to external acts of domination, conquest, settlement and economic exploitation, and to the "regimes of truths" and strategies that underwrite these acts. It is also the inner colonization or alienation of the minds and souls of the colonized and the colonizers (see Fanon, 1967; Memmi, 1967). My point is that the legacy of colonization has always historically meant the targeting of queer sexualities and spiritualities, the crushing of fluid sexual behavior to establish a heteronorm.[1] This heteronorm, of religious and secular powers, is that which seeks to deny and eradicate any fluidity of body and spirit by enforcing a strict sexual dimorphism.

I end with a call for solidarity with variously sexed and gendered persons throughout the world, including men who have sex with men (msm) suffering with AIDS. This solidarity is, in my thinking, the test of an authentic queer spirituality because it acknowledges, first of all, the sexual and spiritual fluidity that exists in all persons (thus making it impossible to delineate a Western version of "just us queers"). According to Sheikh Ibrahim Farajajé,[2] this is the true "beauty" of queer. Moreover, solidarity forces queers around the world to consider the "least of these"[3] —millions of "queer" persons who cannot afford drugs and, as a result, die in vast numbers with their nonqueer brothers and sisters.

True solidarity will mean a change in attitude, a relinquishing of some power and privilege and a real change in political priorities. It will mean the recognition of, for instance, the racism that came along with the suppression of queers of color, queers condemned by the "heathen" "darkness" in which they lived. And it will mean acknowledging the demonization of women and the effeminate.

I visit two poignant examples from queer history that illustrate how the heteronorm was/is established. The two stories that I offer show how this heteronorm is established and enforced in "dark," "heathen," "predatory," effeminate queer populations. One story is from Panama at the cusp of the "discovery" of the New World, the other is from Africa at the cusp of its colonization. I then discuss ways in which our "queer" spiritualities might find positive articulations and manifestations in the journey toward decolonization. Finally, I will suggest that "solidarity" is a profound sign of a decolonized spirit and spirituality. And this solidarity can best and most truly begin, I believe, with a deep concern and activism for those who have little access to drugs and medical care in the AIDS crisis.

Sexual dimorphism is not only a complex ideology, but also is a simple fiction, a construction, whose real purpose is to help produce and sustain the patriarchal state. This state dominates through the use of its metanarratives about the purpose of life (of one man and one woman) and truth. "Decolonization," on the other hand, is that spiritual journey toward wholeness that takes place when bi- and poly-spirited persons meet themselves and their neighbors in the mutuality of oppression. These intersections of oppressions help queers to see where they, body, mind and soul, are colonized, and at the site of these very oppressions can be found a sobering solidarity with fellow "victims." It is ironically here, at the intersection of oppression, that is, that true freedom is found.

My notion of decolonization, then, is simply the reverse of colonization; it is whatever frees the mind, the body, the spirit and the human race from oppression. Moreover, just as one colonization feeds on another colonization—racism on sexism, heterosexism on racism and so forth—decolonization supplants the wide-ranging relationships and hierarchies that work together to oppress queer persons. Decolonization interrupts the orchestration or ordering of oppression. Colonization depends on false binary oppositions, whereas decolonization is fluid and unifying. As colonization tries to compartmentalize—one "agenda" against another, one "race" against another—decolonization takes in the wholeness of life: the personal, the communitarian connectedness, the political, the economic, the religious, the stories told and those yet to be told. That famous succinct equation Martin Luther King Jr. loved so much—that when one person is oppressed, all are oppressed, and he too is oppressed—is, therefore, the ultimate affirmation of spiritual freedom.

Postcolonial giants, such as Albert Memmi (1967), Aimé Cesairé (1972), and Frantz Fanon (1965), while pointing out the dangers and challenges of the quest for decolonization, also affirm the ultimate victory of the colonized. Memmi's (1967) vision revealed his belief that decolonization is, ultimately, deeply personal: "But, regardless of how soon or how violently the colonized rejects his [*sic*] situation, he will one day begin to overthrow his unlivable existence with the whole force of his oppressed personality" (p. 120).

Understanding how the paradigm of colonization works helps "queers" in special ways. First of all, there is the spark of awareness of spiritual-political isolation or aloneness that, ironically, is the beginning of true solidarity with others oppressed. This particular isolation and aloneness is a spiritual place—sometimes symbolized as the "desert"—that, though showing one one's own unique journey, is also a place where all human spiritual striving meets. Second, the awareness of being colonized invites queers to take an honest look into their own history. That, in turn, will expose the subtle ways the "heteronorm" was established over the bodies of queers in the first place. Third, understanding the full range of one's oppression provides a road map, of sorts, out of that oppression. It helps queers to organize themselves against oppressions that have not died but only changed form. A profound assessment of oppression will also not allow us to replace one oppression with another. Finally, in the desert of colonization, past and present, there is found reason to celebrate newfound power and awareness in/of the wonderful giftedness that sexual-spiritual fluidity is, a giftedness that makes queer/bi persons truly beautiful.

THE SODOMITES OF PANAMA

In his expansive work, *The Geography of Perversion: Male-to-Male Sexual Behavior Outside the West and the Ethnographic Imagination, 1750–1918*, cultural theorist Rudy Bleys (1995) began by quoting Black queer theorists Kobena Mercer and Isaac Julien, who wrote: "Historically, the European construction of sexuality coincides with the epoch of imperialism and the two inter-connect" (p. 1). Their point is that sexuality is a construction, a very useful tool, a "foil" that can determine the success or failure of an imperialistic venture. The construction of sexuality, we find, has directly targeted women, people of color, the differently abled and, of course, queers. This is done when the explorer or soldier or missionary or settler constructs categories such as the "heretical," the "cannibalistic," the "diabolical," the "abominable," the "effeminate," "sodomite"[4] and the "dark." Bley's book, as the title outlines, takes an expansive look at the "geography of perversion" created when European explorers and conquistadors came face-to-face with same-sex behavior outside of Europe. Their travelogues, diaries and letters to home created a perverse, dangerous but enticing "geography" in the imaginations of their readers back in Europe; and this determined the policies and strategies of conquest of the church and the state.

One poignant example of this imperialist use of sexuality is the slaughter of the sodomite Indians of Quarcqua in Panama in 1513 by Vasco Nuñez de Balboa. Balboa represents the heroic discoverers from Europe who opened up the closed gates of a new world, a paradise lost, yet a dangerous zone of the uncivilized. Jonathan Goldberg (1993), exploring the construction of "sodomy" and the "sodomite" in history, wrote about this incident in "Sodomy in the New World: Anthropologies Old and New." Two days before Balboa laid eyes on the Pacific, "after killing the leader of the Indians of Quarecqua and six hundred of his warriors, Balboa fed to his dogs forty more Indians accused of sodomitical practices" (p. 4). This murder of the sodomites engaging in same sex gave Balboa, as it were, the spiritual upper hand. He was the not only the bringer of civilization and power, but also a beacon of right behavior, of the heteronorm. Goldberg observed that Balboa saw these murders as a "proto-nationalist" act; Balboa "eliminates and supplants the Indian rulers but appears to be acting as the liberator of the oppressed" (pp. 4–5). In his ritualistic feeding of the sodomites to the dogs Balboa stages for all to see the lie that sodomites were less than dogs, a curse amazingly echoed today by modern rulers like Zimbabwean president, Robert Mugabe.[5] Balboa also stages, for all to observe, the way one conquers: by murdering all queers.

Moreover, those Indians characterized as sodomites and outcasts were likely priests or shamans, "two-spirited"[6] leaders of their people. Perhaps this implies that the power of queers—the spiritual and ritualistic power—was also a threat to Balboa, a possibility that should not escape our attention as we analyze the connection of queers and domination. It should come as no surprise though, gender-variant shamans and priests have long been the target of conquerors. First comes the accusation, wonderfully explored, for instance, in Hebrew Scripture scholar Randall Bailey's (1995) "They're Nothing but Incestuous Bastards: The Polemical Use of Sex and Sexuality in Hebrew Canon Narratives." Bailey's point is that the accusation of sexual deviancy often preceded an active act of conquest by providing the reason and outrage needed. And, of course, the most famous targeting in the Bible is that of certain citizens of Sodom (sodomites) gathered around the divine men and the patriarch Lot (Genesis 19). Balboa very likely knew of this famous story.

Other scholars have illustrated how often those who were targeted were gender-variant persons of the priestly caste or members of a royal court. Randy Conner (1993) wrote:

> In the earliest spiritual traditions known to humankind, gender-variant, homoerotically or bisexually inclined persons served as shamans and priests of goddesses, gods, spirits, and ancestors. With the so-called triumph of patriarchal, monotheistic religions, these men were slaughtered or driven underground, along with female shamans and priestesses. (p. 7)

This is important for us for, again, Balboa's methodology is revealed. He, like so many before him, targets—consciously or unconsciously—these empowered queer personages to establish a new spiritual order: the heteronorm.

A PARABLE FROM AFRICA: STORY OF UGANDA MARTYRS

Sir Winston Churchill and the explorer, Henry Morton Stanley before him, called the kingdom known as Buganda the "Pearl of Africa" (Pulford, 1999, p. 7). As the most centralized and powerful kingdom of the Great Lakes area in East Africa, Buganda was the center of expansion and conflict (Kiwanuka, 1972). It was attractive to many outsiders: a semimythical land where one might find the source of the great Nile River. This kingdom was to eventually become "Uganda," a "protectorate" of the British Empire by 1900. It was the presence of a number of characters and forces—Arabs, European explorers and Christian missionaries—a few years before that date that offer some context for this radical transformation from Buganda to Uganda.

The "Passion of the Uganda Martyrs" begins as the young male royal pages, assembled outside the Kabaka's (the Bugandan king's) ivory court, are about to process into African Christianity's most celebrated martyr-passion narrative. The year is 1886, 4 years before the British annexation of Uganda (Low, 1971, pp. 37–41). The leader of the pages, a certain Charles Lwanga, turns to the others and says "in a firm voice, 'let us go in.'" Rudy Bleys (1995) drew the scenario:

> Mwanga, the leader of the Baganda [or the Ganda people] from 1884–1897 ... maintained a "harem" full of pageboys and resisted Christianization as it became clear that anal intercourse had to be renounced. As gradually more and more boys, who had converted to either Protestantism or Catholicism, refused sexual services to Mwanga and his entourage, a conflict arose. When his favourite pageboy Mwafu resisted as well, Mwanga went into a paroxysm of rage and several boys were killed. (p. 172)

The news of these brutal executions spread quickly to northern Africa and Europe, particularly England and France. Sensational and vivid reports of Bugandan Christians dying for their faith brought the country of Buganda and its Kabaka into the European eye. Newspaper reports spread through Europe, framing the execution as a "persecution" of good Christians in "deepest, darkest Africa." Almost immediately the Christian pages were presented for "canonization" as holy martyrs. The 22 Roman Catholic pages were declared "Blessed" in 1920 by Pope Benedict XV and canonized by Pope Paul on October 18, 1964. The Anglican martyred saints are also highly honored. Indeed, June 3 is Martyrs Day, a national holiday in Uganda; and Uganda is, without a doubt, one of the most profoundly Christianized regions in Africa. The two main shrines to the martyrs are located at the Catholic basilica at Namugongo and at St. Paul's Anglican Cathedral, Namirembe, Kampala.

Mwanga's rage is attributed to the fact that he interpreted the refusal of the pageboys to have sex with him as the work of the antisodomy teachings of the Christian missionaries. And he was not wrong. Christian missionaries, for their part, had indeed been "alarmed by ... well known images" of "sodomy"—particularly anal sex—and had "felt compelled" to sanction Mwanga (Bleys, 1995, p. 186). They felt compelled, that is, to target same-sex anal intercourse between the soon-to-be demonized king and the saintly virgin pages.

Indeed, these royal pages themselves were an envied population because they were the future leaders of the kingdom. They were the noble sons of chiefs who were sent to the king's court to curry favors and win powerful positions. Their bodies also are written upon, as it were, by the missionaries as they sent their reports back to Europe framing Mwanga as the murderer of innocent Christian boys. The sensational production of the martyrdom by these reports and then, almost immediately after, by the beginning of their Cause (their journey to Catholic sainthood) added a powerful weight to this soon-to-be-designated "martyrdom." This was a major coup for Christianity in Africa.

WHO WAS/IS THIS MWANGA?

Today Mwanga has been called "Africa's most famous homosexual" (Ward, 2002, p. 88). The fact that he, like all royals, had wives and children is ignored. So there is little consideration of Mwanga as a bisexual man. I'll return to this. Moreover—and this is important—despite the fact that he was the same age as most of the pages, he is cast as a "pedophile" in the modern fiction of a "dirty old man," a predator. And though we know that same-sex activity was present in the court, it is King Mwanga's "shameful passions" that are exposed[7] and used to shame, or hushed and whispered as an open secret. The dynamic of the "scandal" is one of the ways heteronormativity works. The scandal of it all, for instance, serves to squelch deeper questions about the sexual fluidity of the royal court. Did Mwanga really get this practice from the Muslims in the court—as is claimed by the missionaries[8] —or were same-sex sexual practices a part of this (and other African) cultures before the advent of either the Arab traders or the European settler? How prevalent was same-sex sexual behavior? What were the love relationships of the other men? What of the romance and/or sexual relations of men with men, women with women, women with men. What about the love/sex triangles, the jealousies, the sexual competition, and so on, all of which form the sexual politics of the royal court and, thus, of B/Uganda? These details are eclipsed in importance as heterosexism is established in the land.

Charging Mwanga with "homosexuality" or, in this case, "sodomy" is much more useful to the European missionaries, explorers and entrepreneurs than his apparent bisexuality or his polyamory.[9] To introduce him as a man who had sex with men and women might frustrate the ends of the carefully constructed demonization of Mwanga by the Europeans. And because Mwanga obliged them by carrying out brutal and bloody executions, he remains "Africa's most famous homosexual." This disaster of the Ugandan martyrdom is the most necessary element for Ugandan Christianities' founding story; it is of the utmost theological purpose that Mwanga was only a homosexual. His sexuality produces the inevitable crisis through which a new Christianized, colonized central Africa emerges.

Indeed, Mwanga, years now after he has lost the kingdom of Uganda to the colonial forces, has become a famous stereotype, his name a noun and adjective for a predatory sodomite.[10] An article in the *New Vision*, one of Uganda's leading daily newspapers, by a Ugandan Christian pastor named Martin Ssempa (2005) is revealing. For him, Mwanga is the personification of any non-African, anti-God "agenda." He speaks of this agenda as a "gradual global Mwanga" that is spreading across the world and destroying Christian societies and families, particularly in Africa. He had his own "personal Mwanga experience with a famous Ugandan" (whom he describes but does not name,) who offered him a job only if he would have sex with him. A "personal Mwanga" is, evidently, from his point of view, any predatory male, or any man who makes a pass at him.

Take into account the present controversy over Uganda in the wake of the passing of the Anti-Homosexuality Bill on October 13, 2009 that would, if enacted, broaden the criminalization of sodomy or homosexual acts by providing the death penalty for anyone with previous convictions of sodomy, or who have sex and are HIV-positive, or who engage in same sex acts with minors. Again, Uganda is the worldwide center of a heated debate over sodomy. The passage of this law is unthinkable, but it also proves how "sodomy" is a Christian (and Islamic, to a different way) construct often used as a symbolic even allegorical referent to a larger political agenda, perhaps this time globalization and neocolonialism. That is, this present case is also the result of white, western missionaries, as it were, collecting allies in Africa in order to accomplish and strengthen their spiritual ascendancy.[11] Again, spiritual ascendancy is very important for the heavy task of domination!

It is also important to understand that the homophobic violence in of our stories is only one side of how queers, particularly here queers of color, have been used in European discovery and conquest to establish spiritual ascendancy. The other side is the colonizer's desire, the longing for the dark, "erotic," "exotic," other. As the European came forth from the homeland seeking riches and fame, he also found objects for his erotic imagination. His "colonial desire" and fantasy was to discover and uncover, to experience the naked native, to be devoured by the "cannibal," to have intercourse with an "empty" or "virgin" land, to travel into the "heart of darkness" (Conrad, 1997).

The telling part of these two cases from afar is that both tell the tale of contested sexualities, the tagging of same-sex or mixed-sex behavior as demonic, the targeting of the political arrangements behind these same-sex behaviors as nothing but savagery, all of which were fictions manipulated by the Europeans. It was not, that is, members of the priestly caste of Panama of the 1500s or members of the royal court of late-19th-century Buganda inventing static sexual orientation labels.[12] The facts were much, much more subtle and usually involved men and women engaging in various sexual behavior and gender roles.

EXCURSUS: ACTUAL SAME-SEX PRACTICE IN AFRICA

However, Mwanga's radical alterity and his bisexuality is not the only unobserved or erased reality. "Africa's" body is itself drawn upon and a heterosexist fiction imposed. It is presented in many ways: as proto-hetero, as innocent, as barbaric, as exotic, as decadent. The sexual politics of the court and the martyrdom scene, bloody as it became, reminded the explorer H.M. Stanley of the decadent Roman emperor Caligula (cited in Hoad, 2007, p. 12).

All these depictions helped build imperialist discourse, for strict Eurocentric gender dimorphism and sexual ethics made for a "fiction of purity" that pretty much excluded a majority of the world's population. Fluidity and accepted gender variance must be denied. Yet more and more scholarship is showing that in fact these diversities did exist—in varying ways—in precolonial Africa.

It must be first said that the meanings of same-sex sexual practices and gender variance in Africa are as multiple as are the cultures, erotic spiritualities and "languages of desire" of African people themselves. Men and women of the same "gender" had sex in one social arrangement or another, in precolonial arrangements, in an Arab-style "harem" and later on in boarding schools and in other segregated male and female situations (Murray & Roscoe, 2001, pp. 283–297). It not only existed, it was acknowledged by many Africans as "very common" (p. 35). For instance, cross-dressing and permanent passive roles, as well as passive-active roles among men, are reported in the Nilotic Lango of Uganda, the Teso and the Karamojong of northwestern Uganda and Kenya (Conner, 1993, pp. 36–37; Conner, Sparks, & Sparks, 1997, p. 1). The preexistence of unique African "homosexual" practices might be seen by the presence of terms used for same-sex or gender-variant roles: "Along the Nilotic people of Uganda, gender-variant males engaging in same-sex eroticism were still being called *jo apele* or *jo aboich* in the early twentieth century" (Conner, 1993, p. 40).

Randy Conner and other queer historians want to reclaim, moreover, the connection of past presences of homoeroticism and the sacred in Africa. For instance, two key elements ethnologists have found in African shamanism are "belief in androgynous/gynandrous godhead and the process of gender transformation among practitioners— . . . [which has been] documented in . . . the Akan, Ambo-Kwanyama, Bobo, Chokwe, Dahomeans (of Benin), Dogon-Bambara, Etik, Handa, Humbe, Hunde, Iba, Jukun, Kimbundu, Konso, . . . and Yoruba" (Conner, 1993, pp. 38–39).[13]

SOLIDARITY IN A TIME OF AIDS

Let us now discuss HIV/AIDS. I have to admit being shocked years ago after hearing about the "shock" of so many U.S. doctors when at the international conference on AIDS in Durban (July 2000), South Africa they saw, for the first time, the length and depth of the AIDS pandemic there. I was shocked because these doctors—all noted "experts" on AIDS—were shocked.[14] I thought to myself, "My God, Africa is invisible!" How else to react to such news? How could they not know how AIDS was wiping out whole generations throughout South Africa, destroying the infrastructures of the continent, wasting vast amounts of resources? How could these experts not know about the struggle in South Africa to engage in culturally-relevant education around AIDS, such as condom distribution? One answer is that these White experts from America and Europe (many of them, no doubt, gay, lesbian and bisexual physicians) could care less about Africa; or, perhaps, they would care if they had bothered to find out. Either option involves racism. The other answer is the success of homophobic silencing and erasure in Africa itself.

On the one hand there is the "Gay International," as Joseph Massad (2007) coined it, which gazes upon Africa and so many other countries through its own lens. Although it might have sincere goals, it most often fails to see the "other"—be they African, Arab, Asian—as anything more than the object of their "mission" to bring human rights to all, regardless of "sexual orientation, gender identity, or HIV status" (p. 161). Massad defined the Gay International as those guided by "these missionary tasks, the discourse that produces them, and the organizations that represent them" (p. 161). These organizations are the outreach side of the coin of White gay, lesbian, bisexual, transgender, queer (GLBTQ)—or as Ibrahim Farajajé, among others, calls it, the White lesbigay aristocracy—AIDS organizations whose agendas, even in this country, hardly ever mean sharing of resources or even paying attention to the needs of the Black or Latino/a communities.

On the other hand, what of the homophobia displayed by Africans themselves, a homophobia that largely reflects the victory of the rightist Christian rhetoric of African politicians and bishops who are backed up by powerful Northern (U.S.) allies? (see Hassett, 2007). Theirs is the heterosexist stance that contends that there never was and really still isn't any queer African presence. This heterosexism (or stubborn ignorance) often goes around in the guise of nationalism or pan-Africanism; that is to say, it claims that homosexuality, per se, is a "Western import" and queer populations in Africa, as far as they exist, are dupes of the West. (No one asks about homophobes being dupes.) Indeed, homosexuality is pictured as a genocidal anti-African project, and part of this Western genocidal project or plot is, they fantastically claimed, the very existence of AIDS in Africa!

Of course, some things have changed since that historic meeting in Durban, or so we are led to believe. But even now we see only sporadic attempts to meet the Millennium Development Goals regarding HIV/AIDS or to forgive fallacious "debts" that cripple African nations' health care systems.[15] Moreover, there is no real engagement of the rhetoric of the Right in Africa or in other developing nations; this engagement would be a perfect challenge for U.S. LGBTQ organizations to tackle. Queer scholars of religion and LGBTQ leaders could organize to engage, respectively, the frightening "abomination" speech of African Christian bishops and pastors, as well as the threats to hunt down gays and lesbians by African state leaders.[16] A pandemic must be fought to its end. It cannot be abandoned because those who suffer most are only Black Africans, other people of color or simply the poor. Here at the side of their sisters and brothers Western queers can take the momentum away from the Right wing in this country and Europe. This

Right wing is, at this very moment, forging repressive alliances with African and Latin American nations (see, e.g., Hassett, 2007).

There is much in Africa that could draw the solidarity of bisexuals. For instance, truck driver society there manifests bi behavior (if not bi identity), because these men often are having sex with two sexes and/or genders. This "bi behavior" is often pictured as the ultimate "secret life," the ultimate African "downlow" (McKenna, 1999). However, this is but another stratagem to confuse and scatter support. Indeed, the categorization of some activity or desire as "bisexual," is, as Loraine Hutchins (2007) argued, problematic for many reasons, not the least being because it assumes a dual or bifurcated gender reality in human lives. And what of cross-gendered or transsexual or intersexed persons and communities that belong to both and neither of the dominant gender identities? (Hutchins, 2005). None of the "tags" of these identities necessarily describes actual sexual practices:

> Terms such as "het-behavior," "bi-behavior," "homo-behavior" etc. don't really say much and aren't really accurate because they cater more to people's fantasies or concepts of what such behavior is rather than describe actual acts.... [On the other hand] "penile-vaginal intercourse" is an accurate term regardless of what orientations (het, homo, bi). (L. Hutchins, personal e-mail, January 26, 2007)

And, as we saw in the case of Mwanga, contested sexualities, such as his own, provided rightist discourse with its main discursive and representational weaponry. Who "owns" the various notions and tags of bisexual behavior is of the utmost importance. Manipulating the bisexual's desire helps the Right to demonize "queer" identity in general and Black men (and women) in their downlow sexual practice.

In his "Fluid Desire" essay Farajajé-Jones (1995) posed a few propositions to consider regarding bisexuals and HIV/AIDS. It is amazing how these same issues can be translated into African politics and bisexual politics over the worldwide AIDS pandemic:

> The articulation of a politics of bisexuality and HIV/AIDS interrelate: how the pandemic exacerbates erotophobia and biphobia, how erotophobia and biphobia prevent education and outreach, how the struggles against HIV/AIDS and against bisexual oppression can parallel one another ... [and how] Within most HIV/AIDS organizing, bisexuals remain totally invisible. (p. 119)

Where, indeed, are the dark, hidden, bi-fluid persons in most Western public discourse and media about human rights? How has this silence helped make Africa and the rest of the world, particularly people of color, invisible? The fact is, without any doubt in my mind, that the vast majority of queers in general and bisexuals in particular in this world are still the radically poor and are struggling with HIV/AIDS! They struggle in secrecy and, as such, pass the virus to friends, strangers, and their own spouses (see, e.g., Fleshman, 2004).[17] No substantial international effort has been made to educate people cross-culturally about the use of condoms or other safe(r) sex methods. Is it not then the rightful place of GLBTQ persons in general and bisexuals more than ever before to be there at the side of the vast majority of their brothers and sisters who struggle with AIDS? Is not the gift of bisexuality the ability to announce that neat categories kill? Can the Gay International let go of its controls a bit and allow the silent, silenced voices in Africa and elsewhere a chance to rise? Should not GLBTQ organizations support and follow the leadership of African GLBTQ groups (such as Gays and Lesbians of Zimbabwe [GALZ], Musla-Uganda and Sexual Minorities of Uganda [SMUG]) who struggle to survive, to be seen, and to unearth the complex, deeply cultural causes for "unsafe" behavior? Is it ethical to cast most of our hopes and energy into our own purely western civil rights struggles, like, "gay marriage?"[18] Can a light shine in on a multitude of secret places: households, town councils, churches and schools?

Standing in solidarity with the vast silenced and demonized throngs of bisexed or fluid-sexed of the world is the ethical place to be. That which is ethical is spirit filled. That which is spirit filled is decolonized. And decolonization means our ultimate victory over AIDS. It is not simply a victory of policies and miracle drugs; it is the victory of the spirit over the racism and sexism and heterosexism that perpetuates this disease. Decolonization is our aim, our goal, our fuel. It needs our righteous anger, our best organizing, our most sincere resolution. It has an end; however, for us, the end is far away—and so we must strive each day, one day at a time, to reach that end when body and spirit are free. Free to love all that is queer in us, with us, around us.

EPILOGUE: THE BEAUTY OF "QUEER": FLUIDITY OF THE SPIRIT. A MANIFESTO

It is noble to fight for our spirits, to wage, as Christian evangelicals like to put it, "spiritual warfare." For if we do not stand up for the fluidity of life, love and desire, a hardness settles in and takes over our spiritual ground. We can see this truth in the words of the sage polyamorous thea/ologian and spiritual activist, Ibrahim Farajajé-Jones (2000): "(T)he beauty of the word 'queer' [is that] we can hold more than two things at a time in creative, dynamic tension ... By doing so, we can show how race, gender, class, embodiment, sexuality and spirituality constantly interconnect and intersect" (p. 17).

Farajajé, as an out bisexual scholar, has always striven to be authentically "queer." For him, the beauty of holding on to that term is not to establish any set identity.[19] Rather, he wants to always remind himself that that which is queer always steps outside stable identities and reveals the dynamic fluidity of sexuality and, indeed, sexual politics. For, spirit and spirituality are fluidity itself; they are, as the Christian scriptures describe, like the wind: "It moves where it will . . . thou hearest its sound but dost not know where it comes from or where it goes. So is everyone who is born of the Spirit" (John 3:8).

Challenging domination and contrived binaries is where the journey into the wholeness of spirit begins. It is in the recognizing of ourselves as "one big mix of possibilities of desire just waiting to happen" (Farajajé-Jones, 2000, p. 16). Right after we have escaped through the gates of any of many necessary dominations, we have achieved something deeply spiritual, something that encompasses the whole reality that we call life. When we reject any discourse that empowers the dominators, when we take a strong argument out of their hands, we have arrived, as it were, at a spiritual plane: one that recognizes the oneness of mind and body and soul.

The challenge lies before all who have—no matter their particular identities or desires—experienced Christian erotophobia, somatophobia or Islamophobia.[20] That challenge is to see past the racist "White man's burden," the missionary position, the heterosexist box, the monosexist box, the male supremacist box and the ones queers even place on themselves. In so doing, we are decolonizing our bodies and spirits and preparing ourselves for all the possibilities that desire can create.

NOTES

1. By *heteronorm* I mean the norm established by heterosexism, that infallible regime(s) of "truth(s)" that dictate that all things—and the sacred norms that guide them—are, should be, and must be ruled by the "natural" and organizing principle of reproduction. It includes the criminalization and demonization of non-opposite-sex behavior and the systematic, institutionalized, routine and pervasive exclusion of any truth outside heteronormativity.
2. Ibrahim Farajajé is also referred to in the references as "E. Farajajé-Jones."
3. A reference to the Christian scriptures. Matthew 25 shows Christ at the Last Judgment asking if the disciple had given food and shelter and advocacy to the hungry, the homeless, the imprisoned and finishes with "Whatever you did to the least of these, you did to me."
4. The sodomite is that "citizen" of the mythical city of Sodom. "Constructing" the sodomite means conjuring up the demonization of male same-sex sexuality and gender variance that began in early redactions of the story of the Sodom (and Gomorrah) story in the Hebrew Scriptures (Genesis 19: 29–38), wherein rape of men is implied (Genesis 19: 4–5) and the city is thus destroyed by Yahweh (God).
5. Mugabe, only one of numerous African presidents (such as Uganda's Yoweri Museveni) waging an antihomosexual campaign—heard of the application of the group Gays and Lesbians of Zimbabwe (GALZ) to participate in the country's prestigious international 1998 book fair and it provoked him enough to compare them to "pigs and dogs. . ." and "a scourge planted by the white man on a pure continent." http://news.bbc.co.uk/2/hi/programmes/crossing_continents/143169.stm (accessed March 28, 2010).
6. "Two-spirited" is the concept some indigenous people of the Americas use to describe queer or "gender variant" persons; this term, of course, uses the term *spirit*, but this is not to say that *spirit* means the same in this usage as it would mean in, say, a Catholic academic's mind.
7. And also silenced, the opposite side of the same coin of an "exposé."

8. The martyrdom narrative, which is part history, part saint story, also provides a quasi-anthropological account that reaches backward and claims that precolonial Kiganda (Ugandan) society condemned same-sex practice and roles. One of the main players at the court, Sir Apolo Kagwa, was in fact one of the early sources of Bagandan anthropology and ethnography. He claimed early on that "such practices" were unknown in Buganda before the arrival of the Arabs (Faupel, 1962, p. 9).

9. These would be contained in the missionaries' tag of Mwanga's "polygamy." Not much is said about this as the missionaries decided that sodomy with these young neophytes was the main issue to target.

10. Although, of course, this is not from all sources, such as those who do not wish to throw aspersions on the kabakas.

11. "U.S. Exports Cultural War to Uganda" by Barbara Bradley Hagerty. NPR–January 15, 2010. Retrieved March 29, 2010 from, http://www.npr.org/templates/story/story.php?storyId=122572951&sc=17&f=1001

12. "[Sigmund] Freud and the European sexologists were beginning to do this around the turn of the century," asserted Loraine Hutchins (e-mail conversation, July 5, 2009). Perhaps the missionaries or explorers or scholars were "projecting." Indeed, in the second half of the 19th century a discussion raged in Europe "regarding the nature and origins of homosexuality: whether it was acquired or innate and whether it was to be excused or lamented" (op cit.). Participants in this discussion included jurists, physicians and scientists such as Karl Heinrich Ulrichs—who proclaimed in his theory of "Uranism" that homosexuality was part and parcel of nature—Ambrose Tardieu, Johann Ludwig Casper, Karl Maria Kertbenny, Richard Von Krafft-Ebing, Havelock Ellis, Magnus Hirschfield and John Addington Symonds (Herdt, 1996, pp. 137, 213–239). In such public discussions, these educated European men learned theories of "inversion" and "third sex."

13. Malidoma Somé speaks of the African perception of gender variant persons as "gatekeepers" (Hoff, 1993). This may be another way of acknowledging them as "two-spirit" persons (Brown, 1997) who stand on the cusp between worlds.

14. The exception to this is physicians like the late (2009), eminent African American HIV specialist, Dr. Robert Scott, of Oakland, California.

15. The United Nations Millennium Development Goals [MDG] can be found on http://www.un.org/millenniumgoals/ (accessed March 28, 2010). MDG number six deals with HIV/AIDS and promises to achieve real progress in providing antiretroviral drugs, education to youth, care of AIDS orphans, etc. Regarding the so-called debts owed by poor countries, the organization called Jubilee calls most of the debts in the Global South "illegitimate" and "odious" and it advocates for the forgiveness of these debts. See http://www.jubileeusa.org/truth-about-debt.

16. Websites such as "Behind the Mask," http://www.mask.org.za, give current reports of homophobic attacks on these persons and organizations.

17. I also conducted an interview in 2003 with Patricia Vito who was HIV+, whose husband had given her AIDS, and (later on) with a number of activists in Gays and Lesbians of Zimbabwe(GALZ) who witnessed this sad phenomenon.

18. This is not to in any way deny the importance of the struggle for marriage rights. It's only a challenge to put our priorities in right perspective by remembering what the vast majority of those HIV+ persons who express bi-behavior and bi-desire have to face every day: virulent intolerance (of heterosexism and monosexism), repressive laws, on top of it all lack of medicine.

19. Nor does he take up a contrary stance to the use of the phrase *same gender loving*, which many other Black gay leaders espouse.

20. The fear of and/or hatred of pleasure, the body and Islam, respectively.

REFERENCES

Bailey, R. (1995). They're nothing but incestuous bastards: The polemical use of sex and sexuality in Hebrew canon narratives. In F. Segovia & M. Tolbert (Eds.), *Reading from this place: Social location and biblical interpretation in the United States* (Vol. 1, pp. 121–138). Minneapolis, MN: Fortress.

Behind the Mask. (n.d.). Retrieved October 14, 2009, from http://www.mask.org.za/

Bleys, R. C. (1995). *The geography of perversion: Male-to-male sexual behavior outside the West and the ethnographic imagination, 1750–1918*. New York: New York University Press.

Brown, L. B. (Ed.). (1997). *Two spirit people: American Indian lesbian women and gay men*. New York: Harrington Park.

Césaire, A. (1972). *Discourse on colonialism*. New York: Monthly Review Press.

Conner, R. P. (1993). *Blossom of bone: Reclaiming the connections between homoeroticism and the sacred*. San Francisco, CA: Harper.

Conner, R. P., Sparks, D., & Sparks, M. (Eds.). (1997). *Cassells' encyclopedia of queer myth, symbol, and spirit*. London: Cassell.

Conrad, J. (1997). *Heart of darkness: Complete, authoritative text with biographical and historical contexts, critical history, and essays from five contemporary critics* (R. C. Murfin, ed.). Boston, MA: Bedford Books.

Fanon, F. (1965). *A dying colonialism*. New York: Grove Weidenfeld.

Fanon, F. (1967). *Black skin, white masks*. New York: Grove Press.

Farajajé-Jones, E. (1995). Fluid desire: Race, HIV/AIDS, and bisexual politics. In N. Tucker (Ed.), *Bisexual politics: Theories, queries, and visions* (pp. 119–131). New York: Harrington Park.

Farajajé-Jones, E. (2000). Loving "queer": We're all a big mix of possibilities of desire just waiting to happen. *In the Family, Summer*, 14–21.

Faupel, J. F. (1962). *African holocaust: The story of the Ugandan martyrs*. New York: P. J. Kenedy and Sons.

Fleshman, M. (2004). Women: The face of AIDS in Africa. *Africa Renewal, 18*(3). Retrieved March 29, 2010, from http://www.un.org/ecosocdev/geninfo/afrec/vol18no3/183women_aids.htm

Goldberg, J. (1993). Sodomy in the new world: Anthropologies old and new. In M. Warner (Ed.), *Fear of a queer planet: Queer politics and social theory* (pp. 3–18). Minneapolis, MN: University of Minnesota Press.

Hassett, M. K. (2007). *Anglican communion in crisis: How Episcopal dissidents and their African allies are reshaping Anglicanism*. Princeton, NJ: Princeton University Press.

Herdt, G. (Ed.). (1996). *Third sex, Third gender: Beyond sexual dimorphism in culture and history*. New York: Zone Books.

Hoad, N. (2007). *African intimacies: Race, homosexuality, and globalization*. Minneapolis, MN: University of Minnesota Press.

Hoff, B. H. (1993). Gays: Guardians of the gates: An interview with Malidoma Somé. *M.E.N. Magazine*. Retrieved January 20, 2007, from http://www.menweb.org/somegay.htm

Hutchins, L. (2007). Sexual prejudice: The erasure of bisexuals in academia and the media. In G. Herdt & C. Howe (Eds.), *21st Century Sexualities: Contemporary issues in health, education, and rights* (pp. 135–139). New York: Routledge.

Kiwanuka, M. S. M. S. (1997). *A history of Buganda: From the foundation of the kingdom to 1900*. New York: Africana Publishing.

Low, D. A. (1971). *Buganda in modern history*. Berkeley, CA: University of California Press.

Massad, J. A. (2007). *Desiring Arabs*. Chicago, IL: University of Chicago Press.

McKenna, N. (1999). *The silent epidemic: HIV/AIDS and men who have sex with men in the developing world*. London: Panos. Retrieved October 15, 2006, from http://www.panos.org.uk/images/books/THE%20SILENT%20EPIDEMIC.pdf

Memmi, A. (1967). *The colonizer and the colonized*. Boston, MA: Beacon Press.

Murray, S., & Roscoe, W. (2001). *Boy-wives and female husbands: Studies in African homosexualities*. New York: St. Martin's Press.

Pulford, C. (1999). *Eating Uganda: From Christianity to conquest*. Banbury, UK: Ituri.

Ssempa, M. (2005, June 3). When faith, state, and state-inspired homosexuality clash. *New Vision*. Retrieved March 29, 2010, from http://www.newvision.co.ug/D/8/459/437768/martin%20ssempa

United Nations. (n.d.). *We can end poverty 2015: Millennium development goals*. Retrieved October 14, 2009, from http://www.un.org/millenniumgoals/aids.shtml

Ward, K. (2002, Winter). Same-sex relations in Africa and the debate on homosexuality in East African Anglicanism. *Anglican Theological Review*, *34*(1), 81–111.

BI BOOK REVIEW

Make It Funky Now: The Birth of Funk Studies

Conjuring Black Funk: Notes on Culture, Sexuality, and Spirituality Vol. 1. Herukhuti Sharif Williams. New York: Vintage Entity Press, 2007. 239 pages.

REVIEW BY L. H. STALLINGS
Indiana University-Bloomington, Bloomington, Indiana, USA

"Ain' it funky now!"
James Brown

"And so we became "funky"—like calling ourselves niggers in public."
Stephen Henderson

Upon writing this book review, it's necessary to acknowledge how difficult it was for me to write a review for a book that is marketed toward fields such as Black Studies, Sexuality and Queer Theory, specifically because it surpasses the most radical work in all of those fields. *Conjuring Black Funk: Notes on Culture, Sexuality, and Spirituality Vol. 1* is a collection of creative nonfiction, poetry and essays. It is neither a historical study of Black sexuality nor an empirical study and collection. It accepts race as a major factor in its theories on sexuality in a way that much of White queer studies still refuses to do. In addition, it shares an appreciation of praxis and theory that recalls radical Black lesbian, gay, bisexual, trangender (LGBT) discourses of the 1980s, as opposed to the now-conservative and mainstream Black Queer Studies. Its very structure resists the kind of theoretical posturing Black Queer Studies has become known for. Quite honestly, if categorization must happen, a new category needs to be created for us to understand the importance of Herukhuti's book on sexuality, spirituality and culture as it concerns Black people. Some processed fuckery—that's what Black Queer Studies has become. Funk that's what Black Sexual Studies is, or should I say the study of Black sexual cultures is a discipline called Funk Studies. And it will eviscerate queer and camp until there is nothing left but freaques and funk. Thus, this essay is part book review and part theoretical manifest for the emerging field of studies that I see Herukhuti's book being a part of: Funk Studies.

Herukhuti's contribution to Funk Studies begins with an implicit nod to the radical positionality of bisexuality. In articulating how Black Funk, a Black cultural center focused on sexual empowerment comes to be, Herukhuti asks how and why Black Funk came to be: "When we invert the question of 'why' and 'how,' there are penetrating (see the dick) and enveloping (see the pussy) truths waiting there—why/how did Black Funk create me?" (p. 14). It is this perspective of masculine and feminine, or male and female objects of desire that shape the radical politics of *Conjuring Black Funk*. Rather than an axiologically oppositional framework of ranked binaries, Herukhuti, from the very beginning, insists on the alternative framework of funk, and if ever there were a sexual metaphor or symbolism of funk, bisexuality would be it. It allows the author to make assessments about sexual subjectivity and culture that cannot be made in texts geared toward either or sexual dichotomies and monolithic desires.

Funk, in Black culture, has typically been associated with spontaneity, improvisation, sexuality, the unexplainable and the antibourgeois. In Black music, funk lyrics about sexuality vacillated between subtle double entendres and explicit and frank conversations about sexuality. The performative and cultural aesthetics of funk has tended to resists hierarchical gender and sexual categories and often relies on a bisexual epistemology for its alternative presence and function. When one is funky who can really ever say if you are gay or straight? Intellectual funk projects would, then, move back and forth between theorizing, conversation and practice to sexually educate and liberate Black masses. Right now, Herukhuti's *Conjuring Black Funk* stands as the funkiest piece of writing on Black sexuality and sexual cultures to come out in the last 10 years. Upon first glance at the cover of Herukhuti's *Conjuring Black Funk*, I was a little confused as to why he would feel it necessary to put *Black* in front of *funk*, because any funk that could be conjured has to be inherently Black. Besides, the cover art and design work by Dominguez and Gales visually confirmed the blackness of funk twice over. However, as Stephen Henderson (2000) argued in his essay "Inside the Funk Shop: A Word on Words," words such as funk and soul have been used erroneously and for dubious purposes by The Man:

> Though both of these words have special Black meanings and are, in effect, Black words, they also have "standard" English meanings that both whites and Blacks know. The whites have, however, responded to the vital black meanings in a way which epitomizes their historical response to Black culture. (p. 97)

In briefly discussing the importance of Black English, Henderson's remark on the White historical response to Black culture confronts the West's legacy of stealing, imitating, making bland or destroying Black culture. This is important to remember for the way that Black culture is often appropriated in ways that make it difficult to recall why it was distinctive, radical and nonstatic in the first place. It was the reason George Clinton insisted, "Make my funk the P-funk, I want my funk uncut . . . I want the bomb, I want the P-funk, don't want my funk stepped on" ("P-Funk," 1993). He wanted to emphasize the difference between p-funk (undiluted funk) and diluted versions of funk. This digression about funk is necessary for understanding my valuing of Herukuti's work as Funk Studies, rather than queer theory. Although there has been a White historical response to Black culture, there has been a Black historical response to dominant White culture: assimilate, accommodate or ignore it. Black queerness and Black queer theory/studies remain diluted versions of funk and funkiness. Just as queer articulated marginalized White culture, funk once represented the alternative to mainstream blackness: alternative blackness whose political philosophy was a kind of gender, class and sexual anarchy. Despite Parliament's notion of "one nation under a groove," funk as an intellectual and political manifestation seems to have been dismissed as a cultural fad of the 1970s and early 1980s, especially because it seemed to not have the political staying power of soul ("One Nation Under a Groove," 1993). However, that was when discussions of blackness ignored the symbiotic dynamic between patriarchy and White supremacy. Mainstream Black America embraced funk for its Black roots (its sonic aesthetics, but never its inherent freak politics), which connected to the genre of soul. Yet once those roots branched into Black fruit and Black trees that threatened the monolithic nationalist movements of Civil Rights and Black Power, funk became cultish or assimilation proper. Yet funk acts as the antithesis of mainstream culture, and thus when mainstream culture changes or appropriates the alternative, funk changes. Hence, Funk Studies can go where Black Queer Studies cannot.

BLACK FUNK AS SEXUAL DECOLONIZATION

In the very first chapter of *Conjuring Black Funk*, Herukhuti explains the origins of his book and cultural center:

> In 2002, Black Funk was born. . . . It became clear that a great need existed within people of color communities affected by Western/European colonization and cultural hegemony for empowerment that included a space for sexual healing and sexual liberation. The idea of sexual cultural center emerged as a way to address the need that I perceived. Black Funk became that center. (p. 14)

Black Funk, then, challenges all Black people to continue a process of sexual decolonization that began after emancipation and colonization. It is a process that should be ongoing for years to come, and Herukhuti asserts his center as a place where people of color can "share, research, and explore sexual education, sexual information, erotic aesthetics, and sexual culture from a sex positive, body positive, Afrocentric perspective" (p. 19). So the book, *Conjuring Black Funk: Notes on Culture, Sexuality, and Spirituality Vol. 1*, attempts to take on the restrictions of academic communities and cultural communities that could potentially impede sexual decolonization, as well as create a bridge between the two communities' discourses. In addition to being a community sex activist, Herukhuti also has an advanced degree in sexology. He writes as a participant in the communities he critiques, and one who still believes in theory and the possibility of queerness as a radical identity and field of study.

For me this is the one minor fault with *Conjuring Black Funk*. It forgoes a strategy of fully theorizing the cultural phenomenon of funk embedded in its title and opts for connecting to the more recognizable queer theory. Despite this strategy, Herukhuti's book still amazes and impresses me. If the text itself did not serve as visible evidence of funk (the intellectual practice of it), as I have suggested, then it would fail itself and its readers as a tool of sexual education and decolonization. However, it does not fail as a valuable teaching tool. Herukhuti's (2007) commitment to queer theory is obvious in his innovation of what he calls "Afrocentric decolonizing queer theory," (p. 5) which in conjunction with Barbara Christian's thought on Black folk and theory, as "theorizing," rather than creating a theory (p. 68). Even as Herukhuti states Black feminist thought, Black/postcolonial queer theory, and Afrocentricity as the foundation of his work, the uniqueness of the book stems from the author's early theorizing of conjuring and the text's representation as pure funk.

CONJURING BLACK FUNK

Herukhuti's entire introduction explicitly and thematically addresses the role of conjuring in his text. He makes insightful connections between conjuring and theorizing. Conjuring is theorizing, social hoodoo spells (p. vi), living texts brought to life through reading (p. vii), connections to previously hidden truths and incorporating such truths into one's consciousness (p. vii) and producing thought in action. Because African cosmology insists that subjectivity is always changing and in process, producing active thoughts, rather than final answers and solutions as key, *Conjuring Black Funk* brings a spiritual intonation to the concept of theory and offers an intellectual categorization of conjuring. Such efforts sets Herukhuti's work on Black sexual cultures apart from the queer studies that he sees himself as part of. In White universities, critics discuss theory as strictly an intellectual exercise, but theory is also an inherently spiritual enterprise in that it requires faith, beliefs, concepts and producers of the word. Herukhuti's collection adheres to its own hypothesis that theory can be spiritual and intellectual. In doing so, it risks its conscious connection to queer theory and subconsciously breaks away from the split queer and sexuality studies enact in separating the sexual from the intellectual. That is funky.

SECTION ONE: TEXTS AND GROUPS CENTERED ON SEX

Structurally and ideologically, *Conjuring Black Funk* is accessible without being too simplistic. Herukhuti does not dismiss the complexities of what actual sexual liberation would mean for the sake of empty revolutionary rhetoric or abstract academic theories. The text's chapters are organized in three subject sections: culture, sexuality and spirituality. The first section on culture consists of chapters that examine cultural texts and groups that take up sex as their subject. Herukhuti writes about the representation of sex in the Black gay porn industry, the disturbing audacity of Samuel Delany's *Hogg* (1994), the connection between capitalism and fetishism/Western empires and fetishism, body fascism in the gay community, the "down-low" (DL; its stigmatic existence and misrepresentation), Black pride events, the Million Man March and HIV/AIDS and race. In his discussion of "down-low Black men," Herukhuti's commitment to radical bisexual politics shapes and informs his arguments about accountability by Black men and women in ways that neither J. L. King or Keith Boykin have been brave enough to say.[1] His critique of White normative gender and sexual categories, as well as his commentary on the way in which Black women and men contribute to the ignorant scapegoating of Black bisexuals for the HIV epidemic in Black America, is one of the few assessments to refute the shame, insecurity and moral judgment heaped onto individuals who are neither strictly heterosexual nor homosexual.

In probably the most illuminating chapters of the section, Herukhuti exposes the cultural capital of HIV/AIDS in the hands of racist, homophobic and sexist institutions such as the government and the pharmaceutical industry. As many critics have observed, Black communities' poor response to the HIV/AIDS epidemic has contributed to the rise in HIV/AIDS statistics in Black communities. Herukhuti also notes the way the aforementioned institutions have myopically regulated the way Black communities can address education, prevention and treatment strategies. Moving back and forth between drawing parallels between the prison industrial complex and the HIV/AIDS industrial complex, the author insists that the epidemic cannot be properly fought if we pretend that the same inequities caused by White supremacy rule are passé.

SECTION TWO: CHOOSING ECSTASY AND PLEASURE

Despite the threat HIV/AIDS poses to the general health and well-being of all, Herukhuti, like Samuel Delany before him, still manages to include in his critique of sexuality attention to the role of pleasure in sexuality and sexual wisdom. In what can be seen as emblematic of the provocative, theoretical and practical nature of the text, Herukhuti closes out this first section by attacking the normalcy and sexual entitlement attached to heterosexuals in an era of HIV/AIDS when he proclaims, "'I love fucking without condoms and do so every opportunity that I can.' Now ask me how I do it and you might learn something" (p. 102). That is uncut funk.

Foreshadowed by that final statement at the end of section one, the text's second section on sexuality specifically addresses responses to ecstasy and pleasure. Because the responses to pleasure and ecstasy are often conditioned by social and familial dogmas, Herukhuti chooses an unorthodox and interesting way to start the conversation on sexuality: he focuses on moments or encounters that awaken something in us beyond our conscious and previously learned understandings of sexuality. In those moments, we have a choice. Here Herukhuti does not distinguish or qualify that choice as homosexuality or heterosexuality, but liberation or murder. The act of taking the new learning and remaking the world becomes liberation. Ignoring and silencing the new sensations and consciousness within ourselves and then others through sexual phobias is murder. Yet it is clear that each chapter in the sexuality section is about so-called non-normative sexualities. Herukhuti discusses celibacy as part of sexuality, emotional versus physical uses of sexual pleasure, sexual ideology in the West, love, monogamy, polyamory and Bondage Domination/Discipline Sadism Masochism (BDSM). And as any good funk theorist would do, he recoups and reclaims freak from the clutches of mainstream connotations.

Finally, it is his discussion of sexual courage that highlights the failures of Black Queer Studies and the future possibilities of what Funk Studies can do. He makes an appropriate parallel between the historical racist murdering of Emmett Till and the hushed-up gay-bashings that occurred at Morehouse College. Of the sexual courage that has been lacking in Black America, Herukhuti asks two questions: "How are you transgressing the sexual order and how many Emmett Tills have you made today?" (p. 161). These two questions demand that we make it funky now. In studying Black sexualities and cultures, disciplinary fields, and scholars therein, should not only analyze artifacts that transgress sexual order, but they should also transgress sexual order (that means performing not only physical acts, but the intellectual acts of historical productions and distribution of knowledge).

LORDE'S DEFINITION OF THE EROTIC CHANGES/OUR RELATIONSHIPS WITH EACH OTHER

In the end, the third section on spirituality accomplishes what Audre Lorde (1984) wrote about, the connection between spirituality and sexuality in non-Western cultures and religions. It is this examination of spirituality that returns us back to the bisexual ethos of Black funk. Herukhuti briefly examines the way some African and Native American spiritual traditions can be helpful in relearning and rethinking gender and sexuality. By focusing on the ethereal elements of deities, Herukhuti moves readers away from the traditional boundaries and trajectories of the social bodies, even as he simultaneously acknowledges that our deities may have dicks and pussies. When Herkhuti acknowledges, "I grew up in the priesthood seeing images of divinity that were both male and female. God was female. God was male. God was female and male" (p. 180), he compels readers to acknowledge their sensual godliness in new and less restrictive ways than the white West has envisioned. He also explores how such thinking remains necessary in understanding and accepting trans individuals and communities into larger racialized communities. He also insists upon Black male feminist strategies of reassessing masculine traditions, privileges, and relationships. His attention to the teachings of Audre Lorde impresses upon us to use her definition of the erotic to change the nature of our relationships with one another.

DARE TO MAKE IT FUNKY NOW

In its unapologetic conjuring of bisexual epistemologies that deconstruct binary gender and sexual hierarchies that have impeded sexual liberation and freedom for far too long, *Conjuring Black Funk* courageously asks that we dare to make it funky now. In the end, Herukhuti's early dissection of conjuring remains important, and even though he never explicitly defines or theorizes about "funk," he does allow the text itself to become the funk (the practice of conjuring/theorizing). For full consideration of Black sexual liberation, those interested in ideologies and political philosophies that incorporate class, nation, age and body differences will surely have to elevate funk to the level that George Clinton and Bootsy Collins did. Intellectualize it and politicize it so that it moves beyond a fad or relic of another time. We need only look for it in different spaces than previous years. And though Black intellectual spaces are notorious for coming into or recognizing the theory of Black cultures a little too late; in the case of funk, the rerecognition of funk, as represented by Herukhuti's genre-breaking and thought-provoking *Conjuring Black Funk*, appears to be right on time.[2]

NOTES

1. King's *On the Downlow*, and Boykin's *Beyond the Downlow* in using the discourse of downlow to conceptualize and discuss men who have sex with men limit the radical discourses of bisexual men to discuss and examine bisexuality.

2. In the 1980s, two scholars briefly engaged in a philosophical debate about funk. Toni Morrison briefly played with funk as a tool in her early fiction. In *The Bluest Eye*, Toni Morrison provides a philosophy of funk that is more concerned with behavior than music: "the funkiness of passion, the funkiness of nature, the funkiness of a wide range of emotions" (p. 68). Funk becomes an alternative to controlled behavior, i.e., respectability. Literary scholar Susan Willis later assessed Morrison's use of funk in her essay "Eruptions of Funk: Historicizing Toni Morrison," in which she described Morrison's strategy as countering bourgeois constructions of family and sexuality for Black women.

REFERENCES

Boykins, K. (2005). *Beyond the downlow: Sex, lies, and denial in Black America*. New York: Carroll and Graf.

Brown, J. (2008). Ain't it funky now. On *The Singles*. Volume six, 1969–1970 [CD]. New York: Hip-O Select.

Christian, B. (1988). The race for theory. *Feminist Studies, 14*(1), 67–79.

Delany, S. R. (1994). *Hogg*. Boulder, CO: Black Ice Books.

Funkadelic and George Clinton. (1993). *One nation under a groove* [CD]. Los Angeles, CA: Priority Records.

Henderson, S. (2000). Inside the funk shop: A word on black words. In S. Henderson & W. Napier (Eds.), *African American literary theory: A reader* (pp. 97–102). New York: New York University Press.

King, J. L. (2004). *On the down low: A journey into the lives of "straight" black men who sleep with men*. New York: Broadway Books.

Lorde, A. (1984). Uses of the erotic. In A. Lorde (Ed.), *Sister outsider: Essays and speeches* (pp. 53–59). Freedom, CA: Crossing Press.

Morrison, T. (2007). *The bluest eye*. New York: Vintage.

Parliament. (1993). P-Funk. On *Tear the roof off* [CD]. New York: PolyGram Records.

Williams, H. S. (2007). *Conjuring Black funk: Notes on culture, sexuality, and spirituality*. New York: Vintage Entity Press.

Reading Althaus-Reid: As a Bi Feminist Theo/Methodological Resource

MARGARET ROBINSON

Toronto School of Theology, University of St. Michael's College, Toronto, Canada

This article examines the queer theology of Marcella Althaus-Reid in light of the author's recent qualitative research with bisexual women in the Greater Toronto Area. Althaus-Reid identifies herself as a "queer among queers," and her work builds upon postcolonial and liberation theology. Five themes in her work offer a framework for constructing a bisexual feminist theology: (1) valuing queer culture, (2) sexualizing theology, (3) reframing authority, (4) taking metaphor seriously, and (5) reclaiming the sacred. The author notes the promise and problems in Althaus-Reid's work on these subjects and offers some directions for bisexual feminist theology.

QUEER THEOLOGY AS METHODOLOGICAL RESOURCE

Bisexual women have a complex relationship with Christianity. A study by Darren Sherkat (2002) found that we showed the lowest rate of Church attendance and the second-lowest frequency of prayer. Yet compared with lesbians and gay men, more bisexual women identified with the faith tradition in which we were raised (Sherkat). Why are bisexual women remaining attached to traditions, even as our practice of that tradition dwindles? I believe the answer lies in the lack of a well-developed bisexual feminist theology. This article outlines a method for such a theology based on the work of bisexual theologian Marcella Althaus-Reid. By *theology* I mean a rational and organized discourse on the Divine. By *bisexual feminist theology* I mean not simply a subset of Christian theology (add bisexuality to Christian feminism and stir), but a distinct discourse emerging from the experience of bisexual women. The framework for such a theology can be found in the work of Marcella Althaus-Reid.

I approach this task as a bisexual activist, a working-class feminist, and a Mi'kmaq woman. Like the women in Sherkat's (2002) survey, I feel a connection with a faith that I do not practice (in my case, Catholicism) and with which I have serious problems. This article also emerges out of my decade-long membership in Toronto's bisexual women's community, and out of my recent dissertation study of 40 bisexual women in the Toronto area (Robinson, 2009). It is in relation to this experience and research that I assess the promise of Althaus-Reid's theological framework.

Marcella Althaus-Reid was born in Argentina in 1952 and died in February of 2009. She described herself as a "Latin American woman brought up in the poverty of Buenos Aires," and as a "queer amongst queers" (Althaus-Reid, 2000, p. 9; Althaus-Reid & Isherwood, 2004, p. 104). Her theology is postcolonial, recognizing that Christianity is not simply one religious option among others, but rather has been an integral piece of the colonial project. I find this approach particularly useful for examining the Canadian context. My own ancestors were forcibly converted as part of the military conquest of the New World. As a First Nations woman I am constantly reminded that Canada is a colonized space as well as a colonizing force around the globe. We inherit a colonial master narrative that posits our country as a New Britain and a plethora of counternarratives. Christian dominance, especially as the unexamined horizon of legal, moral and medical discourse, is still a significant social force in Canada. As a psychologically colonizing force it may hold even more sway. A critical consciousness must liberate us from not only oppressive external forces, but also the false consciousness that comes with internalized oppression and unearned privilege.

Some may be properly concerned about the White educated class coopting the discourse of liberation theology to reinforce existing hegemony. The participants in my own study were overwhelmingly White (65%), and 55% were university educated (Robinson, 2009). Yet despite our membership in particular hegemonic groups, bisexual women as bisexuals are not a dominant group. The women in my study struggled against heterosexism, biphobic stereotypes, invisibility and sexist gender norms. Monogamous bisexual women found it difficult to maintain their sense of sexual identity without community support. Monogamous mothers of small children were particularly vulnerable, as the heteronormative pressures of motherhood threatened to overwhelm and erase their sexual identity. Bisexual women of color, poor and working-class bisexual women and trans-identified bis may be so multiply oppressed that participation in bi community (or in research on bi community) is simply not a priority. Bisexual feminist theology must critically examine the mixture of privilege and oppression (race, class, heteronormativity, able-bodied or cisgendered status, etc.) that makes up our daily lives. Although certainly not the most marginalized, bisexual women have numerous oppressions from which we require liberating, and our social location as sometimes insider, sometimes outsider, offers a valuable perspective from which to theologize. Such critical reflection can provide a base of shared knowledge (however tentative and partial) from which we can draw to act more justly with others.

Althaus-Reid (2000, 2003) argued that theology should emerge from our personal experience of transcendence and advocated that women begin the theological process again, discovering God outside of patriarchal relations. Due to the erasure of bisexuality in feminist theology (Robinson, 2009) I argue that bisexual women must engage in this process separately, developing a bisexual theology from the ground up.

Althaus-Reid (2003, 2004) described her theological method as a "critical bisexuality" and named this as a prerequisite for doing theology. This is not to say that a theologian must be bisexual. Rather, she used the term to describe the embracing of subversive readings, instability and fluidity over fixity of meaning. This resistance is made possible by her emphasis on bisexuality's association with threesomes, and polyamory, which displaces the fixation on monoloving—Althaus-Reid's (2003) term for the divinization of monogamy. It is not surprising that Althaus-Reid conflated bisexuality with polyamory; the merger of the two concepts is ubiquitous in the mainstream media, gay and lesbian culture and even bi space itself. Despite this, equating bisexuality with fluidity and multiple partners causes several problems. First, monogamous bisexual women already face challenges maintaining their identity against heteronormativity. Equating bisexuality with polyamory only marginalizes them further. Second, though Althaus-Reid (2003) is correct that bisexuality "cannot be pinned down in a stable or fixed way" (p. 16) this is also true of other sexualities. Their fixity is an illusion. A deeper critical analysis of the conflation between bisexuality and polyamory must occur before their association can be reclaimed as the basis for a theological method. Finally, because Althaus-Reid's critical bisexual theology is a method and not an identity, I have concerns about it being co-opted by nonbisexuals, to our detriment.

If bisexual theology is to develop in such a way as to be a resource for bisexual women, it must, in my view, be an identity-based project, not a methodology. Although this runs the risk of depoliticizing bisexual theology's content it seems to me more vital at this point to avoid the co-opting and marginalizing of bisexuality that has occurred in gay theology, in lesbian theology and in queer theory (Angelides, 2001; Gammon, 2007). I find five themes in Althaus-Reid's work that could form a framework for a bisexual feminist theology: valuing queer culture, sexualizing theology, reframing authority, taking metaphor seriously, and reclaiming the sacred. These themes provide a valuable resource for shaping bisexual feminist theology in ways that correspond with other theologies of liberation.

1. Valuing Queer Culture

Traditional definitions of theological method posit reason as a key element of reflection. In practice, this has included fields such as sociology or anthropology. Yet as Althaus-Reid (2000) noted, the experiences that get included are predetermined by concepts of decency. Liberation theology, she argued, has likewise tended to theologize only the presentable within the life of the poor. By contrast, Althaus-Reid's is a theology after dark, revealing hidden and suppressed experiences and claiming that these too are sacramental (mediating of God's grace). Her portrayal of Latin America is peopled with bisexuals, gays, lesbians, cross-dressers, transsexuals and prostitutes. Her definition of *queer* also includes the poor and socially marginalized, and those heterosexuals whose identity or practice challenges heteronormativity. In the context of this article I follow Althaus-Reid's usage of the term, alert to the danger that *queer* may erase *bisexual*.

Valuing queer culture as a source of revelation is made possible for Althaus-Reid by the immanence of God, which provides free and radical access to the Divine through human experience. In short, we need not search for God; we encounter the Divine in our own circumstances. Instead of placing the burden upon queers to justify countercultural practices, we assume that God works in and through our own traditions. Queer communities are not only an effective mediator of the Divine, but also, for queers of all kinds, a more effective mediator than traditional communities such as the Church because they provide freedom from sexual oppression (albeit limited and partial), and the resources to combat oppression internally and externally. For bisexual women this may include our bi community and the larger queer community in general. The women in my study (Robinson, 2009) had access to and participated in bisexual culture, but 40% also spent time in gay and lesbian space, attending events such as the Toronto Women's Bathhouse, the Dyke March, the Inside/Out film festival, Pride Week or the Michigan Womyn's Music Festival. When we assume that our culture is permeated with the immanence of God the question then becomes what plan do we discern at work for the promotion of justice and human flourishing, and how can we participate in its realization?

One issue that arises if we are to attach theological value to queer culture is its lack of homogeneity. We do not, in fact, share a single international culture with other queers. The closet, for example, figures prominently in Althaus-Reid's work, acting as a constituting element of queer experience. For me, queer experience and closeting seem antithetical to one another. The majority of the women in my study (73%; Robinson, 2009) were out to family and friends. Instead, they faced problems such as achieving and maintaining visibility as bi, countering heteronormativity and sexism, building a support network and accessing bisexual community (Robinson). Instead of elevating a single queer experience as normative a more fruitful direction might be to preserve the multiplicity of our experiences, treating the diversity of our queer culture as a resource rather than a liability.

2. Sexualizing Theology

It is not strictly accurate to describe Althaus-Reid's emphasis on sexuality in theology as new, because for her there is no theology that is not sexual. Traditional theology, Althaus-Reid noted (2004), has based its view of sexuality on an androcentric and misogynistic anthropology. Queer theology must emerge from a feminist anthropology, "where women are in control of their desires and pleasures, and in complete freedom to express themselves sexually with their own bodies, with other women, with men, or both" (pp. 88–89).

If concepts such as justice are to be meaningful, Althaus-Reid (2000) argued that queer theology needs to begin with women's experience of pleasure. "If people cannot honestly incorporate the sexual aspect of their lives into their experiences of the divine," she asks, "then how can they possibly hope to live with integrity and in right-relation with others?" (Simpson, 2005, pp. 99–100). This incorporation is important for bisexual women if we are to navigate between caricatures of us as hypersexual on the one hand and religious constructions of femininity as asexual and reproductive on the other. Yet *women's experience* is a loaded term with a history of marginalizing women, and we must use it with caution. Even within my sample of 40 women in one city, there was great diversity in identity labels, gender expression and the cultural milieu in which they live out their sexuality (Robinson, 2009). Bisexual women's diversity must be preserved or our feminist anthropology will simply propose a new abstract norm against which other (and Othered) women are measured.

Sexualizing theology involves not simply stitching the sexual together with the Divine, but engaging in theological reflection on our sexual experiences, relationships and practices. Although it was not the subject of my study, 17.5% of the women interviewed mentioned spirituality as playing a role in their attachment to their partners. One woman recalled that she and her girlfriend "had some similar spiritual experiences and explorations," and another felt that she and her boyfriend "had a very strong spiritual or even karmic connection right from the start" (Robinson, 2009, p. 186). Sexualizing theology also means asserting that queer women's sexual traditions can have a spiritual impact and religious meaning, even (perhaps especially) when those traditions do not conform to social expectations of women's sexual expression. Such traditions in a Toronto context could include Women's Bathhouse events, sexual play parties such as Bent and activities such as cuddle piling (nonsexual group snuggling). The way in which our sexual practices are also religious requires a redefinition of religion outside of doctrinal lines. If *religion* were defined as humanist author Anthony Pinn (1996) does, as "that which provides orientation or direction for human life" (p. 9), or as Protestant theologian Paul Tillich (1975) did, as our area of "ultimate concern" (p. 15), then we could reclaim its meaning from sectarian monopoly. We could therefore paraphrase the slogan "the personal is political," arguing that the personal is also (perhaps even always) religious.

Yet our experience of sexuality is not unleavened by oppression and social sin. Patriarchy, misogyny, biphobia and other forms of injustice are internalized and form part of our psyche. As theologian Kwok Pui-Lan (2005) asked, "How do postcolonial intellectuals [or any of us who have internalized dominating discourses] begin the process of decolonization of the mind and soul?" (p. 30). We need a theology that liberates us from these internalized discourses (which can undermine our agency, damage our mental health and harm our relationships). Polyamory activists suggest that we also need to be liberated from jealousy and other behaviours that disguise notions of patriarchal ownership as love. We have no access to a "pure" sexuality, untainted by heteropatriarchy, and bisexual theology must begin from a critical feminist standpoint if we are to reduce the risk of simply baptizing oppressive practices. Because oppressive discourses are absorbed into our psyche we must be particularly vigilant not to mistake the acceptance (social and psychological) that comes with conforming for the freedom of liberation.

Althaus-Reid (2000) was alert to the danger of psychological colonization and described queer women's theologizing as a "process of de-hegemonisation" (p. 7). She stressed the need for an analysis of the way women's sexuality has been constructed by heteropatriarchy (Althaus-Reid, 2004). Heteronormative portrayals of women's sexuality have conflated love with sex. This approach has underemphasised the importance of sexual fulfilment for women, redirecting them instead to expressions of love that have been submissive and self-sacrificing. Within Catholicism this approach has been embodied in Mariology (Manning, 1999), which has highlighted Mary's obedience to God, her fulfilment in her role as mother and her patience in the face of suffering. Building upon the Christological maxim that what is not assumed by Jesus is not redeemed (St. Gregory of Nazianz), Althaus-Reid (2004) insisted that if it is to become relevant to women Christology must incorporate insights from sexological research in the United States of America and Argentina. She named the work of Nancy Friday and Susana Finkel as examples.

Constructing a theology that reflects on our sexual experiences of pleasure, and that values our queer culture and its practices may be deemed illegitimate by even the most affirming of Christian congregations. Yet theological illegitimacy is precisely Althaus-Reid's goal. Terms such as legitimate, she argues, are instruments of patriarchal ideology. Her work seeks to "rescue elements of illegitimacy and subversion" in religious ritual and tradition, and in sexual and social practice (Althaus-Reid, 2004, p. 18). This illegitimacy is not reducible to an adolescent contrariness—rather, it is a transformative illegitimacy, which cuts to the root of social expectations of the good, the proper, the right and the holy, revealing that God's values are not the same as hegemonic human values.

3. Reframing Authority

In contrast to the hegemonic theology introduced to Latin America through military conquest and aligned with an oppressive political regime, Althaus-Reid proposed a theology based on a "consensual relationship" with God (Althaus-Reid & Isherwood, 2004, p. 107). To affirm consensuality as a desirable quality for our relationship with the Divine not only encapsulates the theological essence of free will, but also holds out hope that such a value could, through being divinized in this way, come to norm all human relationships. An emphasis on consensual relationships would greater reflect the experience of many in the queer community for whom even the relationships most taken for granted as not chosen, such as family, have been redefined due to neglect, abandonment or expulsion.

A consensual relationship shifts the distribution of power from the Church (or other authorities on the good) to the people in whose marginal and messy lives God is at work. The Holy Spirit, Althaus-Reid maintained (2000), does not limit itself to operating only within channels approved by Church bureaucracy. She proposes a more flexible Holy Spirit, whose presence is saving not only in a soteriological sense (in some spiritual sense or afterlife), but also in present concrete ways, removing our internalized oppression (such as the colonial mind-set) and empowering us to voice our dissent. Such a reframing of religious authority empowers bisexual women to place ourselves at the center of our theology. Rosemary Radford Ruether (1983) argued that the affirmation of women's full humanity must be the critical principle of women's theology. My commitment to freedom for myself and other bisexual women demands that I assert that our personhood is equal to that of others and prioritize our freedom as the starting point of our theology and as the norm by which we assess authority. Following feminist theologian Elizabeth Farians (1972), I agree that "[e]ither religion promotes human development and well being or it is destructive and cannot be representative of the true God" (p. 199).

Consensuality also means adopting a radical suspicion toward Scripture and tradition as it has been received. Althaus-Reid (2004) argued that these categories have been essentially foreign to Latin America and to women. She proposes a theological reassessment of Scripture and tradition based on the religious experience of Latin Americans themselves—in short, not an adaptation of the Bible for indigenous cultures, but a new theology built from the ground up. This rebuilding includes suppressed stories and practices that have been dismissed by Church authorities as primitive, syncretistic or heretical. When the locus of authority is shifted from external (Bible, Church) to internal (community, individual) then many Scriptures become possible.

When bisexual women are placed at the center of our theology, the content of Christian Scripture and tradition can seem very foreign indeed. The theology we inherit from our communities of faith has been a theology by and for men, despite its claims to universality. Even the biblical texts have been selected by men as those that best reflect their understanding of the Divine. Christianity was complicit in the military colonization of North America and continues to be a hegemonic social force today. Catholic arguments against my sexuality that invoke the importance of the family ring hollow for me in light of the residential school system, which systematically destroyed native families. Reframing theological authority means exploring and creating new Scriptural works, and creating canons (however tentative) that embody our own experience of the sacred, evoke the assent of our community and serve as the rule by which we measure our actions.

Alternative revelatory texts could include writing that emerges from the queer community, traditionally secular literature and even (perhaps especially) the text of our own lives. Within bisexual women's community, the first bisexual anthology, *Bi Any Other Name* (Hutchins & Kaahumanu, 1991), has functioned as a kind of Scripture, because bisexual women have looked to it for confirmation of their identity, used it as an authority to argue points of politics, and as an inspiration for building bisexual communities. Carter Heyward (1990) warned against reifying our own perspective on the holy by shutting the theological process down prematurely. "It is wrong," she wrote, "to close the canons at the end of one's own story or that of one's people" (p. 197). We must be open to changes in our Scriptures as the needs (and political awareness levels of our community) change.

At the root of the differences between Althaus-Reid's perception of Scripture and more traditional approaches lies a disagreement on the nature of revelation. The closure of the canon, agreed to by most Christian traditions, assumes that God's direct revelation has ended (having reached fullness in Christ) and can be encapsulated in a collection of authoritative texts. Althaus-Reid assumed that revelation is an ongoing process, which requires embracing new works and abandoning works as their partiality or toxicity are revealed over time. Such a move would have serious consequences for ecumenism, but given the relationship many queers have had with their traditions of origin, it's not unreasonable to ask why we should care.

Althaus-Reid (2004) noted that women's theological struggle may mean "leaving the Church and its alliance with the oppressive state" (p. 81). This may be necessary for bisexual women as most Christian communities are reluctant to even include the bisexual perspective, let alone allow it to take central place in a theological revolution. Although Christianity outside the Church may be possible (or even desirable), as I show in the section below, if our theology changes and those authorized to do theology changes, then our God changes.

4. Taking Metaphor Seriously

A fourth theme in Althaus-Reid's theology is her reexamination of divine metaphor. She demonstrates how particular religious metaphors have promoted heteronormative visions of sexuality. The image of Christ as the bridegroom of the Church, for example, has been used to reinforce claims that heterosexuality and monogamy are normative for all Christians. Taking metaphor seriously requires exploring these and other images from our own perspectives, mining the tradition for new or suppressed meanings.

One of the most interesting developments of this theme in Althaus-Reid's work is her exploration of the use of *monogamy* as divine metaphor. Representations of God as singular, she argued (2003), have baptised other monotraditions: the monotheistic deity in an exclusive relationship with his chosen people, the priest as representative of Christ to the laity, the Pope as head of the Church, the king as head of a Christian empire, and the husband as lord to his submissive wife. Each of these dyads is a hierarchy, rather than a partnership of equals, and each further legitimizes the divine master–slave dynamic. This monothinking has led to the rejection of polyamory in Christian ethics and resulted in a general tendency toward authoritarianism that has often been expressed or reinforced by military violence. What radical reordering might result if God is revealed as multiple, and as blessing multiplicity?

If examined from a queer perspective, Althaus-Reid (2003) suggested, the Trinity could reveal polyamory as a key element of God's nature. This reframing would not only revolutionize sexual ethics, but also influence other areas of theology that have traditionally taken up the monogamous model. Divine polyamory could be a positive concept for reframing the Christian view of the legitimacy of God's covenant with the Jewish people, too long denied by monogamist supersessionism. Polyamory allows the recognition that God has many lovers. Such an approach also holds promise for ecological theology, which has struggled with anthropocentrism. A God whose polyamory includes all living creatures does not place our avaricious desire above the basic needs of his other lovers.

Yet given the challenges reported by monogamous bisexuals in my study (Robinson, 2009; particularly maintaining their visibility as bisexuals), it is not sufficient to simply replace the image of a monogamous god with a polyamorous one. Monogamous bisexual women reported feeling marginalized in bi space by implicit and explicit expectations of polyamory.

This marginalization will only be reinforced by a theology that divinizes the practice. What we require is a reframing of the issues. The problem is not monogamy as such, but the compulsory nature of monogamy: the double standards emerging from heterosexism that posit monogamy as natural for women, and the oppressive nature of its practice within economies of sexual oppression. Althaus-Reid (2003) denounced monothinking, but not the faithfulness, focus, commitment or intimacy of monogamy (pp. 19, 54–55). Bisexual women need a new monogamy and a new polyamory in which our choices are not placeholders in a hierarchy of women. Kwok Pui-Lan (1990) put it well: "In the end, we must liberate ourselves from a hierarchical model of truth which assumes there is one truth above many" (p. 281).

Moreover, there is a problem with treating monogamy and polyamory as completely distinct and opposing categories. The women in my study (Robinson, 2009) did not fall into discrete monogamous and polyamorous categories but used these identities strategically at different points in their lives. Moreover, their definitions of *monogamy* and *polyamory* did not always correspond with the expected; some monogamous women were open to threesomes with their partners, and some polyamorous women were contentedly single or celibate. A theology developed by bisexual women may include a sense of dynamic movement reflecting the strategic transitions of bisexual women themselves.

5. Reclaiming the Sacred

Althaus-Reid applied her hermeneutic suspicion not only to texts, but also to the content of the message—that of a monotheistic male divinity. Traditional theology, she argued (2005), has constructed women as the Other to all that is normative, including God. To discover the Divine apart from patriarchy, apart from the violent dominance and submission of colonialism, and apart from the sexualized violence of heteronormativity is in effect to discover a different God than the one most Christians would recognize. At this point Althaus-Reid exited Christian theology, a concern that bothers her not at all if her choice is between Christian orthodoxy and an authentic God. "We must be proud to be called betrayers," she wrote (2004), "if our unfaithfulness to patriarchal ideology opens up the possibility of discovering God anew" (pp. 3–4).

Althaus-Reid developed the idea of the "queer God," whose face has been hidden and suppressed by heterosexual theology (Althaus-Reid & Isherwood, 2004). This God is not a reformer of the current Church in all its sins (hierarchical, misogynistic, heterosexist, monoloving) but is an alternative to fixed structures of any kind. Instead of the monotheistic father God, which sacralizes compulsory monogamy and male domination, the queer God is a diverse, and dynamic deity whose presence is felt among the outcast, and within intimate human relationships. The queer God can be moved, and far from being absolutely independent and transcendent, "depends heavily on our intimate relationships to configure Godself" (Althaus-Reid, 2003, p. 53). In short, the queer God needs us and thus sacralizes the extent to which we need each other.

Althaus-Reid rejected the authenticity of the God of the patriarchal colonial heterosexist Church, which constructed him in its own image reflecting upon the history of women in Latin America, she noted that "other divinities are not only more friendly, but that there is a 'god' who is one of us: for women she was the Goddess" (2005, p. 267). This other divinity is not simply a female version of God—God in a dress, as it were. Instead, she is as Althaus-Reid (2005) described her "the Other goddess, the Goddess who reads *Capital* and understands the need for agrarian reform" (p. 268).

The prospect of intimacy with a female deity offers intriguing possibilities for bisexual women's theology. Such a relationship, particularly if accompanied by ritual, could be a resource for those women in relationships with men, who find long-term bisexual visibility a challenge. It could also ground celebratory expressions of women's polyamory as reflective of divine love. One example of such a celebration is the Goddess room that has been set up at some of the women's bathhouse events, in which a pagan priestess offers sexual encounters. Women have reported this experience as mediating divine love and community acceptance. At the same time, it seems specific to queer women's community; due to sexism the aspect that makes it sacramental would, I think, be lost if men were included. The psychological effect for women of seeing their own humanity imaged as divine has not yet been fully explored. Although the potential is revolutionary, the history of Mariology within the Catholic tradition ought to make women concerned about what elements of the "feminine" are identified with deity.

Given bisexual erasure, more attention needs to be paid to the sacred quality of being out. I agree with gay theologian Chris Glaser (1998) who argued that "simply being 'out' is a form of ministry" (p. 14). There is a positive value in being out as bisexual and an adequate sexual theology must facilitate this visibility. As I discovered in my research (Robinson, 2009), being out as bisexual requires a community of witness, as our sexuality is often only visible serially, to people we have known for long periods of time. Affirming the social nature of our sexuality highlights the critical role of community in bisexual women's identity development and requires a commitment to building and supporting such communities. This is not a separatist enterprise but occurs amid webs of relationships with lesbians, transsexuals, gay men and nonconforming heterosexuals.

Bisexual Theology Moving Forward

Robert Goss (2002) observed that transgender theology is "further along" than bisexual theology and speculated that this may be "due to insufficient bi activism within communities of faith or to bisexuals not experiencing the degree of exclusion and hostility that transgendered folks do" (p. 252). I see the slow development of bisexual theology as having other causes. Primary among these is the fact that, in most cases, bisexuals do not have our own communities. Communities provide the security and breathing space where people can reflect on their experience and begin the hermeneutical circle which produces theology. To be a bisexual woman in mainstream culture is to be constantly navigating our invisibility and our oppression as bisexuals and as women; this is compounded exponentially if we are also women of color, or members of the poor and working class. Bisexual women in lesbian communities must also navigate invisibility and lesbian biphobia. Only in bisexual community can bisexual women relax in a space where they need not defend or explain themselves and begin the conversations and reflections that produce a uniquely bisexual theology.

To be adequate to the task of meeting bisexual women's needs, theology must also facilitate and support a raised consciousness. Rather than a theology that is blind to social sin, bisexual feminism needs a theology where sexual decisions are made with a conscientized awareness of the social, political and moral context. Mujerista theologian Ada Maria Isasi-Diaz (1990) defined *conscientization* as "a moment of insight which creates a suspicion about oppression" (p. 36). This critical awareness enables the oppressed to grasp the cause of their oppression and envision and enact the praxis required to oppose it. Like coming out, conscientization is an ongoing process, "not something that happens once and for all" (Isasi-Diaz, p. 36). Isasi-Diaz viewed the shift from naïve to critical awareness as a prerequisite for mutuality, for only if we correctly understand the nature of our relationship with another can we relate authentically. A commitment to conscientization as a process is therefore an essential prerequisite to sexual relationships that are based on authenticity, justice and love.

The imagination of conscientized women is a key resource for bisexual feminist theology. Althaus-Reid's queer methodology can provide a framework, but it will take our own awakened imaginations to put meat to the bones, as it were. It may be that an authentic bisexual feminist theology is no longer identifiable as Christian. Theologians such as Althaus-Reid have been willing to follow God out of Christianity if that is where God leads. It is time that bisexual women began to discuss where God is leading us.

REFERENCES

Althaus-Reid, M. (2000). *Indecent theology: Theological perversions in sex, gender and politics*. London: Routledge

Althaus-Reid, M. (2003). *The queer god*. London: Routledge.

Althaus-Reid, M. (2004). *From feminist theology to indecent theology: readings on poverty, sexual identity and god*. London: SCM Press.

Althaus-Reid, M. (2005). From the goddess to queer theology. *Feminist Theology, 13*(2), 265–272.

Althaus-Reid, M., & Isherwood, L. (2004). *The sexual theologian: Essays on sex, god and politics*. London: T&T Clark.

Angelides, S. (2001). *A history of bisexuality*. The Chicago Series on Sexuality, History, and Society. Chicago, IL: University of Chicago Press.

Farians, E. (1972, March). Justice, the hard line. *Andover-Newton Quarterly, 12*(4), 199.

Gammon, M. A. (2007). Troubling the canon: Bisexuality and queer theory. *Journal of Homosexuality, 523*(1/2), 159–184.

Glaser, C. (1998). *Coming out as sacrament*. Louisville, KY: Geneva Press.

Goss, R. (2002). *Queering Christ: Beyond Jesus acted up*. Cleveland, OH: Pilgrim Press.

Heyward, C. (1990). Jesus of Nazareth/Christ of faith: Foundations of a reactive Christology. In S. B. Thistlethwaite & M. P. Engel (Eds.), *Lift every voice: Constructing Christian theologies from the underside* (pp. 191–200). San Francisco, CA: Harpersanfrancisco.

Hutchins, L., & Kaahumanu, L. (1991). *Bi any other name: Bisexual people speak out*. Boston, MA: Alyson.

Isasi-Diaz, A. M. (1990). Solidarity: Love of neighbor in the 1980s. In S. B. Thistlethwaite & M. P. Engel (Eds.), *Lift every voice: Constructing Christian theologies from the underside* (pp. 31–40). San Francisco, CA: Harpersanfrancisco.

Kwok, P. (1990). Discovering the bible in the non-biblical world. In S. B. Thistlethwaite & M. P. Engel (Eds.), *Lift every voice: Constructing Christian theologies from the underside* (pp. 270–282). San Francisco, CA: Harpersanfrancisco.

Kwok, P. (2005). *Postcolonial imagination and feminist theology*. Louisville, KY: Westminster John Knox Press.

Manning, J. (1999). *Is the pope catholic? A woman confronts her church*. Toronto, Canada: Malcolm Lester Books.

Pinn, A. (1996). On becoming humanist: A personal journey. *Religious Humanism, 32*(1/2), 12–28.

Robinson, M. (2009). *Turning points in identity: Bisexual women choosing between monogamous and polyamorous relationships*. Unpublished doctoral dissertation, University of St. Michael's College, Toronto, Canada.

Ruether, R. R. (1983). *Sexism and god-talk: toward a feminist theology*. Boston, MA: Beacon Press.

Sherkat, D. E. (2002). Sexuality and religious commitment in the United States: An empirical examination. *Journal for the Scientific Study of Religion, 41*(2), 313–323.

Simpson, R. (2005). How to be fashionably queer: Reminding the Church of the importance of sexual stories. *Theology and Sexuality, 11*(2), 97–108.

Tillich, P. (1975). *Systematic theology, volume one*. Chicago, IL: University of Chicago Press.

FROM THE ARCHIVES

Bisexual Women as Emblematic Sexual Healers and the Problematics of the Embodied Sacred Whore[1]

LORAINE HUTCHINS

The image of woman as Erotic Priestess or Goddess— sometimes seen also as Sacred Whore—is a central part of new popular sacred sex cosmologies. The Sacred Whore, as we know her, originated during the second wave of feminism during the 70s. She was imagined as an archetype evocative of ancient times when Erotic Priestesses plied their sexual healing arts in temples dedicated to female deities. Since the 1990s an expanding range of people—from sex workers to nurses, massage therapists, ministers, counselors, and New Age tantra practitioners—have all begun to call themselves holy prostitutes or something similar; taking their place among artists, activists and philosophers redefining contemporary cultural constructs of sexuality, spirituality, and the connections between them.

For centuries bisexual women, closeted or not, have been prominent in the ranks of sex educators and erotic healers since we love beyond gender and teach others to serve as societal/erotic change agents as well. However, we often work within a system of heteronormativity and male dominance which eroticizes us more as objects than as representations of divinity. These adverse conditions cause the very sacred sex practices meant to facilitate gender transcendence to instead reify gender and re-enforce constrictive roles of gender and sexual orientation. This article examines current feminist theorizing on The Sacred Whore. It analyzes (1) why she has become embodied now, especially in bi women, (2) the pros and cons of her embodiment, and (3) the prospects for developing inclusive, egalitarian erotic communities within current constraints of gender and sexual orientation that dictate an erotic healer role that is still gender-bound.

[1]This article was originally published in the *Journal of Bisexuality*, Vol. 2, Numbers 2/3, pp. 205–226, 2002, by Harrington Park Press, an imprint of the Haworth Press, Inc.

> When we hold the erotic as sacred, we say that our capacity for pleasure has a value in and of itself, that in fact it is one of the ways in which we connect with the deepest purposes of the universe.
>
> —Starhawk, "The Sacredness of Pleasure" (1995, p. 328)

INTRODUCING THE NEW HOLY EROTICS

Sexual healer is not a common occupational category, at least not one that is currently listed in the Bureau of Labor Statistics' job titles or for which you can receive training and certification at most educational institutions. But if we were to imagine trained sexual healers in today's workplace, what sex would they most likely be? Nurturance and erotic allure are qualities and behaviors currently attributed much more to women than to men. The majority of contemporary sex workers are women. Given these two facts it is quite probable that when most people visualize sexual healers, we see women in these roles. And who better to fill the role of sexual healer than the bountiful, if mythic, bi woman, who cheerfully accepts all comers, in loving and celebratory ways? This essay discusses an emerging new calling or profession being created by—women, many of them bisexual, who both work as sex educators, sex counselors and/or healers, and also identify professionally as *Sacred Prostitutes* or *Sacred Whores*. And try to at least begin answering the question: What does this phenomenon of women as erotic priestesses and sexual healers, particularly bi women as sexual healers, mean for all people in this culture, especially in the context of increased interest in holistic, mind-body integration, and efforts to harmonize sexuality and spirituality? Sacred sexuality is a hot, hip topic these days and the image of Erotic Priestesses is a central part of popular accounts of ancient sacred sex rites. Whether these accounts have any basis in historic fact or not is debatable, but figures such as the Sacred Prostitute or Harlot for the Queen of Heaven are now appearing as the topic of newsstand feature articles. Women acting as Holy Sluts have served the Goddess at the Temple of Love at such large gatherings as Burning Man, the big end-of-summer festival held each year in the Nevada desert outside of Los Angeles (Hutchins, 2001). Therapists integrate tantric techniques advice into their couples counseling. Young people explore music-and-drug- induced trance experiences called "raves." These all night, often outdoor ecstatic dance rituals provide a polymorphous sense of communion, often spiritual as well as erotic. College catalogs offer courses on sex and spirit. It is fairly easy in most big cities now to find one-on-one divine-love-making instruction sessions offered by teachers guided by tantric wisdom, or at least what passes for it in the West. Even once-taboo group erotic rituals are organized through health spas and retreat centers. Sacred sex is the subject of World Wide Websites and television network newsmagazine features, supermarket magazine articles, fashion reviews, and popular novels. Familiarity with sacred sex imagery is even assumed—in everything from *Atlantic Monthly* whiskey ads to mail-order catalog Valentine's Day displays. Whatever terms are used, there is a new popular interest in reviving the ancient arts of erotic spirituality. The sacred sexuality field has expanded; beyond the yoga, massage and New Age meditation arenas, into more mainstream areas such as cable television, Internet chat rooms, and helping-profession associations. Some human service professionals now present sacred sex-themed workshops at psychological research and social work conferences. And several new organizations of sacred sex healers have formed, including at least two different national training programs certifying sacred sex teachers in sexual healing.

People don't necessarily mean the same things when they say tantric sex, sacred sex, or sex magic, but, for better or for worse, distinctions between these varied terms are becoming increasingly blurred. In New Age circles, tantra is often referred to as sexual yoga. But it is really a specific set of Hindu or Buddhist beliefs and practices that originated in ancient India and involve years of devoted study. Sex magic refers to ceremonial uses of erotic energy for various purposes. Sacred sex is more of a catch-all term. However these terms are all used interchangeably to mean anything from erotic calisthenics, to enhanced partner-intimacy or therapeutic spiritual and sexual healing; anything from the pursuit of better orgasms and feel-good ambiance, to seeking connection with the divinity within and beyond oneself. Historically, sacred sex symbology has been rooted in fertility magic; fucking in the fields to make the crops grow, earth goddesses of fecundity and male gods identified with seeds, who often die at harvest and are yearly reborn. Remnants of these cathartic, erotic mystery rituals of release and renewal are evident today in all the places where festivals like Carnival are celebrated. In medieval Europe there was also the Feast of Fools or Saturnalia, and Lupercalia. These rituals usually involved role reversals like peasants being made Queen or King for a Day, as well as cross-dressing and suspension of the usual sexual taboos. Today's sacred sex rituals are by no means all directly derived from these ancient erotic rites, but they also don't emerge out of nowhere; such rituals and beliefs have much historic precedence.

Current interest in sacred sex is fueled by social trends over the past 50 years—increased knowledge about sexuality and sexual diversity, the emergence of sexual liberation movements and mind-body healing methods, and increased interest in more alternative, sex-positive and earth-centered spiritualities. Of all these trends it is sexual liberation movements, and the socio-political space these movements have created, that particularly support the out bi woman as teacher, priestess and healer.

BEING BISEXUAL AND FEMALE IN A MALE-DOMINANT WORLD

As women, we are taught from girlhood that the worst thing we can be called is a slut or a whore. These terms are used to keep us in line. There is a big difference between slut and whore. Sluts give away sex for free. Whores negotiate payment. But in the realm of innuendo and slurs, these terms blur. For men, as it has often been pointed out, there is no real equivalent of the term slut. Sexually active men are more likely praised for their sexual prowess, not disparaged. Stud and even gigolo have entirely different meanings and the notorious double-standard still thrives. Each of us knows instances where women who cross the lines of what is expected are called slut or whore, and often lesbian too, with little regard for the accuracy of these labels. So what are we to make of women who call themselves Sacred Whores? Is this a reversal, a reclaiming, something more? Sometimes the label is Sacred Prostitute, or Quodishtu—the biblical term for the sacred prostitute. I've also heard Holy Slut, Sacred Intimate, Erotic Priestess, Sexual Healer. As a sex educator I identify with this erotic sisterhood, whether or not I solicit cash for my sensual, restorative arts. Why? Because, as a woman I am used to being sexually objectified in this world and as a bisexual woman I am used to being treated differently socially—partly as pariah and partly with deference and honor—just because of my stated identity. As a bi woman in a male-dominated society I am also used to much blurring of lines, not only the lines between gay and heterosexual (where I live), but also the lines between what is sexual and what is "not," what is therapeutic and what is erotic, what is free and what is bartered/purchased. All these lines are sometimes quite indistinct in intimate communication between people, especially between women and men. Furthermore, we bisexual women are so used to being called sluts, being accused of promiscuity and indiscriminate desire (whether it is true or not) that it is not that much farther a step to capitalize on what we are accused of, to commercialize the exchange of sexual services, and/or to even elevate them to the status of spiritual calling—as in the case of women who call themselves "Sacred Whores." But making erotic exchange a sacred healing act also raises many new problems and questions. Whether we charge money for our services is only one of them.

We women who openly love without regard to gender, or despite it, or beyond it, or simply inclusively love people, must regularly fight against having our desires suppressed or invalidated. Therefore, developing comfort with, and an assertiveness about, our sexuality are usually survival mechanisms we have internalized and depended upon for so long that we hardly even realize them. Still, we learn to self-consciously scrutinize our own (and other's) sexuality, probably more than most women; another attribute that serves us well if we become sex-workers, holy or not. We have to be self-conscious about our bisexuality, or else we'd settle for merely passing as heterosexual, or gay, according to with whom we were in relationship at the time, or which community felt more like home. Since we instead become used to asserting ourselves sexually by going against the norms and learning to live somewhat "outside the box" just to be able to assert our pleasure-direction without interference or misunderstanding, it makes sense that we're also likely to be pioneers in other areas of sexuality—such as in sex-related professions—sex counselors and researchers, massage therapists, erotic dancers, etc. Being ostracized, or at least objectified, as sexual outlaws—women who won't conform to social expectations and norms—also makes it easier for us to become the stand-out sexperts extraordinaire, the erotic teachers and artists who have become the initiators and leaders of new cultural trends. Think of Betty Dodson, Maggi Rubenstein, Annie Sprinkle, Carol Queen, Barbara Carellas, Kate Bornstein, Joann Loulan, Kim Ayres, Jill Nagle, Elise Matheson, Lani Ka'ahumani, Susie Bright, Tristan Taormino, Cecelia Tan, Pat Califia—all bisexually behaving, most also bisexually-identifying—who are some of our best sex teachers in the national LGBT community. (And this is only a partial list.)

Yet bisexual women's assertiveness, particularly in regards to sexual behavior, is coded *male* in a larger society where men more often initiate sex and women more often don't. However, *because* we are still women in a male-dominant society, our ways of being sexually assertive are gender-limited. For example, women are regarded as nurturing, passive and deferential, even if as the subset—bisexual women—we are somewhat gender deviant. The same erotic assertiveness that makes us the modern-day equivalents of good geishas or courtesans—professional dominatrixes, hands-on sex educators and masseuses, erotic dancers—can also ghettoize us. While these kinds of erotic service positions can confer a unique kind of power and authority—they also present problems related to sexual-objectification, of living in a culture where sex and spirit are seen as divorced from each other, even in opposition. Bi women are also multiply Otherized as members of sexually objectified groups— women and queer people at least, sometimes also as people of color. And all these groups are more associated with the body, with the earth, than the dominant groups, who are, in a mind/body dichotomized world, conversely associated with the mind, with maleness, with whiteness, with heterosexuality, and with spiritual, political, and economic power over "others." These ways of gendering sexuality, power and spirituality in turn all affect how we "read" the current phenomena of women who enact/express aspects of our sexual and/or professional lives as erotic priestesses, sexual healers, sacred whores.

ORIGINS OF THE SACRED WHORE ARCHETYPE

Perhaps you've never heard of anyone calling themselves a Sacred Whore. Or perhaps you thought she existed only in antiquity, as an archetype, a temple priestess dedicated to Aphrodite or Venus, but not someone who walks today's busy streets or hangs out her shingle on the Internet. I first encountered the term Sacred Prostitute in the late '70s and '80s, in the works of two feminist writers named Merlin Stone and Deena Metzger (Metzger, 1989; Stone, 1976). They wrote about historic and/or fictitious characters, who may have lived as Sacred Whores in ancient times, although Metzger entreated us all to integrate a bit of the Sacred Whore into our contemporary daily lives as a way of becoming more whole. Over the last decade, between the late 1980s and now, people in New Age spirituality circles, human potential and therapy circles, feminist spirituality practitioners and feminist sex workers have all begun to popularize the term Sacred Prostitute or Sacred Whore.[1] In these U.S. circles probably several hundred people, mostly women, many of them bisexual, identify deeply with the Sacred Whore archetype, whether or not they work, as sex workers, in a business sense. This is in itself unusual. When was the last time in history that women began intentionally identifying with those most ostracized of their class and when women with middle-class professional educations began identifying with and using the same techniques in their workplace (and/or bedroom) as their sisters with less options?

It is a dramatic change to take the Sacred Whore out of history books and into contemporary workplaces as well as in social/recreational, support, and spiritual community spaces. And it is my contention that this would not have happened without the current interest in connecting sex and spirit, or, what some call the sacred sexuality movement. Sacred sexuality beliefs and practices are part of a larger mind/body movement focused on holistic healing, beliefs rooted in the need to re-integrate sex and spirit. The contemporary Sacred Whore is one of the roles for women within the communities of those interested in and practicing sacred sexualities. Until sacred sexuality communities began to develop an interest in sexual healing and erotic priestessing over the past two decades, the Sacred Whore was merely a non-embodied archetype, a part of classics study and feminist spirituality lore. Sacred Whore imagery depends upon a more positive image of women's divinity than exists in most western religious traditions. It is rooted in an image of woman as Goddess that has emerged, or re-emerged, as part of feminist, New Age, Neo-Pagan, and Eastern-influenced Goddess spirituality traditions, within the last 30 years.

But to what extent is eroticized Goddess imagery shaped by contemporary men's desires, by men historically, by women historically and/or by women contemporarily? How much is the Erotic Priestess something inherent in the eternal female aspects of spirituality, and how much is it something culturally projected upon us? In a sexually oppressive world there is sometimes a fine line between celebrating sexuality and being the repository, or target, of its celebration. When I first began this research into contemporary U.S. sacred sexualities I knew, as witches and children do, that pleasure's root *is* sacredness. But I thought the Wiccan "Charge of the *Goddess*"—*all acts of love and pleasure are My acts*[2]—*and* the sex-positive focus of certain Hindu and Buddhist traditions like Tantra and Taoism were theological anomalies, at least in the developed Western world. That was before I found out that many religions hold erotic imagery at their secret, mystic cores. For instance, the original Hebrew temple in Jerusalem, the one that was destroyed in antiquity, had highly erotic art in its inner sanctum.

Still, in the Bible one does not easily find holy women who were comfortably and powerfully sexual on their own (much less bisexual). In fact, women are often blamed for bringing sexual knowledge (Eve's apple) into the world. The biblical harlot is that woman most looked down upon, that woman most associated with the body, with the earth, with sin. Like bisexuals today, "(T)he harlot is a kind of legal outlaw, standing outside the normal social order with its approved roles for women, ostracized and marginalized, but needed and therefore accommodated ... the harlot not only demands a price, she controls the transaction ... a reversal of the normal sex roles ... ambivalence pervades the whole relationship" (Bird, 1997, p. 206). This "ambivalence that pervades the whole relationship" between whores and men is an ambivalence particularly about women who step outside the gender norms and dare to act with sexual agency and/or to put a price on sexual exchange. Bisexual women stand outside the normal social roles and act with sexual agency. We are often regarded as promiscuous sluts, whether we actually take on that identity ourselves or not.

But being holy is a very different thing. We as women, bisexual or not, have only traditionally been honored as partners of men in heterosexual and monogamous matrimony, if at all. We certainly have not been revered as independent holy sexual beings. There is still, in this age thousands of years after Biblical time, no autonomous role for women spiritual leaders, bisexual or otherwise, that is both holy AND sexual. So collapsing these two polar images—erotic and spiritual—into one, as the image of the Sacred Prostitute does, is both profoundly disturbing, and fascinating. The Sacred Whore or Sacred Prostitute is, depending upon how you look at it, either appalling and impossible, or a powerful, enigmatic statement about reclaiming female wholeness in a broken world.

It is important to note that Merlin Stone, the first contemporary feminist scholar to investigate usage of the term Sacred Prostitute, asserts in *When God Was a Woman* (1976) that it is actually a mis-translation artifact, resulting from white male scholars' misunderstanding and/or distorting of women's ancient sexual and religious roles:

> The sacred sexual customs of the female religion offer us another of the apparent ties between the worship of the Divine Ancestress as it was known in Sumer, Babylon, Anatolia, Greece, Carthage, Sicily, Cyprus and even in Canaan. Women who made love in the temples were known ... as "sacred women," "the undefiled.".... The use of the word "prostitute" ... leads the reader to a misinterpretation of the religious beliefs and social structure of the period. (Stone, 1976, p. 157)

Though Stone clearly eschewed terming the temple priestesses "sacred prostitutes," it caught on as a term, probably because it juxtaposed sacred and profane, calling directly into question current sex and spirit splits. Stone wrote in the '70s, during the flower of the feminist Goddess movement; several years after the first classics—Mary Daly's *Beyond God the Father* (1977) and Carol Christ's *Womanspirit Rising* (1979)—were published, and several years before the major works of Starhawk (1979, 1982, 1995), Monica Sjoo (1992), Barbara Walker (1983), Margot Adler (1986) and others were released. After *When God Was a Woman* and other feminist spirituality books became more widely read, something interesting happened: the Sacred Whore walked right out of history books and into real life. My hunch is that 1985 is Her rebirth or embodiment year.

The year 1985 was a significant turning point, for a number of reasons; 1985 was the year Rock Hudson died and AIDS awareness broke into the general public's consciousness. Along with a generalized panic about how to make sex safe, and in the wake of remembering how profoundly sex and death relate, came both an accompanying impetus to take sex more seriously and increased public permission to long for sexual healing more openly. With this came a stronger awareness that the roots of sexuality are, and always have been, sacred to the core. This all fueled an interest in tantra and other forms of sacred sexuality rituals, which over the next decade (1985–1995) would begin to be more widely taught in U.S. cities. By the mid-80s the movements against sexual harassment, rape and abuse had also created increased societal awareness of our profound cultural needs for healing around sex. In 1985 women of all sexual orientations were beginning to express sexual agency and autonomy. It was a time when the feminist anti-porn and domestic violence movements gathered steam and radical Christian Rightwing groups also began mobilizing mainstream backlash against us.

At this time two interesting and very different new pieces of writing on sexuality and spirituality came out: (1) the Naaid Press anthology, *Lesbian Nuns,* was excerpted in *Penthouse Forum* magazine (June 1985), and (2) feminist poet Deena Metzger's article "Re-Vamping the Holy Prostitute" was reprinted in *Utne Reader* (1985). When Barbara Grier, publisher of Naiad Press, made the controversial decision to sell the *Lesbian Nuns* excerpt to a mainstream pornography venue she was roundly criticized by many in the feminist community, especially since she sold the excerpt to *Penthouse* without the knowledge or consent of the book's contributors or editors. However, the results of her decision to garner publicity for *Lesbian Nuns* was that it spotlighted many men's, and women's, longstanding erotic fantasies about nuns, and undoubtedly brought the book to new and wider audiences. The conflation of women as *both* sexual and spiritual beings was not only at the heart of *Lesbian Nuns'* popularity, it was also key to the fascination with Metzger's thesis.

Metzger, however, spoke of embodying the erotic priestess/sexual healer imagery in ALL people, not just women religious. In the early '80s Metzger had first presented her ideas in an address to the Conference of Feminist Art and Culture at California State University, Long Beach (Metzger, 1985). Invoking basic concepts from the U.S. women's spirituality movement, she said that "(t)he original whore was a priestess, the conduit to the divine, the one through whose body one entered the sacred arena and was restored. Warriors, soldiers, soiled by combat within the world of men, came to the Holy Prostitute, the *Quedishtu,* literally meaning 'the undefiled one,' in order to be cleansed and reunited with the divine" (Feuerstein, 1989). Her speech, entitled "Re-Vamping the World: On the Return of the Holy Prostitute," was the kind of speech everyone photocopied and passed around. Eventually the alternative press digest, *Utne Reader,* reprinted Metzger' s speech. In the issue following its release *(Utne Reader,* 1985), a whole section of commentary and letters had to be devoted to response.

Contemporary sacred prostitute imagery emerged during this period of overall reclaiming of women's positive erotic and spiritual imagery. The blossoming literature of the women's spirituality movement and feminist sexuality resources produced many beautifully erotic books that verged on the spiritual—Betty Dodson's *Liberating Masturbation: A Mediation on Selfloving,* Tee Corinne's *Cunt Coloring Book,* Dolores LaChapelle's *Sacred Land/Sacred Sex,* Judy Grahn's *Another Mother Tongue,* and Diane Mariechild's *Lesbian Sacred Sexuality* are all examples.

Books specific to sexual healing itself—as a feminist and holy profession—have been less numerous, but *The Sacred Prostitute: Eternal Aspects of the Feminine* (Qualls-Corbett, 1988) and *Women of the Light: The New Sacred Prostitute* (Stubbs, 1994) have both established the historic and modern basis of feminine archetypes of sexual healing. Jungian psychoanalyst Qualls-Corbett (1988) focuses on the elemental erotic nature of the feminine, explored through her clients' dreams. The dream analysis portion of her book is sandwiched between reflections on sacred prostitute imagery, both historic and modern. While most religious imagery in the U.S. separates mind from body and distinguishes spiritual love from physical love, making spirit "superior," goddess spiritualities do not have this split. In her section "The Demise of Sacred Prostitution," Qualls-Corbett (1988) explains that "Over time, the temples of love gave way to the house of the Lord, radically displacing woman's role in religious rites .... Profane prostitution continued to flourish, and woman's sexual nature was associated with it or judged by it. No longer seen as a gift of the divine, woman's sensuality was debased and exploited. The very qualities for which woman once had been considered sacred now became the reason for which she was degraded. ... No longer was the feminine envisioned as the source of physical delight and spiritual ecstasy—an overall feeling of inner harmony" (Qualls-Corbett, 1988, pp. 42–43).

Kenneth Ray Stubbs released *Women of the Light: The New Sacred Prostitute* twenty years after he first met bisexual artist, sex educator, teacher and healer, Betty Dodson, whom he cites as its inspiration (Stubbs, 1994). *Women of the Light* features Dodson and eight other women who integrate erotic spirituality and healing into their work and lives. Their professions range from porn star and group-sex hostess to sex surrogate, call girl and masseuse; from meditation teacher and nurse to artist and priestess. Stubbs ends the book with a resource section listing places where one can obtain training to become a "wo/man of the light," emphasizing that all the women in the book "are of service to both genders and there are men of the light who do likewise" (1994, pp. 239–240). The implication is that people who work as sacred prostitutes or erotic healers see their calling as unbound by gender, that they are open to clients regardless of gender, and thus, at least in some senses, are beyond the usual constraints of dichotomous sexual orientations or preferences, i.e., *bisexual*. Although not all the women in his book identify as bisexual, many of them do.

San Francisco anthropologist Lee Gilmore is currently researching the historic as well as the contemporary Sacred Whore. She interviewed women working professionally as sacred prostitutes who model their work on what they know or imagine about erotic priestess/healers from ancient times. She is now extending this work into doctoral research, studying Akkadian, the ancient middle-eastern language in which many of the original so-called "sacred prostitute" references were first found. There was definitely some form of sexual activity occurring within a cultic context throughout the ancient Near East, she says, but "the dilemmas engendered by countless layers of biased and misinformed translations are exacerbated by the paucity of data available, leaving the roots of the association between priestesses and prostitutes unexposed and rendering definitive conclusions impossible." However, Gilmore says that "(t)he very possibility that the border between the sacred and the profane was non-existent in the cultures of antiquity asks us to reconsider this division, turning back on our own questions and categories" (Gilmore, 1998).

PROBLEMATICS OF THE EMBODIED SACRED WHORE

Ten years ago when Lani Ka'ahumanu and I solicited contributors to *Bi Any Other Name* (1991), bisexual porn star and performance artist Annie Sprinkle offered us her "Sex Guidelines for the 90s." In this piece Sprinkle introduced the new term "sacred prostitutes," praising them as guides who empower people to "visualize a safe and satisfying future for your sex life and the sex lives of people of future generations." But she said that sacred prostitutes only existed in cultures past, "such as the ancient Taoists and Tantrics, some Native American tribes, some geisha, and the Sacred Prostitutes from ancient cultures like Sumeria and Mesopotamia" (Sprinkle, 1991). Between then and now, she and other bisexual women sex activists, including some of the other women contributors to *Bi Any Other Name,* have begun to identify professionally as erotic healers or sacred whores. Concurrently, a number of bi women had begun to organize with workers in the sex industry and found that some of them were beginning to visualize their work as much more than a source of income, as a sacred, healing calling. Even women who didn't identify as political activists—in the New Age movement, the neo-pagan movement, in therapeutic healing networks and in bodyworkers and women's spirituality therapists circles—were also becoming more confident in declaring their sexuality and their spirituality openly and seeing this as an asset rather than an individual shame or quirk. In my own research I interviewed several women who entered the field of Sacred Prostitution through first working as certified massage therapists, or as sex surrogates who consult with psychologists to help sexually dysfunctional clients. All of these different kinds of women, many of whom are bisexual, are popularizing sexual healing as a mode of service and devotion, spreading this philosophy beyond the sex industry into New Age, neo-pagan and other spiritual circles, as well as into the helping (human service) professions. But women, depending upon our education, our credentials, our economic statuses, our orientations, our relationships, and our class backgrounds, perform our sexual healing efforts differently. And whether we see Sacred Prostitution as an avocation, a vocation, or an attractive option in any form, usually relates not only to our preference and aptitude, but also to our economic options and opportunities.

In these past ten years, feminism and sex work, once seemingly separate universes, have begun to dialogue actively. Carol Queen tells the story of how the National Organization for Women moved significantly—from strongly opposing all forms of prostitution to being more open to understanding the points of view of feminists involved in sex work and organizing sex workers. Carol says that a crucial bridge for this new understanding came from women involved in the women's spirituality movement, that is women who understood intuitively how erotic healing could be regarded as and experienced as a sacred and respectable, non-exploitative act.[3] In a little over ten years the act of erotic healing has moved from fanciful ancient history, to, at least in some parts of the country and culture, a possible and enacted modem role. Albeit still small, yet now complete with a set of real life practices utilizing a variety of hands-on curative and nursing approaches such as breathing exercises, guided imagery meditation, conscious touch, and intimate communication/relationship coaching. The sexual positions of the kama sutra are still part of this but not the most important part. And since these approaches exist, much like bisexuality, on the margins of what is understood or acceptable, they have come to embody much of the same exotic, eroticized allure. Some of my contemporaries, both women and men, tend to romanticize the Sacred Prostitute. This both interests and frightens me. Metzger inspires people to bring the sacred and the erotic back together, to help people treat each other as divine beings. But her ideas can also be used to excuse violent, abusive men, men who would go to a "sexual healer" to be "cleansed and forgiven" as a way of being socialized back into "civilization" (Metzger, 1981). Women have been serving men this way for thousands of years without making men less violent or inspiring them to revere the feminine. I like the idea of women being more in control in sexual relations. Replacing the commonplace image of Eve as male temptress with the image of woman as authoritative priestess, civilizer and sexual healer is definitely an improvement. But presenting these images unconnected from a political movement for sexual equality, unconnected to a serious strategy to transform religious and social norms, will, I fear, change only women (and only a few of us, if that), not men. Why? Absent a critique of men's roles and actions, women's erotic power remains merely romanticized. And without scrutinizing the economics of sex work and other inequities in the waged labor of women and men, we will continue to make the Sacred Whore part of a gender ghetto. We certainly won't get the sexual healing from men that we deserve, nor will they be encouraged or learn how to give it to us or to each other. The sweet, compliant, healing whore re-enforces images of women as essentially different from men, of us as sexual nurturers, as non-threatening geisha/courtesans, as ameliorative influence tempering (but not morally or politically challenging or changing) a harsh, unjust world. Yes, there is a revolutionary element to Sacred Prostitute imagery that supports women as leaders of spiritual institutions and women as free agents sexually. But unless institutions and men's roles change dramatically, along with the visualization of new roles for women, I don't see us getting very far. I also don't see us, within current constraints, being able to create much free social space for large groups of women to act as sexual healers for each other, though I long for this.

Citing Metzger's work, for instance, yoga scholar Georg Feuerstein notes that she "explores ways out of the current anti-sexual stance of our contemporary society" and that her thoughts on the holy prostitute are "not applicable to women only," since "men and women alike must rediscover the sacredness of sexuality and 'revamp' (that is, refurbish) their outlook on life to include the sexual and the spiritual dimensions" (Feuerstein, 1989, p. 70). Absolutely. But what's lacking is an accompanying social justice agenda, an articulation of the intermediate steps from here to there. Sexual servitude is not, by definition, holy. Erotic healers are not meant to be items of entertainment or objectification. The feminist scholarship and activism of the past several decades has helped create a world in which women's sexuality and sexual agency is empowered enough for these kinds of images to be openly expressed and debated. That is great progress. But as women, bisexual or not, we still walk in fear, suffer hate crimes, are regularly battered and raped. The small group of people who call themselves erotic healers and endeavor to teach people how to reclaim sexuality and connect it to spirituality and intimacy are essential. This work is a central part of women's liberation, all people's liberation. But it cannot work in a vacuum, it cannot work without other political changes toward equality and social justice. I will close by exploring a bit further why this particular vocation of sexual healing, despite or because of its current contradictions, has become attractive to some very talented, intelligent bi women, and how what we teach about integrating sex and spirit is part of the most hot, incisive erotic/political commentary of our time.

THE POLITICS OF SEXUAL HEALING TODAY

What does it mean for bisexual women to be at the forefront of a new tradition of women as sexual healers? Are we priestessing with the authority of office, in communities we have equal voice in governing, and with the power to change things; or are we merely serving the unequal status quo by performing erotic/nurturing roles that pacify and distract people from seeking more far-reaching change? I suspect it's a bit of both and that individual situations need to be evaluated with these questions in mind. Genuine sexual healing need not involve exchange of money and often doesn't. Genuine sexual healing is also not your ordinary sex work transaction, even when it does involve exchange of services for money. It is not about the quick satisfaction of horniness, or being "serviced," although it may be about being "served." However, who serves whom is the key to the imagery-reversal of the Sacred Whore. The Sacred Whore is the Goddess embodied. Her clients enter her inner sanctum as worshippers, not as her employers or customers. She honors them as seekers and devotees. It's an attempt to turn the whole whore/john relationship upside down and around. True sexual healers teach more than they satisfy. They teach people breathing, relational, and visualization skills. Their work is hands-on, spiritual and therapeutic. Yet since they sometimes touch people's genitals for erotic purposes they are classified as sex workers under most existing state laws. The small but increasing number of people, mostly women, many of them bi, who come to this work sometimes come to it from traditional sex work but they tend to be more educated than the average prostitute. They often augment their sexual healing focus with training from allied health and other helping professions—integrating bodywork, massage, hands-on touch, relational exercises, meditation, and tantric breathing techniques to teach clients to love their own bodies, and to seek sacred erotic intimacy with others, in concert with spiritual beliefs rather than in conflict with them. These sexual healers often see themselves as part of a larger movement or community practicing sacred sex—learning tantric lovemaking and meditation skills, ritual sex magic or other neo-pagan earth-worshipping forms of expressing erotic spirituality in embodied ways.

What I found researching sacred sex circles over the past several years is that the pressure of heteronormativity can often serve to rigidify and reify gender expectations rather than to fulfill sacred sexuality's stated goal of transcending gender. For instance, visualizing women as erotic priestesses is attractive, but, in a heterosexual context, representing us as the nurturing centers of sexual energy can tend to re-enforce men's dependence upon women for meeting their sexual needs, rather than to become more nurturing themselves. Men still caught in sexual shame do indeed need encouragement to honor women erotically, but they also need to experience their own bodies as wholly divine. If our commitment to sacred whoring comes from a feminist and progressive social justice analysis, then we must subject our desire to serve as sexual healers to evaluation and begin to see what parts we play and can play within the larger society as we endeavor to legitimize pleasure, love beyond gender, and reunite eros and spirituality. As Annie said to me recently, "It is important to create safe space and to be appropriate. It can be beautiful, and it can be dangerous. Always remember we are playing with fire." Metzger's call for us all to consider ourselves sacred prostitutes is problematic because she issues this call to a world where prostitution itself is still a function of male supremacy and the double standard is defined by and controlled by men. However, as women redefine our own sexual options and realize we can openly love women as well as, or instead of, men, this can expand the possibilities and paradigms of marriage, family life, and relationships considerably. And when part of this expanded paradigm involves re-visualizing who and how we worship, bringing Goddess imagery back into religious services, and feminine meanings back into divinity, then possibilities and options for women and men, for all people, increase. But in the meantime, it's also true that the contradictions, political tensions and conflicts increase as well.

I am interested in how the women's spirituality movement, and feminist organizing within the sex industry, have combined forces in a way that influences certain sectors of alternative medicine, mental health and institutionalized religion to all consider sexual healing as worship and legitimate therapeutic intervention, as erotic rites—of passage and of community. I have attended conferences where I have seen erotic priestess/sexual healer imagery being adopted by some psychoanalysts, sex educators, body workers, nurse practitioners, and clergy. The Sacred Prostitute imagery is expanding beyond the feminist community to certain parts of the gay men's community and New Age self-improvement circles as well. Sacred Whores are in the forefront of those artists, activists and philosophers redefining cultural constructs of sexuality, producing what Shannon Bell calls, "a strategic genealogy that undermines and displaces the modern construct of the prostitute" (Bell, 1994, p. 19). I am not sure that the Sacred Whore DOES displace the modem construct of the prostitute, in any place other than a few post-modem academics' minds. However I think that the concept of women as BOTH erotically and spiritually powerful can help heal our culture as a whole, but only if the performance of this healing role is seen as part of a larger critique of gender and power, both temporal and divine.

I first started studying contemporary U.S. groups doing erotic ritual by asking how women and queers, some of the classes of people traditionally most eroticized and sexually-objectified, fared in these groups. What I found was that women and queer people are contributing some of the most interesting innovations. The idea of the all-accepting, non-gendered, or multi-gendered, Sacred Whore is just one of them. All-women's and all-men's sacred sex rituals can be empowering and restorative regardless of the orientation of those involved. Women and queer people in sacred sexuality circles are also often in the forefront of experimenting with rituals to reclaim self-pleasuring touch and in expanding the format of sacred lovemaking—from a male/female dyad-only-form into a form that includes that, and much more. I explore these forms more extensively in my dissertation, *Erotic Rites* (Hutchins, 2001). Briefly, these include: (1) a valuing of sexual sovereignty and self-love, of one's own relationship with oneself as divine, (2) a sense of mutual ministering arising out of egalitarian erotic massage circles, less focused on gender-roles than on the roles of giver and receiver, and including practices such as Sacred Spot Massage which involves hands-on-penetration for men as well as women and full-body, multi-orgasmic-training for both sexes, and (3) the creation of erotic communities larger than the couple where sexual energy is experienced and expressed in ritualized, group-guided ways. As lesbian ethicist/theologian Kathy Rudy says: "Many urban-based gay male, lesbian, and mixed-gender sexually radical communities . . . are in the process of providing for us a new kind of ethic based not on individuality, but rather based on community" (1999, pp. 133–142). Visualizing women, and men, as Sacred Whores seems, at present at least, to be a key part of many newly-forming erotic communities where sacred sexuality is practiced in a variety of forms. While the Sacred Whore as embodied archetype somewhat disturbs me, I also continue to love and cherish her. Sometimes she reminds me of the wounded healer in myself, that part that is brave enough to teach from her own vulnerability and incompleteness, while reaching down into her strength and power completely too. I love feeling my erotic power deeper in my being and helping others tap their own erotic energies too. And I love creating the sacred spaces that make this possible. I won't give these things up. But I will stay vigilant about how gender roles function in these situations, as well as other power differences of differential privilege sited in orientation, race, age, class, etc. It is easy to settle for sensual, fanciful distractions that appear to merge sex and spirit, while serving to distract us from the inequities we want to right in the first place and the more inclusive erotic communities we could have. Unless we find ways to make erotic healing rituals more available to more people, at a variety of levels suitable to different needs, and woven into resistance movements that profoundly change people for the better, we will never have what we really need: a community of sacred erotic healers who practice beyond current gender constraints and the constraints of all oppressions. This bi feminist settles for nothing less.

NOTES

1. Any quick World Wide Web search engine scan will yield many links to sites containing discussions of sacred prostitution and advertisements by those who work as sacred prostitutes. There have also been a number of articles in New Age and women's magazine print publications in recent years. See my dissertation for more such citations.

2. Starhawk, *Spiral Dance,* pgs. 90–91.

3. Lee Gilmore, *The Whore and The Holy Woman,* 1998. From the Carol Queen interview in Chapter Four: "The Living Sacred Whore."

REFERENCES

Adler, M. (1986). *Drawing down the moon: Witches, druids, goddess-worshippers and other pagans in America today.* Boston, MA: Beacon Press.

Anonymous. (1985). Lesbian nuns: True confessions of homosexuality in the convent. *Penthouse Forum, 14*(9), 32–38.

Bell, S. (1994). *Reading, writing and re-writing the prostitute body.* Bloomington, IN: Indiana University Press.

Bird, P. A. (1997). *Missing persons and mistaken identities: Women and gender in ancient Israel.* Minneapolis, MN: Augsberg Fortress Press.

Califia, P. (1997). The dominant woman as priestess and sacred whore. In P. Califia & D. Campbell (Eds.), *Bitch goddess: The spiritual path of the dominant woman.* San Francisco, CA: Greenery Press.

Christ, C., & Plaskow, J. (1979). *Womanspirit rising: A feminist reader in religion.* San Francisco, CA: Harper & Row.

Corinne, T. (1975). *Cunt coloring book.* San Francisco, CA: Last Gasp Books.

Curb, R., & Manahan, N. (1985). *Lesbian nuns: Breaking the silence.* Tallahassee, FL: Naiad Press.

Daly, M. (1977). *Beyond God the father: Toward a philosophy of women's liberation.* Boston, MA: Beacon Press.

Diamant, A. (1997). *The red tent.* New York: St. Martin's Press.

Dodson, B. (1974). *Liberating masturbation. A meditation on self-loving.* New York: Bodysex Designs.

Fabian, C. (1997). The Holy whore: A woman's gateway to power. In J. Nagle (Ed.), *Whores and other feminists* (pp. 44–64). New York: Routledge Press.

Feuerstein, G. (1989). *Enlightened sexuality: Essays on body-positive spirituality.* Freedom, CA: Crossing Press.

Gilmore, L. (1998). *The whore and the holy woman: Ancient and contemporary myths of the sacred prostitute.* Unpublished Masters thesis, California Institute of Integral Studies, San Francisco, CA.

Grahn, J. (1984). *Another mother tongue: Gay words, gay worlds.* Boston, MA: Beacon Press.

Hutchins, L. (2001). *Erotic rites: A cultural analysis of contemporary U.S. sacred sexuality traditions and trends.* Doctoral Dissertation, Union Institute, Cincinnati, OH.

LaChapelle, D. (1998). *Sacred land: Sacred sex: Rapture of the deep: Concerning deep ecology—and celebrating life.* Silverton, CO: Finn Hill Arts.

Lemer, G. (1986). Origins of prostitution in ancient Mesopotamia. *Signs, 11,* 236–254.

Mariechild, D., & Martin, M. (1995). *Lesbian sacred sexuality.* Oakland, CA: Wingbow Press.

Meador, B. D. S. (2000). *Manna: Lady of the largest heart—Poems of the Sumerian high priestess Enheduanna.* Foreward by Judy Grahn. Austin, TX: University of Texas Press.

Metzger, D. (1981). *The woman who slept with men to take the war out of them.* Culver City, CA: Peace Press.

Metzger, D. (1985). Revamping the world: On the return of the holy prostitute: A controversial proposal for the next step in feminism. *Utne Reader, 11,* 120–124.

Qualls-Corbett, N. (1988). *The sacred prostitute: Eternal aspects of the feminine.* Toronto, Canada: Inner City Books.

Rudy, K. (1999). Sex radical communities and the future of sexual ethics. *Journal of Lesbian Studies, 3*(3), 133–142.

Sjoo, M. (1992). *New age & armageddon: The goddess or the gurus? Towards a feminist vision of the future.* London: The Women's Press.

Sprinide, A. (2001). *Hardcore from the heart: The pleasures, profits and politics of sex in performance.* New York: Continuum.

Sprinkle, A. (1991). Beyond bisexual: Sex guidelines for the 90's. In L. Hutchins & L. Kaahumanu (Eds.), *Bi any other name: Bisexual people speak out* (pp. 103–107). Boston, MA: Alyson Publications.

Sprinkle, A. (1997, March 15). *Sex work as a spiritual path.* Unpublished paper presented at the International Conference on Prostitution, Van Nuys, CA.

Starhawk. (1979). *The spiral dance: A rebirth of the ancient religion of the great goddess.* New York: Harper and Row.

Starhawk. (1982). *Dreaming the dark: Magic, sex, and politics.* Boston, MA: Beacon Press.

Starhawk. (1995). The sacredness of pleasure. In N. Tucker (Ed.), *Bisexual politics: Theories, queries and visions* (pp. 325–329). Binghamton, NY: The Haworth Press, Inc.

Stone, M. (1976). *When God was a woman.* San Diego, CA: Harcourt, Brace & Jovanovich.

Stubbs, K. R. (1994). *Women of the light: The new sacred prostitute.* Larkspur, CA: Secret Garden Press.

Walker, B. G. (1983). *The women's encyclopedia of myths and secrets.* New York: Harper & Row.

Bi bell: Spirituality and the Sexual Intellectual

L. H. STALLINGS
Indiana University, Bloomington, Indiana, USA

Currently, there is very little research and scholarship on spirituality and bisexuality in Black American life and culture. Although numerous books and essays on Black theology, Black liberation theology and spirituality exist, these collections' singular focus remains on the politics of race. Only recently has there been a growing trend to study gender and sexuality as part of these theologies. Even then the attention to bisexuality in dominant models of religion and spirituality for Black Americans is rare. In this article, the author proposes that searching outside the typical configurations of spirituality unveils spiritual traditions that readily incorporate bisexuality for Black people in the United States. Specifically, I argue that the act of writing serves as an alternative spiritual tradition for Black intellectuals interested in deconstructing the false divides between spirituality, sexuality and the intellect. Analyzing the work of bell hooks, the author argues that writing as spirituality promotes and fosters bisexual subjectivity. This subjectivity creates mechanisms for combating sexual dysfunction in the lives of Black women.

I think that the concept of women as BOTH erotically and spiritually powerful can help heal our culture as a whole, but only if the performance of this healing role is seen as part of a larger critique of gender and power, both temporal and divine. (Hutchins, 2002, p. 222)

Much of my work is written to create a context of healing. Words have the power to heal wounds.... Writing becomes then a way to embrace the mysterious, to walk with spirits, and an entry into the realm of the sacred. (hooks, 1999, p. 130)

What role does intellect play in shaping spiritual traditions that embrace various genders and sexualities? In this article, I argue that it destabilizes the binaries that exist in religious, political and intellectual discourses on sexuality and the body. The opening epigraphs imply that bridging the discursive gap between intellect and spirit may offer a wide range of healing possibilities, especially for women. However, in Black communities this has been easier said than done. Black people have relied on spirituality to heal themselves from the ravages of racism and White supremacy, but the cure for the sexual dis(ease) caused by the legacy of slavery and apartheid in the United States continues to be delayed by religious beliefs. Michael Eric Dyson, in "When You Divide Body and Soul, Problems Multiply: The Black Church and Sex" (2001), defined sexual disease and its cure, stating the need to develop a theology of eroticism that "frees Black Christianity from guilty repression and gutless promiscuity" (2001, p. 319). Dyson revises Audre Lorde's earlier call to wisely use the erotic. He claimed that in Black America "there is a profound kinship between spirituality and sexuality" and asserted that "black singers Marvin Gaye, the artist formerly known as Prince, and R. Kelly" are a segment of secular Black culture that has consistently explored the intimate link between spirituality and sexuality (pp. 317–318). Despite that Dyson does address homophobia, the theology for such erotics has been slow to form outside of secular arenas. Furthermore, critic Marlon Moore (2009) indicated that "to date contemporary religious-political discourse still assumes a mutually exclusive binary in which 'people of faith' are set apart from gay/lesbian communities; an antagonism that situates queer sexual identities in the inferior ideological position" (p. 12). Moore does a superb job of demonstrating how African American lesbian, gay, bisexual, transgender, queer (LGBTQ) fiction articulates ways of being queer in traditional and nontraditional spiritual spaces. She assessed already traditional religions and spiritual myths such as Christianity, vampirism and nature and their articulations of the 'soul' and then demonstrated how African American writers revise or queer those constructions of the soul. Moore's contributions come in that she, like Dyson, revealed that the secular, creative fiction rather than music is not the only space where Black queer people have theorized themselves and their spiritualities. Adding to Moore's work, I argue that critical writing acts as an unacknowledged spiritual tradition, more sacred than secular, which promotes liberating sexual subjectivities for Black women. I ask, what is the role of the Black female bisexual intellectual in creating spiritual traditions that examine numerous and varied sexualities practiced within, alongside, and in response to spiritualities for Black women? Using the work of bell hooks as a focal point, I riff on Dyson's title and suggest that when you link body, soul and mind, sexual healing is possible. Understanding that writing is an ethereal interzone where all three entities intersect, I assess how bisexuality has been expressed and practiced within the spiritual tradition of confessional and critical writing.

In many dominant models of religion and spirituality, ideologies and traditions are formed by messiahs, prophets, shamans, priestess and popes. These traditions are maintained by teachings taken from holy books and documents such as the Bible, the Koran, the Torah, the Avesta, the Tripitaka, the book of Confucius or the Tao. In some spiritual traditions 'love of wisdom' and 'love of God' exist in opposition to each other. Likewise in Black secular tradition, the same holds true. When presenting wisdom from her spiritual doctrine of Baduizm, neo-soul singer Erykah Badu (1997) proclaimed that "most intellects do not believe in gods, but they fear us just the same." Badu assumed a philosophical divide between the spiritual and intellectual. She is not alone in believing that intellectual work and spiritual work are axiologically positioned. Historically, the book of Genesis in the Bible has served as a parable about how knowledge of the world can be a detriment to the moral and spiritual salvation of humanity.

To construct empowering political identities and self-sustaining sexual subjectivities, Black writers and critics invested in queer subjectivity have had to strategically move away from philosophies in which intellect and spirit remain separate. Decades before Dyson insisted upon a theology of erotics, writer and critic Audre Lorde (1984b) successfully wrestled the erotic and eroticism away from pornographic designs to produce a lasting document "Uses of the Erotic" that remains intellectual, spiritual and sexual in scope. Uninhibited by the traditional binary splits of the political/personal or spiritual/political, Lorde (1984) theorized of the erotic:

> For the bridge that connects them is formed by the erotic—the sensual—those physical, emotional, and psychic expressions of what is deepest and strongest and richest within each of us. . . . The sharing of joy, whether physical, emotional, psychic, or intellectual, forms a bridge between the sharers which can be the basis for understanding much of what is not shared between them, and lessens the threat of their difference. (p. 56)

Throughout that essay, Lorde spoke of creative energy, and though some might think this alludes merely to poetry and fiction, the essay itself demonstrates creative energy. The spiritual tradition she was invoking in discussing the erotic was writing, be it fiction, poetry or criticism. The link to understanding the eroticism and spiritual ethos of critical and nonfiction writing comes in understanding its purpose in creating a subject, or in religious terminology gods and goddesses.

In *Black Women, Identity, and Cultural Theory: (Un)becoming the Subject*, critic Kevin Quashie (2004) discerned the difference between identity and subjectivity for Black femaleness and suggested that "subject is a more fluid term ... a thing whose indeterminacy is both freedom and peril ...; and identity is about placement, a sense of repeatability, a way a thing is put into a place" (p. 7). Quashie's point is relevant to this special issue's concern with bisexualities and spiritualities because Black intellectuals' discourses on subjectivity and Black women, as is argued throughout this article, are very often spiritual work. Their spiritual work has too often been overlooked for the political goals of creating identity that is privileged in contemporary intellectual labor.

Writing is a daunting model of spirituality. After all, there is not one foundational holy book that establishes principles to follow. Polytheistic in many aspects, writing incorporates its own spiritual ideology, rituals, sacred spaces, conversions and dogma. Paper and ink take the place of temples, mosques and churches. In consideration as to what sexualities are practiced alongside or within spiritualities and traditions, writing is often seen as a tool to record and convey the 'real' spiritual ideologies. Yet the act of writing can and has often been positioned as a spiritual tradition. Black women in the United States have relatively few traditional spiritual institutions that embrace non-heteronormative considerations of spirit and body like bisexuality or sacred sexuality. Even when non-Western traditions become incorporated into Black women's contemporary spiritual explorations, heteronormative values remain foundational.[1] Perhaps this is why critiquing and writing about the fiction, nonfiction and poetry of Black women serves as a viable substitute for Black women intellectuals seeking alternative spaces to worship and praise supreme beings that reflect the self back, in addition to providing a space where spiritual conversion and rebirth around sexuality and gender can take place. Writing does not simply teach individuals to worship and praise gods. It teaches individuals how to be gods, or see God in self.[2] More than intellectual work or leisurely pleasure, Black female writers and their readers replace holy books with texts produced by Black women writers. These writers and scholars have referred to Black women's writing as divination, praise songs and ancestral presences.[3]

However, to better understand writing as a spiritual tradition that allows various sexualities to be practiced within or alongside it, it remains important to remember that writing produces and creates subjectivity in atypical ways not often associated with sacred spaces. In his discussion about the girlfriend as a metaphor of Black female relationality, Quashie (2004) introduced an unheralded bisexual subjectivity/conduit for Black women writers and scholars:

> Through a discourse of otherness some Black women scholars represent selfhood as the dynamic relationship between one woman and her other, her girlfriend. This relationship is dynamic particularly because the boundaries of self, metaphorically but also literally, are disrupted,

> severed, transcended; the self and its girlfriend become contagious and sometimes indistinct subjects. ... In this context subjectivity is an "ungoing unsettling process" that makes chaotic grace of the material and spiritual edges that normativities would to calcify. (p. 16)

Quashie's theory about the girlfriend may not appear to be especially linked to bisexuality as an identity, but it does connect with bisexual subjectivity. In assessments of bisexuality, noted critic E. D. Daumer (1999) proposed, "that we assume bisexuality, not as an identity that integrates heterosexual and homosexual orientations but as an epistemological as well as ethical vantage point from which we can examine and deconstruct the bipolar framework of gender and sexuality" (p. 159). The girlfriend represents a particularly intimate model of friendship and romance that is capable of deconstructing bipolar frameworks of gender and sexuality. Before Quashie used the girlfriend to support his work on Black women, its potential for nonheteronormative sexual subjectivities had been the subject of many song produced by Black singers and songwriters: From Prince, Queen Pen, and Nicky Menaj to Alicia Keys and Pebbles, the potential for the girlfriend to be a trusted confidante or a betrayer is shaped by the sexual desires and genders of those involved. The girlfriend, as articulated by Quashie, remains a sexually ambiguous epistemology and an otherworldly subjectivity within Black women's writing. To complete the process of building a selfhood, Black women must deconstruct notions of gender and sexuality through their otherness. bell hooks remains an unacknowledged teacher of bisexual epistemologies rooted in spirituality.

CONFESSION IS GOOD FOR THE SOUL

bell hooks was my Luther Vandross. For years I'd theorized about hooks' sexual politics and identity with no concrete evidence from her or her works. However, unlike Luther fans I finally got my answer. In *Wounds of Passion: A Writing Life*, bell hooks (1997) identified as bisexual when she reveals a confession that she made to a male lover: "From the very beginning I tell him I see myself as bisexual" (p. 165). Later on she follows up that statement with a judgment about her fashion obsession as one interlinked with the seduction of men and women: "Fashion for me and my roommate then was all about ... the art of seduction. We begin with the vamp motto that *there is no man or woman that cannot be had*" (p. 196). These admissions are significant because they satisfy general curiosity about the writer's life, but most importantly because *Wounds of Passion* explicitly demonstrates the way in which bell hooks' writing is a series of uncovering bisexuality. By now, many feminists know that Gloria Watkins aka bell hooks created her pseudonym by invoking an ancestral presence, taking her grandmother's name. More than a pseudonym, her self-naming was the first way in which hooks enacts her bisexuality and writing as a spiritual tradition. bell hooks, the girlfriend of Gloria Watkins, becomes a liminal subject, of which Quashie (2004) noted: "The liminal, the self-centered, the self-created: these are bodies of divinity and this practice is one of spiritual subjectivity (p. 79). She simultaneously pays tribute to her ancestors while also laying the groundwork to create a new self. Despite that her work decenters the binaries of gender and sexuality, hooks chooses to stake a claim to bisexuality after she has established herself as a cultural critic. hooks' self-reflection back through a confessional mode of writing emphasizes the necessity for Black women to obtain a vision of a self always in process and (un)becoming.

It was Ann Burns's (1997) book review of *Wounds of Passion* in *Library Journal* that drew me back to hooks after an extended break from reading her work:

> In this sequel to *Bone Black*, hooks ... returns to her painful childhood, to the oppressive South, to her abusive father, and then moves on to a relationship with someone who shares her intense desire for writing and sexual enjoyment. ... As in her previous book, hooks moves from first to third person, allowing the reader to eavesdrop on her innermost thoughts, *hear of her bisexuality*. (p. 94, italics added)

I admit that I was interested in hearing "of her bisexuality" since I'd been wondering about the possibility of it for years without really understanding why I felt so strongly that she should, no had to come out, say something about her own sex life that would showcase the practicing of a radical praxis that she theorized about in so many works. It wasn't the mentality of claiming one for the bi team, but rather something in the way she seemed unafraid to emphasize the importance of sexual desire and spirituality in her theories on racism, classism, sexism, eroticism, gender, popular culture, love, while seeming to always withhold where these insights were arising. It is a reflection that many of us who do work in gender and sexuality studies, queer studies, gay and lesbian studies, find ourselves engaging in with the works of others as well as our own. Can we write about dismantling binary systems of gender, heterosexism, homophobia and patriarchy as frequently and passionately, as someone like hooks does, without admitting the practice of how we do so in our own lives? Of course many people, regardless of sexual orientation, would argue quite simply yes. However, it is not that simple. Confessional writing reveals the correlation between spirituality, sexuality and subjectivity and the tensions between public and private spheres that might impede connecting all three. Confessional writing negates the fixedness of identity and makes a space for the liminal, whereby bisexuals can create and revise their subjectivity.

In *Wounds of Passion*, hooks (1997) discussed her sexuality with regards to Black female/male sexual relationships, interracial sex, student/mentor–teacher dynamics and bisexual objects choices. In the process, she implicitly makes a case for readers to reject Western metaphysics of gender and sexuality, as well as answer or confirm questions about her own personal sexual identity. Each concern is necessary to demonstrate how hooks' writing intends to heal the dis(ease) around Black women's sexualities and desires. According to Barbara Omolade (1994), this sexual dis(ease) is fostered by the historical way in which sex between Black people and "all aspects of their lives were considered in the dominion of the public, white master/lover's power" (p. 57). Most of hooks' writing depends upon a confessional tone that can usurp the dominion of the White public. The confessional mode of writing makes it possible for hooks to blur the line between private and public spaces, place or identify herself as bisexual, and creates a subjectivity that can simultaneously, as Hutchins (2002) advised, critique larger orders of power and be temporal and divine. Because hooks (1992) insisted that "we must make the oppositional space where our sexuality can be named and represented, where we are sexual subjects—no longer bound and trapped" (p. 77), writing must become more than a discursive act, it must be a form of spirituality that can embrace bisexuality. Raised as a Baptist, and now a Buddhist, hooks (1993) elaborates on the space:

> Despite the sexism of that segregated black world, the world of spirituality and magic was one where black women teachers, preachers, and healers worked with as much skill, power, and second sight as their black male comrades. Raised in such an environment, I was able to witness and learn. (p. 9)

Wounds of Passion offers the most obvious representation of hooks (1997) using her writerly gift as a spiritual tradition where bisexual subjectivity is promoted as important to liberating selfhood. When hooks reveals why she uses the first- and third-person narration in *Wounds of Passion*, she acknowledged the importance of her decision:

> The inclusion of the third person narrator who has both critical insight and an almost psychoanalytical power that enables critical reflection on events described is an act of mediation. When we rewrite the past, looking back with our current understanding, a mediation is always taking place. I give that mediation a voice rather than mask this aspect of any retrospective reflection on our lives. (p. xxii)

hooks not only moves between first and third person to showcase her mediation, she also utilizes italics to differentiate the voices and inflects nuanced tones into each voice to showcase her sexual evolution thus far. From the very beginning, hooks testified that she will provide information that she has been less than forthcoming about all along:

> Despite the growing popularity of confessional writing many works by black writers evade subjects still deemed taboo, particularly issues of sexuality... [O]ur autobiographical narratives are often marked by a stern control and reserve. Often one leaves these works with only a limited awareness of the writer's life. It may be that the conventional narrative form of the autobiography lends itself to this obscuring of the inner reality and consciousness of an author. (p. xix)

hooks could have simply added analysis of critical essays and nonfiction to support this statement. Yet she chooses instead to confess her bisexuality and note the public interest in her life and the lives of other African Americans. She admits that the Black public sphere may have contributed to her unwillingness to make such confessions earlier in her career. Notably, when hooks is concerned with using writing as a tool of political identity, bisexuality remains absent. However, when hooks reflected on writing as a spiritual tradition new spaces are uncovered and bisexuality privileged.

Despite her straight-girl mainstream appeal, hooks has written to aid in the creation of sexual subjects who are no longer bound and spiritually wounded, and that task began long before *Wounds of Passion*. bell hooks' narratives are floetic[4] critiques of race, gender and sexuality. She spoke of race, gender and sexuality as the social constructs they are without minimalizing the real and historical experiences of oppressed bodies. She wrote about sexuality like someone who actually enjoys the act, and not just writing about the representations of the act. Her writing itself becomes an act of desire and sex, as well as a graceful meditation on the rapture and ecstasy of writing. For example, hooks' *Teaching to Transgress Education as the Practice of Freedom* (1984) serves as compelling evidence as to how her mission for self-hood for nonheteronormative sexualities moves her into intersectional territory of intellect, spirituality and sexuality. Taking on the taboo subject of teacher–student relationships and sexuality, hooks discussed the ways in which eroticism functions in the classroom for herself and her students by sharing her experiences and publishing excerpts from student journals. In one case, hooks detailed what happens when she received a phone call from a school therapist about one of her male students who feels that he has been mistreated by her in the class:

> I did not know who the student was ... but later when he identified himself in class, I realized that I was erotically drawn to this student. And that my naïve way of coping with feelings in the classroom ... was to deflect (hence my harsh treatment of him), repress, and deny. (p. 192)

Because hooks' books thematically address self-help and self-hood, modes of confession function in the same way that the voyeuristic gaze would work. Readers anticipate confession and receive some pleasure from reading or writing it. Ironically, confession has often been acknowledged as cathartic and a way to receive divine forgiveness in Judeo-Christian tradition. Yet confession in bell hooks' self-help books is where the act of desire and sex begins. Her willingness to confess what might be characterized as sensational experiences from her life and then intellectually analyze them becomes the graceful meditation. Writing, Audre Lorde (1984) noted, remains a useful tool of eroticism (p. 58). The act of writing can create new spiritual and sexual subjectivity for the professor, writer and student. "To restore passion in the classroom or to excite it in the classrooms where it has never been, professors must find again the place of eros within ourselves and together allow the mind and body to feel and know desire" (hooks, 1994b, p. 199). Writing's ability to compel us to observe the world around us, engage our senses, and surrender to what we see and feel means that it moves far beyond acting as an intellectual exercise. Bridging the gap between the intellectual, spiritual and sexual moves us into other arenas of sexual healing.

IN THE BEGINNING, THERE WAS CONFESSION, DIVINATION AND DIFFERENCE

hooks' agenda of self-help also fits into proscribed notions of ancient divination. Creating a phenomenology of divination for the African diaspora, Evan M. Zuesse (1975) asserted that "forms of divination may be grouped into two polar categories, which we may call 'possession' and 'wisdom' types, with perhaps a third form, intermediary or prior to the other two, which is 'intuitive'" (p. 159). Intuitive divination is when the specialist can ascertain without "possession or esoteric sciences" the client's problem (p. 162). Because hooks writes nonfiction and criticism, she may utilize all three. hooks (1999) expanded on her own perception of her healing gift, when she admitted, "spirituality has always been the foundation of my experience as a writer" (p. 125) and "writing has been for me one of the ways to encounter the divine" (p. 126). Although she does not throw koala nuts or bones, read signs of nature or discern tea leaves or entrails patterns, she does rely on ancestral voices. As if she were a descendant of the Fon from ancient Dahomey, bell hooks uses writing to divine on Black women's genders and sexualities. In her very first exploration of Black women's cultural and historical lives, bell hooks (1981) deconstructed how race becomes prioritized in constructions of self in ways that tend to devalue other elements of identity:

> Contemporary black women could not join together to fight for women's rights because we did not see "womanhood" as an important aspect of

> our identity. Racist, sexist socialization had conditioned us to devalue our femaleness and to regard race as the only relevant level of identification. (p. 1)

Womanhood may have been one element, but as gay/lesbian and queer studies revealed, sexual desire and orientation were other factors. hooks continues a tradition of praxis and theory that begin with the likes of Toni Cade Bambara and Audre Lorde before her. She reads the discourses of White supremacy patriarchy, and divines how to confront the problem.

Early in her career, hooks' critique of power in regards to Black women's sexuality attributes the spiritual displacement that causes body and soul divisions to the legacy left by the institution of slavery. In *Ain't I a Woman: Black Women and Feminism* (hooks, 1981) much of the discussion around sexuality concerns the sexual exploitation and rape of African American women during slavery, with hooks also exploring the continued devaluation of African American women into the 20th century. In explaining how white power is deployed through sexual control, hooks (1981) noted, "White colonizers sought to suppress sexuality because of their deep fear of sexual feelings, their beliefs that such feelings were sinful, and their fear of eternal damnation" (p. 30). hooks also highlighted the new developing nation's social discourse on sexuality that depends on an othering of the Black body:

> At the onset of their arrival in the American colonies, black women and men faced a society that was eager to impose upon the displaced African the identity of the "sexual savage." As white colonizers adopted a self-righteous sexual morality for themselves, they eagerly labeled black people as sexual heathens. ... One white politician urged that blacks be sent back to Africa so that white men would not fornicate or commit adultery. (1981, p. 33)

These early considerations of race and sexuality serve as initial explorations that would lead hooks into more radical discussions of sexuality and spirituality. When hooks disposes the legacy of White supremacy, she finds her stride in discussing the major anomalies of Black women's sexual and spiritual life. Black women's malaise occurs when the forces of racism and patriarchy divide body and soul. She asserted in *Rock My Soul* (2003),

> Black people who embrace a more fundamentalist Christian doctrine, with its binary focus on good and evil, dark and light, chosen and unchosen could no longer look to religion to provide a healthy basis of self-esteem. By investing in a belief system that not only deemed some folks worthy and others unworthy ... black folk were essentially internalizing the Western metaphysical dualism that was already used to affirm and uphold domination. And even when black people did not absorb all this thinking, it created confusion and contradiction that were and

> are emotionally stressful. That stress has been apparent in the arena of healthy self esteem about the body and sexuality. (p. 110)

Rather than dismissing the usefulness of spiritual well-being, hooks returns to it in various ways. hooks (1993) proposed a bisexual narrative that counters the doctrines of parasitic dualisms and detrimental binaries in dominant Black religions:

> Lesbians, bi-sexual, and black female sex radicals challenge those black women trapped in the confines of a hurtful oppressive heterosexist eroticism to recognize that we have choices. In urging us to reconsider our relation to our bodies, as well as the bodies of other black women, the field of eroticism was expanded and with promise of greater passion and pleasure. (p. 114)

In suggesting that Black women's eroticism has been specifically influenced by a culture of domination, hooks determined that difference acts as an affirmative intercession in the lives of Black women. In speaking about desire and difference, hooks (1992) explained that "exploring how desire for the Other is expressed, manipulated, and transformed by encounters with difference and the different is a critical terrain that can indicate whether these potentially revolutionary longings are ever fulfilled" (p. 22). For many Black women to find God in self and love her fiercely, bell hooks' works suggest that it is important to embrace bisexual epistemologies and subjectivities.

ANCESTORS, THE NEW WOMAN AND THE ABSENT NARRATIVE OF BISEXUALITY

In *Remembered Rapture*, hooks (1999) ended her personal treatise on the writer at work by invoking ancestral figures who have cleared the path for her to create her bisexual narrative. Zora Neale Hurston, Ann Petry, Lorraine Hansberry, Toni Morrison, and Toni Cade Bambara have each contributed to destroying Western metaphysics of binary genders and sexualities by creating their own spiritual worlds so that Black women can recoup and sustain empowering sexual selves. In a discussion on the importance of Lorraine Hansberry to her own writing life and work, hooks (1999) recalled of Hansberry: "She represented the 'new woman'—the woman I wanted to become. Experimental, free, determined to live life on her own terms" (p. 211). Hansberry serves as an ancestral mooring for hooks. In discussing the ancestors as "an abiding, interested, benevolent, guiding presence that is yours and is concerned about you, not quite like saints but having the same sort of access, none of which is new information," Toni Morrison (1984) attended to the way in which ancestors are "benevolent, instructive, and protective, and they provide a certain kind of wisdom" (p. 343). hooks' attention to the subjectivity of the "new woman" also connects to bisexuality. Helene Cixous' and Catherine Clement's *The Newly Born Woman* (1986) suggests that bisexuality exists in two forms. The first form heavily influenced by Freudian foundations is defined as a "fantasy of a complete being, which replaces the fear of castration and veils sexual difference" (p. 84). The second form appears all the more relevant to considerations about women of color: In this latter case, bisexuality becomes "the multiplication of the effects of desire's inscription on every part of the body and the other body" (p. 85). For hooks' entire canon of writing there is, in deliberations on the interzones of sex and writing, a concern with the fantasy of a complete being that veils sexual difference, as well as desire's inscription on the self and the representation of self (that other) by dominant society. She seeks to experiment and create her new terms for Black women becoming subjects. Bisexuality, for hooks, acts as a yam for Black women's subjectivity. hooks (1993), in calling upon the familial influence of Toni Cade Bambara to produce her first explicitly self-help book, *Sisters of the Yam*, explained that the sisters of the yam must draw power from a deep rooted source, "Yams provide nourishment for the body as food yet they are also used medicinally—to heal the body" (p. 13). Bisexuality acts as a rooted source of difference that can change the way Black women relate to their gender and sexuality. It provides nourishment for the body, but the pleasure and eroticism derived from sex nourishes and heals the body as well. Once nonhierarchical choices are made available, Black women are provided with new ways of reading difference. Alternative models of difference enable Black women to break free from the grip of cultural heteronormativity.

hooks' *Remembered Rapture* (1999) mirrors the language of spiritual conversion and sexual surrender: "Written words change us all and make us more than we could ever be without them. Still the being we become in the midst of the very act of writing is only ever intimately present to the one who writes" (p. xvi). Although it may seem to represent a binary of writer and other, hooks' words showcase how writing functions as a liminal gap for numerous possibilities to form simultaneously and in the same space. This does not mean that all narratives are bisexual. hooks' narratives become bisexual narratives primarily when they are concerned with writing sexuality as a narrative that can be revised, rewritten and edited. Marjorie Garber (1995) argued that "bisexuality is not an 'identity' (or a figure or a trope) but a narrative, a story" (p. 87), whereas E. D. Daumer (1999) continued to speak of it as a "force that is able to shed light on the gaps and contradictions of all identity, on what we might call the difference within identity" (p. 159).

For years the glaring omission in hooks' critical works was her own sexuality, but just as the confessional strategies within her writing create a spiritual plane for bisexual subjectivity, bisexuality expands traditional notions of free will, and what hooks does with that free will is create pussy rituals to heal Black women.

PUSSY PRAISE SONGS

Long before the new queer theory school erupts, hooks (1992) wrote numerous works that project writing as spirituality dependent upon sexuality: "Desired and sought after, sexual pleasure alters the consenting subject, deconstructing notions of will, control, coercive domination" (p. 22). Remembering that subjectivity is where intellect, spirit and sexuality traverse, spiritual conversion through sex occurs when Black women can use the spiritual tradition of writing to enact (dis)identifications with their other selves. Quashie (2004) maintained that

> this practice of pairing with an/other and oscillating between states of (dis)identification yields a liminal identity, a subjectivity that is material and corporeal but which also transcends the limits imposed by corporeality, visual culture and colonization—a selfhood that challenges the normative construction of "self." This liminal subjectivity is not exactly an achieved state, instead it is a series of uncoverings. (p. 78)

The final meditation in exploring how hooks' divination fosters bisexual subjectivity occurs when she creates rituals of (dis)identification through pointed and purposeful use of the vernacular term *pussy*. During these "pussy praise songs," she quietly, but consistently, constructs her own queer voice that finds pleasure and power in pussy, while exposing the heterosexism and patriarchy that makes accessing such pleasure and power almost impossible. Too often in scientific, secular and sacred sexuality discourses, the womb and the vagina are represented as sacred parts and spaces of the female body, primarily because they ensure and sustain the creation of life. The nonreproductive parts of female genitalia: the vulva, clitoris, and lips, all encompassing to form pussy, are implicitly aligned with the profane. hooks (1997), in *Wounds of Passion*, offers an interpretation of the way masculine society thinks of pussy: "Pussy had no power, no color, but dick now that was tied to meaningful manhood, to notions of privilege and choice and power . . . But pussy was pussy; it had no color and allegiance" (p. 165). How does one do away with the very negation of pleasure, and therefore erotic power, posed by such ideologies? Mockingly hooks turns such masculine raps upside down, assigns new value to pussy by creating rituals around using the word in ways that highlight free will and bisexual object choices.

hooks' "Whose Pussy is This?" in *Talking Back* (1989), "Selling Hot Pussy" in *Black Looks* (1992), "Power to the Pussy" in *Outlaw Culture* (1994a), and *Wounds of Passion* (1997) hone in on the power that arises when women acknowledge and express their own autonomous sexual desires. hooks' deliberate use of the word pays homage to this power. Usually when *pussy* is used in conversations about female sexuality, it is done so in a vulgar, derogatory way that locks discussion of female sexuality into traps of misogyny and heterosexuality. However, in each of the essays, where hooks has purposely used and called attention to pussy through her use of it in essay titles, its usage has been to offer an alternative to heterosexist discussions of female sexuality and empowerment.

In *Talking Back*'s "Whose Pussy Is This?" hooks (1989) discussed the importance of heterosexuality in early representations and discussion of female sexual liberation choice in women's sexual relationships:

> At that time, the conceptualization of female sexual liberation was informed by a fierce heterosexist bias which saw sexual liberation primarily in terms of women asserting the right to be sexually desiring, to initiate sexual relationships, and to participate in casual sexual encounters with varied male partners. (p. 136)

hooks begins a weighty process of dismantling the strict binaries of male/female and heterosexual or homosexual. She admits to other possibilities for women.

hooks (1989) further explored this manifestation in Black cultural representations of Black women when she criticizes Spike Lee's *She's Gotta Have It* for its problematic representation of the Black female lead's experience:

> As Jaimie rapes Nola and aggressively demands that she answers the question, "whose pussy is this," this is the moment of truth—the moment when she can declare herself independent, sexually liberated, the moment when she can proudly assert through resistance her sexual autonomy (for the film has highlighted her determination to be sexually active, to choose many partners, to belong to no one. (p. 139)

hooks' previous point about the limitations placed on women's sexual liberation is proven true, for Nola does not claim herself but gives herself away and submits out of force or choice by answering the question with "yours." In her rejection of Spike Lee's story of Black women's sexual liberation, hooks makes certain to reject the masculine ownership of female bodies and sexual pleasure. As she stated (1993) in *Sisters of the Yam*, "the realm of black heterosexual expression is rarely a place where black females learn to glory in our own erotic power" (p. 119). But the coup d'état of the pussy praise songs happens when she explains what radical female sexual liberation looks like. Her explanation provides a ritual space necessary for healing.

Continuing her analysis of Spike Lee's (1989) film, hooks used another influential film to counter Lee's version of female sexual liberation:

> In perfect contrast to *The Color Purple*, wherein same-sex relationships between women are depicted as a source of mutual, non exploitative erotic affirmation that serve as catalysts for self-development, the lesbian sexual in *She's Gotta Have It* is negatively portrayed. It does not represent an alternative to destructive heterosexual practice. (p. 140)

hooks forcefully explained that real sexual liberation would entail more than an overthrowing of a dual-gendered system, it would also mean throwing off the shackles of dual sexual orientations that privilege heterosexuality. hooks performs a viable privileging of same-sex desire in this piece.

In another work, *Black Looks'* "Selling Hot Pussy," hooks (1992) again created a space for female sexual agency in voicing her appreciation for what she sees as empowering oppositional images to Lee's film in the black British film collective Sankofa's *Passion of Remembrance*:

> In one playfully erotic scene, two young black women, a lesbian couple, get dressed to go out . . . looking at their images in the mirror, exulting in their black female bodies . . . their pleasure, the film suggests, emerges in a decolonized erotic context rooted in commitments to feminist and anti-racist politics. When they look in the mirror and focus on specific body parts (their full thick lips and buttocks), the gaze is one of recognition. (p. 76)

In both cases, hooks scoffs at the premise of product and ownership that comes with the male use of female sexuality and the word *pussy*. Her praise song reclaims ownership of female sexuality away from men and gives it back to women by returning to the dynamic relationship between the self and other. In both her reflections on same-sex desire in conjunction with the vernacular, she ensures the presence of female sexual agency. Indeed, when the titles of her essays include *pussy*, they hint at, from the very beginning, an interest in same-sex desire as a viable radical force, movement, subjectivity and site of autonomous pleasure for women and their girlfriends. Undoubtedly hooks' pussy praise songs are made possible by the potential of writing as a spiritual institution and bisexuality as its most useful epistemology. hooks' canon of academic and self-help texts are based on an ethos that recognizes a multiplicity of difference, and from the interplay between those distinctions we observe that words can heal.

NOTES

1. Take for example the ways in which noted spiritual advisor and Yoruba priestess Iyanla Vanzant (1993) had incorporated ancient Yoruba spiritual principles into her spiritual and self-help works, while

removing or ignoring the radical implications of gender and sexuality from that spiritual tradition. In addition, Alexxys Tylor's (n.d.) notorious cable access/you tube–syndicated show on vagina power uses some version of sacred sexuality to discuss how Black people can sexually empower themselves in the most heteronormative ways possible.

2. In Ntozake Shanghe's (1997) *For Colored Girls Who Have Considered Suicide When The Rainbow is Enuf*, the phrase "i found god in myself/ & I loved her" is repeated throughout the play (p. 63).

3. Alice Walker (2003) relies on nature to draw a connection between writing and spirituality in *In Search of Our Mothers' Gardens*. Karla Holloway's *Moorings and Metaphors: Figures of Culture and Gender in Black Women's Literature* (1992) uses African concepts of ancestors. Mae G. Henderson's "Speaking in Tongues" (1989) and Marjorie Pryse's and Hortense Spilliers' *Conjuring: Black Women, Fiction, and Literary Tradition* (1985) make direct correlations between writing and spiritual rituals.

4. Floetic is a stylistic descriptor based on the R&B duo Floetry and their neo-soul sound of blending rhythmic poetry with jagged sensual sounds.

REFERENCES

Badu, E. (1997). On and on. On *Baduizm* [CD]. New York: Kedar Records.

Burns, A. (1997). Wounds of passion: A writing life. *Library Journal, 122*(16), 94.

Cixous, H., & Clemente, C. (1986). *The newly born woman*. Minneapolis, MN: University of Minnesota Press.

Daumer, E. D. (1999). Queer ethics: Or the challenge of bisexuality to lesbian ethics. In M. Storr (Ed.), *Bisexuality: A critical reader* (pp. 151–162). New York: Routledge.

Dyson, M. E. (2001). When you divide body and soul, problems multiply: The Black church and sexuality. In R. P. Byrd & B. Guy-Sheftall (Eds.), *Traps: African American men on gender and sexuality* (pp. 308–327). Bloomington, IN: Indiana University Press.

Garber, M. (1995). *Vice versa: Bisexuality and the eroticism of everyday life*. New York: Simon & Schuster.

Henderson, M. G. (1989). Speaking in tongues: Dialogism and the Black woman writer's literary tradition. In C. A. Wall (Ed.), *Changing our own words: Essays on criticism, theory and writing by Black women* (pp. 16–37). New Brunswick, NJ: Rutgers University Press.

Holloway, K. F. C. (1992). *Moorings & metaphors: Figures of culture and gender in Black women's literature*. New Brunswick, NJ: Rutgers University Press.

hooks, b. (1981). *Ain't I a woman: Black women and feminism*. Boston, MA: South End Press.

hooks, b. (1989). *Talking back: Thinking feminist, thinking Black*. Boston, MA: South End Press.

hooks, b. (1992). *Black looks: Race and Representation*. Boston, MA: South End Press.

hooks, b. (1993). *Sisters of the yam*. Boston, MA: South End Press.

hooks, b. (1994a). *Outlaw culture: Resisting representations*. New York: Routledge.

hooks, b. (1994b). *Teaching to transgress education as the practice of freedom*. New York: Routledge.

hooks, b. (1997). *Wounds of passion*. New York: Henry Holt and Co.

hooks, b. (1999). *Remembered rapture: The writer at work*. New York: Henry Holt and Co.

hooks, b. (2003). *Rock my soul*. New York: Atria Books.

Hutchins, L. (2002). Bisexual women as emblematic sexual healers and the problematics of the embodied sacred whore. *Journal of Bisexuality*, *2*(3), 205–226.

Lorde, A. (1984). Uses of the erotic. In A. Lorde (Ed.), *Sister outsider: Essays and speeches by Audre Lorde* (pp. 53–59). Freedom, CA: Crossing Press.

Moore, M. (2009). *Queering the soul: Homoerotic spiritualities in African American literature*. Unpublished doctoral dissertation, University of Florida.

Morrison, T. (1984). Rootedness: The ancestor as foundation. In M. Evans (Ed.), *Black women writers (1950–1980): A critical evaluation* (pp. 339–345). New York: Doubleday.

Omolade, B. (1994). *The rising song of African American women*. New York and London: Routledge.

Pryse, M., & Spilliers, H. J. (Eds.). (1985). *Conjuring Black women, fiction, and literary tradition*. Bloomington, IN: Indiana University Press.

Quashie, K. (2004). *Black women, identity, and cultural theory: (Un)becoming the subject*. New Brunswick, NJ: Rutgers University Press.

Shanghe, N. (1997). *For colored girls who have considered suicide when the rainbow in enuf*. New York: Scribner.

Tylor, A. (n.d.). *Vagina power*. Available at: http://vaginapower.ning.com/ and http://www.youtube.com/user/alexyktylor

Vanzant, I. (1993). *Acts of faith: Meditations for people of color*. New York: Fireside Press.

Walker, A. (2003). *In search of our mothers' gardens*. Ft. Washington, PA: Harvest Books.

Zuesse, E. M. (1975). Divination and deity in African religions. *History of Religions*, *15*(2), 158–182.

Nonmonogamous Bisexuality as the Practice of Spiritual Freedom in *The Color Purple*

Marlon Rachquel Moore
University of North Carolina Wilmington

"Celie, he say, you have my sympathy. Not many women let they husband's whore lay up in they house" (Walker, *Color Purple* p. 55). With these words, laced with indirection and scorn, Celie's father-in-law articulates the perception and judgment of the rural Black community in Alice Walker's 1982 novel, *The Color Purple.* His words are spoken to Celie but aimed at his son, Albert; for Celie has no authority in her marriage and, consequently, has no say in where her husband's other lover may lay. The focus of the father-in-law's critique is the *ménage a trois* in which Albert oversees Celie as she nurses Shug, Albert's beloved mistress and mother of his 'outside' children, back to health. While it scandalizes the good Christian folk in the small Georgia town, the living arrangement is only the beginning of the queering, or destabilization of black sexual norms, that Shug's presence imbues: Shug and Albert are longtime off-and-on lovers who were "as hot for each other as two pistols" (p. 270) and, on the occasion denounced by the father-in-law, had engaged in noisy sex in the bedroom and stealthy passion on the side of the porch within Celie's earshot.[1] Meanwhile, Shug also sparks a sensual flame with Celie which culminates in a lesbian affair and facilitates Celie's spiritual empowerment. Eventually Shug abandons Albert, but returns to his house with her own husband, Grady—only to exit again with Grady, Celie and another woman, called "Squeak," in tow. Shug deposits and, for awhile, financially supports them all in her home in Memphis. Through these romantic affairs and domestic arrangements, Shug represents bisexual nonmonogamy, an expression of sexual fluidity that is situated in the novel as a type of liberated selfhood. Consequently, the kinship network Shug constructs attests to her erotic power and, when contrasted with other characters, marks her as the most liberated and self-actualized character in the narrative.

Because Celie's life and (dilemma of) voice are at the center of the narrative, most critiques of *Color Purple* analyze it from the perspective of her journey from "ostensible nothingness" (Wasserman p. 301) and "into a state of bliss and restoration" (Hankinson p. 320). Many writers have also identified how Walker posits a patchwork of black female strength and self-love in Celie's life from which she is able to stitch together her own identity and self-worth. It is also well established that Shug's role in Celie's life as mentor and "professor of desire and self-fulfillment" (Berlant p. 214) is particularly crucial to Celie's transformation. This essay builds on those observations and adjusts our lens ever-so-slightly by zooming in on the particularities of Shug's transformative power and the implications of her transgressive sexuality.

Shug's sexual, emotional, and affective life is a complex configuration that requires some meditation. To be clear, I do not use the terms "bisexual nonmonogamy" and "queer" synonymously. Stating that Shug queers black sexuality, as I do above, is not the same as asserting that Shug is *a* queer. Queer is useful as a critical lens because it refuses fixed notions of sexuality; a queer methodology privileges the slipperiness and context-based possibilities of human interaction. It opens up a text to multiple readings and, as a verb, "to queer" allows me to describe the havoc Shug's character wreaks on dyadic notions (good/bad or hetero/homo) of black sexuality. Yet as a category of sexual identity or community moniker, queer problematically obfuscates the differences between types of sexual and gender nonconformists. In its attempt to resist all notions of fixity, as Cathy Cohen points out, "queer politics has served to reinforce the dichotomy of heterosexual and everything 'queer'" (p. 438). To say that Shug is a queer would simply be insufficient.

Shug's inclinations could also be described as polyamorous. Polyamory is "the assumption that it is possible, valid and worthwhile to maintain intimate, sexual, and/or loving relationships with more than one person [at once]" (Haritaworn, *et al.* p. 518). Clearly, this is Shug's perspective: Once in Memphis, Shug moves her female lover in a room across the hall from Shug and Grady's marriage bed; and Grady begins a romantic relationship with Squeak, which Shug acknowledges.[2] Therefore, Shug does exhibit a polyamorous disposition; however, it is important not to mute the bisexual nature of her affinities—same-sex attraction is not a presumed aspect of multi-partner lifestyles. I could also use the term "bisexual polyamory," but practitioners of polyamory insist that the designation implies something more than a nonmonogamous perspective on sexuality.[3] Elizabeth Sheff distinguishes it from other multiple-partner arrangements this way:

> It differs from swinging in its emphasis on long-term, emotionally intimate relationships and from adultery with its focus on honesty and (ideally) full disclosure of the network of sexual relationships to all who participate in or are affected by them. Both men and women have access to additional partners in polyamorous relationships, distinguishing them from polygamy. (Sheff p. 253)

Polyamory as defined by practitioners is not applicable because Shug's lovers do not necessarily enter into relationships with her fully aware of the sexual network in which she operates.

Shug's interactions also reflect an African relational style called mati-ism, while her liminality invokes the Queen B(?) figure of African American folklore.[4] In the essay, "Mati-ism and Black Lesbianism," Gloria Wekker traces mati-ism from present day Afro-Surinamese culture to precolonial West African social traditions. It is a group dynamic in which one woman moves among several male and female partners that may not be aware of each other. Importantly, mati as a cultural phenomenon has no negative connotation. It simply is. Among mati women, a claim to a particular sexual orientation is irrelevant; the same is true of outness or disclosure of the relationship to others. Mati same-sex relationships are often characterized by their intergenerational nature and mentoring aspects, instead of differences in gender roles, such as butch-femme, though such gender expression differences are also visible in some cases.

Similarly, the African American Queen B(?) figure is a woman whose sexual politics indicate "the dismissal of false bilateral ordering of sexuality" (Stallings p. 170). She is a trickster figure who, like the Bad Man/Nigga of folklore and popular culture, is heroic because she operates outside of legal and/or moral boundaries. The variations of Queen B(?), which are the bitch, bulldagger, or bee, "[present] female omnipotence through sexual desire, sexual freedom and independence" (Stalling p. 172). Walker participates in the Queen B(?) tradition in the characterization of Shug as a woman who fulfills her immediate sexual and emotional needs with men but does not depend on or cling to them. Shug is, in her own words, "high natured" (p. 250) and prioritizes her erotic attractions where and whenever they occur. She bounces in and out of Albert's life as she pleases, and the marriage contract with Grady is not treated as an iron clad, monogamous 'till death do us part' arrangement. The crowded house in Memphis becomes a "domestic, sensual, and spiritual space" (Russell p. 206) in which Grady and Celie share Shug as a romantic partner, while Grady is also enticed by Squeak. In most cases, these conflicts and overlaps would lead to disharmony; instead, life in Shug's house is depicted as an idealistic communal arrangement wherein food, music, and physical intimacy blend with ease. Celie narrates that

> Nobody cook like Shug when she cook. She get up early in the morning and go to market. Buy only stuff that's fresh. The she come home and sit on the backstep humming and shelling peas or cleaning collards or fish or whatever she bought. Then she git all her pots going at once and turn on the radio. By one o'clock everything ready and she call us to the table. [...] Us eat and eat, and drink a little sweet wine and beer, too. Then Shug and me go fall out in her room and listen to music...Us lay with our arms around each other. (p. 210)

Shug lives up to her stage name, the "Queen Honeybee," and the Memphis estate is her hive. Through these various erotic openings, intersections and diversions, Shug embodies the disruption of monosexual discourses and unidirectional models of sexuality represented by heterosexuality, homosexuality, and monogamy. As the review above reflects, there is a spectrum of terminologies and styles of nonnormative sexualities available to help articulate Shug's emotional/erotic/romantic penchants. I use the term "nonmonogamous bisexuality" in hopes of capturing the specific design of her fluidity. Also, because bisexuality is underrepresented as an orientation and identity in the field of sexuality studies, it is strategically important to say its name. I propose that nonmonogamous bisexuality is articulated in *The Color Purple* as a type of blueswoman evangelism.

The moniker "blueswoman evangelist" signifies the multi-layered, intersectional relationship between the transformative powers Shug exerts in her private life, and the public ministry of the Blues music she performs.[5] Her blues consciousness is a secular religion, a liberation theology which informs her sexuality; they are branches of the same tree. In *Blues Legacies and Black Feminism*, Angela Y. Davis identifies three areas of African American life that were transformed dramatically in the post-Emancipation experience: the possibilities for travel, individual education, and the freedom to choose sexual partners. Because of these profound changes in the life of the black masses, travel and sexuality are ubiquitous themes in Blues lyrics. So blues consciousness was shaped by and gave expression to this social transformation. Furthermore, because Blues is an aesthetic of the psycho-emotional life—composed of moans, hollers and an overall churchy aesthetic—it is considered the secular counterpoint to spirituals. According to this logic, if the spiritual is God's music, then Classic Blues, its sonic twin, belongs to the Devil.

However, African American expressive culture defies the simple sacred/profane binary. Jon Michael Spencer, author of *Protest & Praise*, argues that Blues music's location outside of the church setting reflects its function as an expressive extension or variation of intense spiritual engagement. Spencer contends that "Christian religion was the sacred history...of blues people [while] blues and blues life subsisted within the larger sphere of Christianity" (p. 109). That is, there are blues people who are church folk, and there are blues people among the jook-joint crowd (of course, some are both); either way, the blues (as mood or philosophy) precedes utterance and is intrinsic to all spiritual striving. "God was the reference source in times of blueness, whether petitioned by the churched in black spirituals or by the unchurched in blue spiritual" (Spencer p. 112). Spencer explains the deeply religious experience of blues performance:

> It was the bluesman's religious demeanor that rebaptized profane space for the sake of the unchurched black blues community. Saturday night in the "juke houses" was their sacred time and place for the communion of blues confession, what Albert Murray designated "a ritual of human existence" and the "truth of black experience" as preached to them in the blues, was a way of rendering meaning to the cosmos by being brazenly truthful about it. (p. 113)

Blueswomen, particularly, represented love and sexuality in ways that often blatantly contradicted mainstream ideological assumptions regarding women and being in love. The lyrics speak of women's frustration with cheating men, the loneliness and jealousy of being the other woman, good and bad lovers, intimate partner violence, homosexuality, suicide, violent revenge, drunkenness, incarceration and poverty (Davis pp. 8-11). Although African American culture functions in a way that often blurs the line between sacred/profane spaces and performances, most church folk are invested in maintaining a clear rhetorical distinction between them. Therefore, lifestyles of the most famous blueswomen represent an unchaste, unholy, 'nasty' womanhood, as is illustrated in the novel.[6] Blueswomen were doubly debased by their participation in Blues rhetoric because the lyrics often speak of romantic love but not in the idealized terms of mainstream love songs.

Walker situates Shug in the Blues tradition by linking her to Bessie Smith, the first real superstar in African American popular culture. "First Shug sing a song by somebody name Bessie Smith," Celie writes, "She say Bessie somebody she know. Old friend" (p. 72). The invocation of Smith's legacy is key to understanding Shug's position among the other women in the story. Bessie Smith is believed to be linked sexually to her professional mentor, blueswoman Ma Rainey, whose lifestyle demonstrates elements of female masculinity, open marriage, polyamory and mati-ism (Phillips and Stewart p. 23). Smith was "known for traveling with a coterie of women-loving women, including a male impersonator, [and] she indulged her diverse sexual palate at buffet flats." (Phillips and Stewart p. 33).[7] Smith defied prescribed female roles and operated outside of moral boundaries. "In many regards," Jana Braziel observes, "Smith...embodied the very stereotypes continually (and negatively) associated with bisexuality—promiscuity, fickleness, lack of commitment, unpredictability, and illicit disregard for consistent or constant same sex and/or different-sex identifications (pp. 6-

7). Walker combats the negative views of bisexuality by illustrating the ways fickleness and unpredictability are not inherently destructive traits. With Shug, the messiness and chaos of love and sex are nutrients in a garden of growth and healing. Her relationships exemplify the human complexity that June Jordan extols in her defense of bisexuality, a speech entitled "The New Politics of Sexuality."
Jordan writes,

> Bisexuality invalidates either/or formulation, either/or analysis. Bisexuality means I am free and I am as likely to want and to love a woman as I am likely to want and to love a man, and what about that? Isn't that what freedom implies? If you are free, you are not predictable and you are not controllable (p. 14).

Shug is neither predictable nor controllable in her relationships with Albert, Celie or Grady. She maintains her sexual autonomy and allows others theirs. After Grady and Squeak move away together, Shug strikes up an intergenerational romance with Germaine, a nineteen-year-old flutist in her band. She is nearly sixty. She recognizes that the age difference is taboo when the woman is the older partner but she doesn't subscribe to patriarchal masculine privilege. She describes him as "a baby" that is "A third my age. A third my size. Even a third my color" (p. 251). Nonetheless, she "got to have it" (p. 250) and so begs Celie for patience and understanding as the mating ritual runs its course.[8]

Shug's blueswoman theology insists that an appreciation of sensual pleasures is the foundational principle of humanity's relationship to God. This is the distinction she draws between the church folk and bluespeople. The difference, as Shug bluntly states, is that the Blues performance puts "singing and dancing and fucking together. That's the reason they call what us sing the devil's music. Devils love to fuck" (p. 115). Shug recognizes that bluespeople embody the unfettered pursuit of pleasure and gratification which Christianity-based practices, as portrayed in the novel, consider an ungodly indulgence of the flesh. The phrasing of "singing and dancing and fucking" highlights the rhetorical lines drawn in mainstream Christian cultures between the sensual pleasure one can experience while dancing and singing in church, and the pleasures associated with singing and dancing in a dimly lit, sexually-charged club environment.

But religious catharsis requires a similar letting loose, as we say in the south, of self-consciousness and involves a similar build up and climax to that of dance floor space. Murray notes that church songs generate paroxysms of ecstasy far exceeding anything that occurs in the blues gathering (quoted in Spencer p. 108). Often these scenes begin during the praise and worship portion of the program in which music-making is the locus of spiritual activity. Singing and clapping lead to the ecstasy of being touched by the Spirit—a submission to spirit possession which is seen as one's obedience to Jesus, the believer's 'bridegroom,' made manifest on the body.[9] Religious ecstasy in the arms of Jesus takes many forms. Some people fall to the floor in a trance and begin to speak in tongues. Others jerk spasmodically, jog or dance in the grip of the Holy Spirit until they are physically spent. When Shug argues that devils put singing and dancing and fucking together, she is contrasting it with singing and dancing and catching the spirit. I would argue that there is only a *perceived* difference in the energetic current that flows through the sensuality in the church space and the fluid energy in the club atmosphere.

In *Race Rules: Navigating the Color Line*, Michael Eric Dyson eloquently illustrates this point. Dyson traces the buildup and persistence of energy from the clapping, swaying and dancing induced by the choir that spreads through the building, to the pitch and fervor of the sermon, and including the parade of well dressed bodies traipsing to the collection table and podium for announcements. The black worship service is, for Dyson, a ritual of religious arousal (pp. 88-89). Shug's statement reveals how the religious arousal that Dyson describes is veiled or denied in the church. "Singing and dancing and fucking" revises the church perspective in which singing, dancing and praising is the proper trio. Yet, as Dyson corroborates, the club atmosphere can mirror the emotionalism, physical release, and bodycentric culture of a passionate Black church service. The difference lies in the discourse: erotic energy in church is not recognized as such, while the spirituality of sexual energy is presumed in the Blues. Angels and devils are both spiritual beings, after all.

Shug's blueswoman theology contradicts her own formulation of the sacred/profane dichotomy by folding the religious ecstatic moment into the erotic ecstasy of orgasm. First, she reconfigures the Creator as an It, which removes the masculine gendering. In doing so, she discursively evaporates the patriarchal justification for women's bodies and loyalties to always be under control of men, whether those men are their husbands, fathers, or the masculine Holy Trinity. "Men and their religions have tended to make love for anything and anybody other than themselves and their Gods an objectionable thing, a shame" Walker writes in *The Same River Twice*, "But that is not the message of Nature, the Universe, the Earth or of the unindoctrinated Human Heart, where everything is profusion, chaos, multiplicity, but also creativity, containment and care" (pp. 171-2). It is Walker's Pagan interpretation of the "message of Nature [and] the Universe" that Shug brings to Celie in a way that equates sexual ecstasy with spiritual ecstasy, a blueswoman's theology which includes homoerotic and masturbatory experiences.

Shug testifies that when she found It, it was on a day when she "was sitting quiet and feeling like a motherless child, which I was, [and] it come to me: that feeling of being part of everything..." (p. 195). It is a testimony of emotional development. The confession of being a "motherless child" underscores Shug's state of disconnection: she is motherless figuratively because of her nasty woman outsider status in the community, and literally because she is shunned by her biological family. That she was sitting quietly suggests a meditative or prayerful state during which her connection to and clearer understanding of her inextricable link the Universe descended upon her. Shug laughed, cried, and "run all around the house" (p. 196), behavior that mirrors the religious ecstatic moment described above. Shug echoes her "singing and dancing and fucking" formulation by insisting that the spiritual breakthrough feels "sort of like *you know what*... [as she is] grinning and rubbing high up on [Celie's] thigh" (p. 196 my emphasis). As her hand moves up Celie's thigh, Shug stimulates Celie's body in order to open her mind to the lesson of receiving God. As Jesus is savior and bridegroom, Shug is spiritual leader and romantic partner. In order to understand what "you know what" means to Celie, we must examine an earlier scene in which Shug introduces Celie to the prospect of clitoral orgasm:

> Listen, she say, right down there in your pussy is a little button that gits real hot when you do *you know what* with somebody. It git hotter and hotter and then it

> melt. That the good part. But other parts good too, she say. Lots of sucking go on, here and there, she say. Lot of finger and tongue work. (p. 77)

The omission of gendered pronouns in this definition of orgasm creates imaginary space for Celie to insert Shug as the "somebody" to do the "finger and tongue work" in her pussy. Yet, Celie will be the first to actually touch herself there. After this conversation, Celie tearfully masturbates while listening to Shug and Albert make love (p. 79). The first time the two women actually engage in sexual intimacy, the details are left out. Celie simply says they kiss and touch each other. So, for Celie, the only logical reference to "you know what" when Shug rubs her thigh is the "little button" at the tip of Shug's fingers. By touching Celie's thigh during her testimony, Shug invokes the sexual pleasure Celie associates with those hands and claims that pleasure as an act of thanksgiving, praise and connection to the Creator. In blueswoman theology, "God love all them feelings" (p. 196) and so same-sex love and "you know what" are valid spiritual experiences which can bring one closer to the Creator.

The narrative shatters the ideological barriers between (nonnormative) sexuality, and spirituality, and struggles to undo antagonisms between bodily pleasure and spiritual strivings that were part of Celie's doctrinal education. But this insistence on the sacredness of pleasure is a painful tenet for Celie to live by, for it means that she must accept Shug's pursuit of other lovers. When explaining to Celie why she must follow her desire for Germaine, she acknowledges Celie's lesbian orientation while asserting her own bisexual inclination: "He's a man. [Celie] write on the paper. Yeah, she say. He is. And I know how *you* feel about men. But I don't feel that way. I would never be fool enough to take any of them seriously, she say, but some mens can be a lots of fun" (p. 250, emphasis added). Shug is a devil who loves to fuck and is freer because of it. Though she knows Celie is hurt by it, Shug honestly and openly insists upon her right to indulge her desires with other people. According to Shug's gospel, unidirectional sexuality is but one orientation among many. Spiritual freedom is practiced as one's openness to the gifts of the Universe or a conscious participation in Creation. The absence of Christianity's narratives of restraint and guilt creates space for the exploration, affirmation even, of Celie's lesbian identity *and* Shug's nonmonogamous bisexuality. Still, Shug seems more fulfilled overall than Celie. As I stated earlier, Shug stands apart in the grand scheme of the novel as always already spiritually and sexually arrived. Her function in the text is to teach the others how to live and love freely.

Among the cast of characters in *Color Purple*, except Sophia perhaps, Shug has no lesson to learn about life, friendship, or God. She is the teacher in every scenario. So much so, that even her absence is instructional. Shug is as capricious as she is powerful, and she often chastises her devotees. She brings love and then withdraws it, teaching the profound lessons of the blues (Marvin p. 422). While Shug travels with Germaine, for example, Albert and Celie bond through their mutual yearning for her. As Albert waxes philosophical about his lifelong devotion to Shug, he makes plain the differences between his discontentment and Shug's satisfaction:

> All I ever wanted in life was Shug Avery, he say. And one while, all she wanted in life was me. Well, us couldn't have each other... I got [the wife his father approved of]. Then [Celie]. [And] All them rotten children. She got Grady and who know who all. But still, look like she come out better than me. A lot of people love Shug, but nobody but Shug love me. (p. 282)

Because he acquiesced to his father's demands for a respectable daughter-in-law, and even though he and Shug continued a clandestine affair, Albert suffers spiritually and feels deprived of meaningful love. Shug, on the other hand, is not preoccupied with traditional romantic devotion. She indulges her desires with other men and "who know who all" in the name of self-love. Albert represents those of us who listen to the regulatory voices around us, those produced by society, family, and/or religion, and internalized/perpetuated by loved ones, while we stifle, suppress, deny, or silence our own inner voice, that which speaks through desires (Simcikova p. 51). Shug sermonizes for a transformative paradigm, one in which we free ourselves from self-denial and the desire for mainstream acceptance. Shug personifies this message of emancipatory, revolutionary love.

In Walker's paradigm, "love is *the* revolutionary emotion, partly because it cannot be limited, cannot be compartmentalized, cannot be controlled" (quoted in Simcikova p. 126). In Shug's absence, Albert's humanity expands. In his state of newfound spiritual clarity and intimate friendship with Celie, he falls in love with Celie and proposes they re-marry, "this time in the spirit as well as in the flesh" (p. 283). But Celie is a lesbian and, more importantly, does not entertain the possibility of another lover. So she, too, is frustrated, lonely, and jealous without Shug. Eventually, though, Celie's inner voice breaks through the solitude and imparts the wisdom of emotional commitment by which Shug already lives:

> Sometimes I feel mad at her. Feel like I could scratch her hair right off her head. But then I think, Shug got the right to live too. She got a right to look over the world in whatever company she choose. Just cause I love her don't take away none of her rights. [...] I miss her friendship so much that if she want to come back here dragging Germaine I'd make them both welcome, or die trying. (p. 268)

The blueswoman evangelist is the center of the erotic vortex and benefits the most when her followers recognize her power, which is her deeply instilled sense of freedom. So through temporary moments of loss, they learn to love her without possession. Shug is the politicized ideal of the bisexual in that she is neither emotionally destructive nor spiritually restrictive. She models a life of love and spirit which reframes desire "in porous, nonexclusive ways" (Storr p. 146). When she returns to Celie and Albert, the *ménage a trois* that Albert's father so disdains is naturally reconstituted. At the novel's close, their love flows in multiple directions and carries with it the promise of liberation and wholeness.

NOTES

1. The noisy sex occurs in the novel, while the porch scene occurs in Walker's adaptation for Steven Spielberg's movie version. I realize that they are not the same text; however, Walker is the author of the novel, screenplay and of all the characters. Her vision of these relationships is consistent. The screenplay, "Watch For me in the Sunset," is published in *The Same River Twice: Honoring the Difficult* (Scribner, 1996) p. 91.
2. In Albert's house, Grady makes "goo-goo eyes at Squeak and Shug sorta tease him about it" (p. 115) and in the passage which Shug tells Celie about her affair with Germaine, she claims to be relieved that Grady finally "lit out after Mary Agnes" (p. 249) which is Squeak's proper name.

3. For practitioners and ethnographers who discuss the importance of consent and open communication in polyamorous communities, see the work of Serena Anderlini-D'Onofrio, Elisabeth Sheff, Dossie Easton, and Janet Hardy.
4. L.H. Stallings introduced the use of the question mark in her explication of the Queen B(?) character as a way to signify and discuss the multiple uses of the trope and "to highlight the fluctuating position of this outlaw figure in African American culture" (p. 170). The "B"-word in the phrase "queen b(?)" can indicate bitch, bulldagger, or bee depending on context.
5. My assertion of a "Blues ministry" draws from the school of thought, primarily pursued in the 1970s, which asserts a theological essence of Blues music: James Cone, *The Spirituals and the Blues: An Interpretation* (New York: Seabury Press, 1972); Paul Oliver, *The Meaning of the Blues* (New York: Collier Books, 1966); William Ferris, *Blues from the Delta* (Garden City, NY: Anchor/Doubleday, 1979); Rod Gruver, "The Blues as Secular Religion," *Blues World* 29 (April 1970).
6. Celie narrates a church scene in which the preacher "take [Shug] condition for a text. He don't call no name but he don't have to. Everybody know who he mean" (pp. 43-4).
7. Phillips and Stewart define buffet flats as private parties which featured an assortment of illegal activities, erotic shows, and sex acts (p. 33).
8. Celie is heartbroken by Shug's relationship with Germaine. As I will show, Celie is a lesbian and is devoted sexually and emotionally to Shug. Shug's nonmonogamous nature serves to teach Celie how to love without claiming possession.
9. The imagery and symbolism of marriage is applied to Christ and his followers. Christ, the Bridegroom, has chosen the church to be His bride (Ephesians 5:25). Her responsibility is to be faithful to Him (2 Corinthans 11:2; Ephesians 5:24). At the Second Coming of Christ, the church will be united with the Bridegroom, the official ceremony will take place (Revelation 19:7).

REFERENCES

Berlant, Lauren. "Race, Gender and Nation in *The Color Purple. Alice Walker: Critical Perspectives, Past and Present*. Henry Louis Gates, Jr., ed. New York: Amistad Press, 1993.

Braziel, Jana Evans. "Bye, Bye Baby": Race, Bisexuality, and the Blues in the Music of Bessie Smith and Janis Joplin. *Popular Music & Society* 27.1 (Feb2004): 3-26.

Cohen, Cathy. "Punks, Bulldaggers and Welfare Queens: The Radical Potential of Queer Politics?" *GLQ: A Journal of Gay and Lesbian Studies* 3.4 (1997): 437-485.

Davis, Angela Y. *Blues Legacies and Black Feminism: Gertrude "Ma" Rainey, Bessie Smith, and Billie Holiday*. New York: Pantheon Books, 1998.

Dyson, Michael Eric. *Race Rules: Navigating the Color Line*. New York: Random House, Inc., 1996.

Ellison, Ralph. Living With Music: Ralph Ellison's Jazz Writings. Robert G. O'Meally, ed. New York: Random House, 2001.

Hankinson, Stacie Lynn. "From Monotheism to Pantheism: Liberation from Patriarchy in Alice Walker's *The Color Purple*." *Midwest Quarterly* 38.3 (Spring 97): 320-328.

Haritaworn, Jin, et al. "Poly/logue: A Critical Introduction to Polyamory." *Sexualities* 9.5 (2006): 515-529.

Hull, Akasha Gloria. *Soul Talk: The New Spirituality of African American Women*. Rochester (VT): Inner Traditions International, 2001.

Jordan, June. "A New Politics of Sexuality." *Progressive* 55.7 (July 91): 12-14.

Marvin, Thomas F. "'Preachin' the Blues': Bessie Smith's Secular Religion and Alice Walker's *The Color Purple*." *African American Review* 28.3 (Fall94): 411-422.

McKever-Floyd, Preston. "Tell Nobody But God: The Theme of Transformation in *The Color Purple*." *Cross Currents* 57.3 (2007): 426-433.

Phillips, Layli and Marla R.Stuart. "Nontraditional, Nonconforming, and Transgressive Gender Expression and Relationship Modalities in Black Communities." *Black Sexualities: Probing Powers, Passions, Practices, and Policies*. Juan Battle and Sandra L. Barnes, Eds. New Jersey: Rutgers University Press, 2010.

Razak, Arisika. "Her Blue Body: A Pagan Reading of Alice Walker Womanism." *Feminist Theology 18.1* (2009): 92-116.

Russell, Danielle. "Homeward Bound: Transformative Spaces in *The Color Purple.*" *Dialogue* 5: *Alice Walker's The Color Purple.* Kheven LaGrone, ed. New York: Rodopi Press, 2009.

Simcikova, Karla. To Live Fully, Here and Now: The Healing Vision in the Works of Alice *Walker*. Lanham: Lexington Books, 2007.

Spencer, Jon Michael. Protest & Praise: Sacred Music of Black Religion. Minneapolis: Fortress Press, 1990.

Stallings, L.H. *Mutha is Half A Word: Intersections of Folklore, Vernacular, Myth, and Queerness in Black Female Culture.* Columbus: Ohio State Press, 2007.

Storr, Merl. "Epistemologies of the Fence." *Bisexuality: A Critical Reader*. New York: Routledge, 1999.

Walker, Alice. *The Color Purple.* New York: Harcourt Inc., 1982.

— *The Same River Twice: Honoring the Difficult*. New York: Scribner, 1996.

Wasserman, Jerry. "Queen Bee, King Bee: *The Color Purple* and the Blued." *Canadian Review of American* Studies 30.3 (2000): 301-317.

Wekker, Gloria. "Mati-ism and Black Lesbianism: Two Idealtypical Expressions of Female Homosexuality in Black Communities of the Diaspora." *Journal of Homosexuality* 24.3/4 (1993): 145-158.

The Third Precept: Toward a Buddhist Ethics of Bisexuality

Lisa Keele
Clayton State University

Buddhism is a religion with which one can engage at many levels. People of many religions, and those who believe in no religion, have found solace and personal benefit in the teachings and practices of Buddhism. Magazines and self-help books recommend Buddhist-style meditation for the general reduction of stress and mental well-being. The writings of the Dalai Lama have touched people all over the world. Committing oneself to the religion in a more serious way, such as taking vows to officially become a devotee of the religion, however, involves more than meditating for personal well-being; it involves, among other things, vowing to practice the religion regularly, and vowing to uphold the ethics of the religion to the best of one's ability.

The purpose of this article is to investigate exactly what Buddhist ethics means for those identifying as bisexual. Of course, bisexuality is a multifaceted thing, and there are as many ways to be bisexual as there are bisexual people. Those who identify as bisexual but live in monogamous marriages with members of the opposite sex will find few religions ethically condemning their sexual practices. There are few, if any, Buddhist writings which condemn or even address particular sexual orientations or identities; but rather, Buddhist ethics advocates certain practices and deems other practices as unethical. I wish to investigate what Buddhist ethics has to say about two practices which some, though not all, bisexuals engage in: particularly, same-sex relationships, and polyamory, the practice of having more than one lover at the same time. It seems at first glance as though both of these practices are explicitly forbidden by Buddhist ethics. However, I will argue that at least some interpretations of the third precept— the part of Buddhism which explicitly forbids "sexual misconduct" — can not only permit same-sex lovers and polyamorous relationships, but can actively guide a person through the ethical issues which may arise.

This paper will have three parts. The first part will be a brief overview of Buddhist beliefs and ethics, with particular attention paid to the teachings involving sexuality in general. The second part will be an examination of some of the Buddhist writings which condemn same-sex sexual practices and sex outside of legal marriage. The third part will be an argument that these practices can in fact be embraced in such a way which upholds the core beliefs of Buddhism.

PART I: BUDDHISM AND SEX

Sexuality is a vexed issue for Buddhism in general. Many believe it is best avoided or limited. Buddhist monks are completely celibate, and often suspicious of all sexual activity, though they admit that sexuality is a necessary part of non-monastery life, and that most Buddhists are householders (i.e., non-monks). The suspicion toward sexuality stems from the core beliefs of the religion. At the base of Buddhist ethics and beliefs are the four noble truths, which many Buddhists adhere to as the heart of the religion itself. The four noble truths are:

1. All living beings suffer.
2. The cause of suffering is desire.
3. Suffering can cease.
4. Freedom from suffering can be attained by following the eight-fold path.

Among the tenets of the eight-fold path is the dedication to Right Action; Right Action means, among other things, following the Buddhist precepts.

The precepts are a list of actions to avoid; the list of precepts differs depending upon what level of commitment to Buddhism one practices. There are more stringent precepts for monks and nuns than for householders, for example; there are also special lists for laity who wish to spend some time, a month, for example, engaged in their religion at a deeper level. The basic list, traditionally applicable to all lay Buddhists, has five precepts, which are the basis of Buddhist morality:

1. Avoid killing or harming living creatures.
2. Avoid stealing.
3. Avoid sexual misconduct.
4. Avoid lying.
5. Do not ingest intoxicants.[1]

The more stringent precepts for monks and nuns begin with these five, though the third precept is strengthened to celibacy. All five are subject to interpretation, and all five are regarded as important. The fifth, ingesting intoxicants, is sometimes called the "master vice," as it can lead to a lack of mindfulness which therefore leaves a person more open to breaking the other precepts as well.[2] However, the first three are particularly emphasized in Buddhist scripture. The Magga-vibhanga Sutta describes Right Action as consisting only of the first three: "And what, monks, is right action? Abstaining from taking life, abstaining from stealing, abstaining from sexual intercourse: This, monks, is called right action."[3] The Maha-cattarisaka Sutta analyzes the importance of Right View, another branch of the eight-fold path, in terms of these three precepts: "Of those, right view is the forerunner. And how is right view the forerunner? One discerns wrong action as wrong action, and right action as right action. And what is wrong action? Killing, taking what is not given, illicit sex. This is wrong action."[4]

The focus of this paper is the third precept, and interpretations of what exactly 'sexual misconduct' entails. However, it is important first to note that wariness about sexuality for Buddhism has its roots in the second noble truth, which is not only fundamental to Buddhist practice but also to the Buddhist world view. The problem faced by all sentient beings, in Buddhist analysis, is suffering; the cause of this suffering is desire. Of course, what is meant by desire is much broader than simple sexual desire, or even carnal desire (that for food, drink, fun, etc.), but rather, it refers to any activity or emotion which ties oneself to this world in unhealthy attachment.[5] Desire takes all forms and shades. The suffering caused by physical pain, for example, is multiplied and made worse by our desire to be healthy and well. When one has a toothache, in addition to the physical pain itself, one often suffers from an intense desire for the pain to stop, to get back to normal life. This impatience with things in life which strike us as less than desirable, the longing for things we believe are worthwhile which we do not possess, and many of our deepest fears, such as the fear of dying, all fall under the category of 'desire.' All of these forms of desire cause suffering, according to Buddhist doctrine.

However, lust is indeed one of the desires warned against, one which is seen as causing a great deal of suffering. There is a high tendency for sexual desire to lead to unwise choices, and to attachment. There is no doubt that sexual desire can be overwhelming, can easily overpower our attempts to be mindful, fully present, and detached; perhaps few other emotions and desires have the tendency to pull us away from the present moment more than sexual desire (intense anger is another such emotion, and thus, anger is also warned against, and violence forbidden by the first precept).

Thus, the root of the prohibition against sexual misconduct is the second noble truth; sexuality is seen as drawing us away from our spiritual selves, immersing ourselves in the sea of desire and craving, and is really best avoided, or at least controlled. That said, outside of the monastery, sexual conduct is allowed; the question which now faces us is what precisely the third precept forbids. The rest of this paper will investigate what is meant by sexual misconduct, and under what interpretations it forbids same-sex relations and polyamorous behavior, and why.

PART II: THE CASE AGAINST

In many traditional and modern interpretations of the third precept, both of these forms of sexuality are forbidden. In these interpretations, in essence, sexual expression is permitted only within the context of legal married life between a man and a woman, for the purposes of procreation, and is otherwise to be avoided. Venerable Yin-Shun, a modern Chinese Buddhist monk, interprets the third precept along just such lines.

> "Do not engage in improper sexual conduct." If a man and a woman agree to be husband and wife by means of publicly recognized rites, with the approval of guardians and not in violation of secular laws, then sexual contact between husband and wife (which is an important element of family formation for the continuation of posterity) is proper and not sinful. Even in cases where the other partner consents, sexual conduct is improper for laypeople if it is not permitted by the Buddha Dharma [...], not allowed by secular law, or not agreed to by the related guardians. Buddhist lay devotees should abstain from such contact.[6]

Buddhism is known for being such an open and accepting religion in many respects, it may at first seem shocking to see a sexual ethics expressed which is so conservative;

restricting sexuality to acts between one man and one woman, within the bounds of a legally and publicly recognized marriage, and even necessitating the approval of guardians. For Yin-Shun, the reasons behind these prohibitions are neither cultural nor simply traditional; rather, he posits serious ethical concerns:

> Such contact not only harms the other person's abilities to make choices free of external influences, but it is also evil conduct that ruins the harmony of families and disturbs the order of society.[7]

Yin-Shun is not the only one to hold such a strict view of the third precept. This attitude, restricting sexuality to legal marriage between a man and a woman, appears in many ancient and modern Buddhist texts. Most interpretations of the third precept specify that adultery—defined as sexual contact outside of the context of marriage—is strictly forbidden. Notice that Yin-Shun specifies these prohibitions hold even when all parties in the situation agree. He is not simply condemning lying to or cheating on one's legal partner, but all extra-marital sexual behavior, however consensual. This interpretation thus leaves open the possibility of same-sex relationships provided that you live in a society which legally recognizes same-sex marriage, and you happen to be in such a marriage, but explicitly forbids polyamorous relationships, with the sole exception of those who live in a society which legally approves of polygamous and polyandrous marriages, and that you wish to marry all of your partners before engaging in sexual behaviors.

However, even if the legal definition of marriage is expanded beyond the one that Yin-Shun and the "Defense of Marriage Act" puts forth (i.e., marriage between one man and one woman), Buddhist literature goes beyond this. Some interpretations of the third precept specify a wide range of sexual acts which themselves count as 'sexual misconduct' regardless of whether there is a legal and socially approved marriage or not. Specifically, sexual relations between same-sex partners are forbidden by these interpretations. In the *Dakini Teachings*, for example, which are meditations on Buddhist thought and principles attributed to Padmasambhava dating back to the 8th century, the third precept is given full interpretation, and presents an elaboration on what 'sexual misconduct' means in many directions. To quote just part of this elaboration:

> The essence of the third physical non-virtue, sexual misconduct, is the act of engaging in intercourse with an object of desire with whom one has no authority to do so. When divided, there are the following kinds. 1. It is unsuitable for a commoner to have intercourse with someone under the guardianship of a king, such as his queen. 2. It is unsuitable to have intercourse with someone prohibited by the law. 3. In India, it is unsuitable to have casual intercourse with someone under the guardianship of parents, since men and women not in their own household are protected by their parents. 4. It is unsuitable to have intercourse with someone protected by "civilized principles," which means someone with whom it is shameful, such as a mother or a sister. [...]
>
> There are also occasions on which it is unsuitable to have intercourse even with your rightful companion. 1. It is unsuitable to have intercourse at an inappropriate time such as on the full moon, new moon, and the eight day. 2. It is unsuitable to have intercourse in an inappropriate location, such as in the presence of a shrine for

> the Three Jewels. 3. It is unsuitable to have intercourse in an inappropriate orifice, such as engaging in the manner of animals.[8]

Here we see a parallel with some of Yin-Shun's prohibitions, such as his 'guardianship' requirement, as well as the legal requirement;[9] the specificity of this elucidation to time and place are apparent in the prohibition against sexual conduct between commoner and queen, and specifying that the guardianship clause is relative to India's social structure. Most important for our purposes is the last requirement, which specifies that sexual conduct using the "inappropriate orifice, such as engaging in the manner of animals" counts as misconduct. As far as I am aware, this is the oldest example of the "wrong orifice" theory of sexual misconduct in Buddhist thought.[10]

His Holiness the Dalai Lama seemed to have this interpretation in mind when he debated the acceptability of same-sex sexual relations with gay activists in the 1990s. During a meeting in 1997 between the Dalai Lama and a group of gay and lesbian Buddhists, clergy, and human rights activists, he urged tolerance and respect for sexual minorities, and opposed "violence and discrimination based on sexual orientation."[11] However, while he expressed strong disapproval of societal discrimination, he reiterated his belief that same-sex sexual activity is classified as sexual misconduct, and therefore forbidden by the third precept. In fact, he stated that the "wrong orifice" definition of misconduct ruled out any form of sex other than penile-vaginal intercourse. In his own words, "Even with your wife, using one's mouth or the other hole is sexual misconduct. Using one's hand, that is sexual misconduct."[12]

The Dalai Lama insists that sexual orientations are never wrong, simply certain sexual activities. He also distinguishes between Buddhists and non-Buddhists. "If someone comes to me and asks whether it is okay or not, I will first ask if you have some religious vows to uphold."[13] Thus, for non-Buddhists, and those who have not taken other vows against sexual activity, or same-sex sexual activity, there is nothing wrong with identifying as bisexual, or having same-sex lovers. It is only if one has vowed to uphold the precepts, as even lay Buddhists do, that such activity becomes immoral.

Mind you, under such an interpretation of the third precept, same-sex activity is still classified as sexual misconduct, even though the Dalai Lama sees no reason to condemn non-Buddhists for breaking this precept. However, even while noting this as a statement of compassion and acceptance from His Holiness the Dalai Lama, it is still rather unsettling that the most famous Buddhist monk would openly state that having same-sex lovers is immoral. It leaves those who identify as gay or bisexual in the same bind as do many religions; they are free to practice sexual activity in line with their inclinations only if they either abandon their religion, or know that this activity is immoral and will lead to punishment (in the case of Buddhism, the consequences of breaking the precepts include accumulating very specific types of karma which will lead to suffering in later incarnations, and will ultimately delay one's ability to approach enlightenment and the release from suffering).

Thus, traditional Buddhist texts as well as modern Buddhist interpretations of the third precept explicitly forbid polyamorous practices, as well as having same-sex lovers. It is worth considering how this interpretation affects those who identify as bisexual, on a personal level; especially those who also identify as Buddhist. First, however, it is worth elaborating upon the Dalai Lama's claim that this attitude toward sexuality does not and should not impede the pursuit of social equality for all, and the development of an attitude of compassion toward all people. Like Christianity, Judaism, and Islam, Buddhists do believe that the spiritual consequences for our actions affect all human beings equally, whether or not they believe in the religion (i.e., a Christian believes that non-Christians are judged under the same rubric as believers; a Buddhist believes that negative karma attaches to non-Buddhists and affects them in the same manner). However, the Buddhist belief in reincarnation tends to produce more room for error, if you will. While a Christian typically believes that a person has one life to earn his or her place in the afterlife, and thus might believe that helping non-Christians convert to the 'correct' belief system and lifestyle is of the utmost importance, a Buddhist typically believes that a person has countless lifetimes to 'get it right,' and that most people, including most Buddhists, will not succeed in attaining Nirvana or enlightenment during this life.

Thus, many Buddhists, including the Dalai Lama, advocate compassion toward all people; judgment is not a useful approach to take. Notice above that the Dalai Lama explicitly condemned discrimination and violence against sexual minorities, and prefaced his remarks on the "wrong orifice" interpretation of sexuality with the comment, "If someone comes to me and asks whether it [i.e., same-sex sexual activity] is okay or not, I will first ask if you have some religious vows to uphold."[14] Thus, while a non-Buddhist will accrue the same amount of negative karma for breaking the third precept, this is an expected and normal part of human life, and the doctrine of reincarnation dictates that the only metaphysical ramification for this is the necessity to reincarnate—which most non-Buddhists would have to do anyway.

While the advocation of respect and tolerance for all, regardless of sexual orientation, is laudable, the conservative interpretation of the third precept poses a problem for those who identify as bisexual and also Buddhist. First, recall that in general, Buddhists do not demonize those who identify as bisexual, or any other sexual orientation. Prohibitions are against particular actions, not against personal identity. Therefore, a bisexual Buddhist is free to identify as both, and restrict her or his sexual actions to those allowed by this interpretation of the third precept, with no karmic ramifications. If one wishes, however, to become polyamorous, or to have a relationship with a person or people of the same gender, one is explicitly acting against Buddhist ethics, according to this interpretation of the third precept. As in all religions, of course, one is free to accept or ignore the various prohibitions and recommendations; few of us practice any religion with perfection, and Buddhism is much more forgiving of those who 'get it wrong' than many other religions. Of course, one who believes in Buddhism will also most likely believe in the metaphysical ramifications of breaking the precepts. However, whether one chooses to obey the third precept, or break it and suffer the metaphysical consequences, it is discouraging and disenfranchising to learn that one's religion considers one's honest expression of love and desire to be fundamentally unethical. This interpretation could drive one to refrain from taking Buddhist vows altogether, or to take vows, but take them less seriously, knowing that one is going to break the third precept.

It is also detrimental from the view of self-acceptance and mental well-being. Suspicion of sexuality in general is the lot of many Buddhists, given the second noble truth (that the cause of suffering is desire). Religiously codifying the preference of one sexual orientation and one sexual act over all others, however, could conceivably add to internalized biphobia and other difficulties with self-acceptance,[15] and could give those who are already biphobic further justification for their irrational view. The stance of many in the queer community is that there is nothing fundamentally unethical with same-sex sexual activity or polyamory; this interpretation of the third precept states exactly the opposite, and as such is a barrier to self- and societal-acceptance. This may be particularly disappointing for those who were drawn to Buddhism precisely because of its reputation as a more tolerant religion in general.

However, famously, Buddhism has many paths to enlightenment, and, as one of the world's oldest living religions, many interpretations of key precepts have arisen over the millennia. In the next and final section, I will argue that not only are there interpretations of the third precept which do not pose such a bleak picture for those who identify as bisexual and Buddhist, but also that Buddhism can provide an ethical guide for navigating the sometimes stormy waters of bisexuality.

PART III: TOWARDS A BUDDHIST ETHICS FOR BISEXUALS

Assuming that we do not wish to give up, declare polyamory and same-sex sexual activity immoral, and go our merry non-Buddhist ways, is there room in Buddhism for those who follow an alternate sexual-orientation path? I believe there is, and will attempt to lay out the foundations of a Buddhism-based ethics applicable to bisexuals below.

The first point to note is that in Buddhism, the monastery life is not seen as religiously higher than lay life; monks may live a life of purposeful self-denial, but Buddhism does not expect everyone to follow the same path. While the emphasis on celibacy and world-denying behavior in which monks engage may seem as though it makes any sexual activity at all immoral, and that therefore, only procreative sex is acceptable, many Buddhists, including monks, do not advocate this point of view. The Buddha himself discussed a middle path, declaring life-denying lifestyles as well as pleasure-indulging ones equally far from the correct path. As the Venerable Yin-Shun (the same monk who gave us our one-man-one-woman definition of sexual misconduct, above) writes,

> When Sakyamuni Buddha turned the Dharma-wheel, he began by revealing the Middle Way—the practice of neither asceticism nor pleasure seeking. He considered both extremes incapable of leading the body and mind to a normal state, and hence not conducive to liberation.[16]

Thus, Yin-Shun does not view a completely life-denying lifestyle as a better, holier lifestyle than that of the pleasure-seeker, but rather, both monks and laity must temper their natural inclinations toward denial or indulgence, respectively, and try to walk the middle path. The laity are not further away from true Buddhism by nature of their world-engaged path.

> In order to accommodate those who wanted to continue life's pleasures, the Buddha allowed disciples to remain laypersons. [...] Although they lived as laity, they practiced the Buddha's true Dharma, taking refuge in the Three Treasures, keeping the five precepts, practicing meditation, and attaining wisdom. As long as they kept the resolution to renounce and as long as living a full lay life did not

> hinder their practice, they were still able to become liberated from birth and death.[17]

The important parts of the above passage for our purposes are as follows: first, the Buddha did not forbid life's pleasures to the laity. Second, the laity are capable of becoming enlightened and liberated from suffering *without ever becoming monks*. There is no need to become world-denying and celibate in order to proceed in one's own spiritual development. Buddhism has alternate paths, both of which lead to the same end, if followed with all due seriousness.

Thich Nhat Hanh, a Vietnamese Buddhist monk and peace activist, discusses the required celibacy of monks in similar terms, declaring that it is not the ideal which laity fail to reach; thus, required celibacy for some is not a moral proclamation on the worthwhileness of sexuality in general, but, simply, a practical restraint, as pursuing an active sexual life detracts too much from monastery life. Therefore, sexuality is not only available to laity, but also something to be enjoyed and cherished, within certain constraints. As he writes in *Being Peace*,

> Traditionally, Buddhist monks were celibate for at least three reasons. The first is that the monks in the time of Buddha were urged to practice meditation for most of the day. [...] If a monk had to support a family, he would not be able to perform his duties as a monk. The second reason is that sexual energy had to be preserved for meditation. [...] The third reason Buddhist monks observed celibacy is the question of suffering. [...] Aware that having more children in his society would be to make them suffer, the Buddha urged the monks not to have children. I think that during the past 2,500 years, Buddhist monks in many countries have helped curb the birth rate. That is quite important.[18]

Far from advocating the monastery path of celibacy as the higher road, then, with lay people allowed to have sex merely for the sake of conception and furthering the human race, Nhat Hanh views celibacy as a more practical course for those who wish to dedicate their lives to meditation. Importantly, he also believes that bringing children into the world should only be done with great deliberation, by those who are able to spend the time and resources caring for them adequately. This is not a moral judgment on the superiority of celibacy, nor does it convey a suspiciousness of sexuality or sexual activity. In fact, he says directly in his discussion of the second reason for celibacy that, "Buddhist monks observed celibacy, not because of moral admonition, but for conservation of energy."[19]

In fact, Nhat Hanh believes that our love for other people can bring us closer to mindfulness, and that the most fulfilling kind of love is one where both practice Buddhist principles, which brings them closer together. In *You Are Here*, he advises,

> The first miracle of mindfulness is our true presence – being here, present, and totally alive. Then, if you are really here, something else will also be here: the presence of the other. [...] When the other person realizes that his or her presence has been recognized and confirmed, he or she will blossom like a flower. To be loved is to be recognized as existing.[20]

Nhat Hanh believes in a practice he calls "Engaged Buddhism."[21] He advises against using Buddhist monasteries as a retreat from the world, and believes in actively working toward making the world a better place. He also advocates developing an active appreciation of the good that is in this world, even while maintaining appropriate levels of non-attachment. This view is expressed clearly in his statements on love and mindfulness, above: while he recognizes that attachment leads to suffering, he still advocates a middle path, refusing to deny the existence of love, beauty, and the suffering of others, advising rather that we engage with it in appropriate ways.

Interestingly, while the Dalai Lama and others who promote the conservative interpretation of the third precept focus on the capacity of sexuality to produce children, Nhat Hanh does not believe the production of children to be an unquestionable good; producing children can add to the suffering of the world, and one should do so only within the context of the committed ability to raise them well. Sexuality, for Nhat Hanh, has another goal altogether; to produce love and community in the world, and to connect to others who can support us on our spiritual journeys. This leads to the obvious question, given the topic of this paper: what, precisely would appropriate sexual engagement look like, if we are not to take a life-denying, only-for-procreation attitude toward sexual behavior? Nhat Hanh has his own expansion of the third precept, which he delivers in the form of a meditation upon the precepts.

> "Aware of the suffering caused by sexual misconduct, I vow to cultivate responsibility and learn ways to protect the safety and integrity of individuals, couples, families, and society. I am determined not to engage in sexual relations without love and a long-term commitment. To preserve the happiness of myself and others, I am determined to respect my commitments and the commitments of others. I will do everything in my power to protect children from sexual abuse and to protect couples and families from being broken by sexual misconduct."[22]

Note, this says nothing about following the laws of the land, or about how many people should be involved and what gender/sex they all are. Instead, it focuses on avoiding harming others through sexuality. Do not harm children, and in fact, protect them from others. Respect yourself, and your partner. Act from love and commitment, not from simple lust. Do your best not to harm society, families, or partners. If you have made commitments, honor them; if others have made commitments, honor those as well.

This interpretation of sexual misconduct can be applied equally to same-sex, opposite-sex, and multiple partner relationships, to relationships which do or do not produce children, to serial monogamy, even. It does not specify what type of sexual activity one participates in within these respectful relationships, nor which orifices are the 'correct' ones. What this interpretation clearly bars is casual sex, lying, cheating, and behaving in such a way that you do not take adequate safety precautions, or precautions against the emotional or physical harm you may do to others. Many of these precepts are reflected explicitly in the ethos embraced by the polyamorous community[23], and many are adhered to by those in same-sex relationships.

Interestingly, while His Holiness the Dalai Lama specifies, as we saw above, a very different interpretation of the third precept, Nhat Hanh's interpretation is very much in line with the underlying ethics the Dalai Lama discusses. As the Dalai Lama writes in *How to Practice*, "the main principle of Buddhist morality is to help others and, if that is not possible, at least to do no harm."[24] Compassion and *ahimsa* (non-harm) form the foundation of the Dalai Lama's ethics. Specific details aside, including levels of commitment to Buddhism and interpretations of the meanings of each precept, helping and avoiding harming others is central; Thich Nhat Hanh makes this foundation explicit in his interpretation of the third precept.

Another modern Buddhist monk, Shravasti Dhammika, agrees with Nhat Hanh's interpretation; that the heart of the third precept is to avoid harming others through one's sexuality, and to avoid breaking other precepts, such as by lying. He argues that specific genders, orifices, or legal arrangements are not implied by basic Buddhist teachings. In his blog, he writes, "Buddhism judges acts, including sexual acts, primarily by the intention (*cetana*) behind them and the effect they have. A sexual act motivated by love, mutuality and the desire to give and share would be judged positive no matter what the gender of the two persons involved."[25] Or, one presumes, the gender of the three or more people who may be involved in a larger polyamorous family, assuming that each relationship was motivated by the same spirit of love, mutuality, and respect.

Thus, while Buddhism, like many religions, contains specific prohibitions against sex outside of marriage, certain sexual acts, and same-sex relationships,[26] by focusing on the heart of Buddhist ethics, compassion and *ahimsa*, one can develop an ethics for polyamorous and same-sex activity. Thus, it is quite possible to both identify as bisexual and develop one's own way of approaching that sexual identity, within the scope of Buddhism itself, as Thich Nhat Hanh has demonstrated in his compassion-based elucidation of the third precept.

Developing a Buddhist ethics of sexuality along these lines opens up a wide range of possibilities for those who identify both as Buddhist and as bisexual. The primary advantage is the lack of a discriminatory framework, where same-sex sexual activity and sex outside of a legal, culturally binding marriage are automatically viewed as immoral. Thus, this interpretation does little to reaffirm biphobic attitudes or contribute to internalized biphobic responses; under the more liberal interpretation of the third precept, all expressions of sexuality can not only be ethical, but welcome, and a fulfilling part of a Buddhist life. Adopting this approach to the third precept goes further than simply refraining from adding to the sense of discrimination and judgment many who identify as bisexual feel, however. That is, the advantages of this interpretation go beyond the negative advantages, of not advocating harmful self- and world-views. There are positive benefits to be gained from this interpretation as well, in that the compassion-based interpretation provides one with a positive moral framework.

Thus, one who identifies as Buddhist and bisexual, and agrees with this interpretation of the third precept, can take Buddhist vows as a lay person[27] without conflict, and can use the third precept as she or he uses the other precepts, to guide his or her moral journey through life. A Buddhist bisexual, then, should base relationship decisions on the principle of compassion, *ahimsa* (the principle of non-harm, and the first precept), and the principle of honesty (the second precept). Sexual activity which causes harm to those involved, through a neglect of safety precautions or through a disregard of personal feelings, then, would count as sexual misconduct. The typical conception of 'cheating,' that is, having multiple partners without the explicit consent of every partner, would count as sexual misconduct as well as a breach of the fourth precept forbidding lying. Sexual interaction with children counts as sexual misconduct, obviously, and also breaks *ahimsa*.

Casual sex is forbidden, under this interpretation, even if it is approached with honesty, respect, and with appropriate safety precautions. I presume this is due to the strength of the second noble truth: desire is the cause of suffering. Casual sex is viewed as simply an indulgence in desire, without building a longer, compassionate, loving relationship, the connection which Nhat Hanh views as the essential role of sexuality within a relationship. Thus, while this interpretation does not take a stance on the gender of one's partner or particular sex-acts performed, clearly, a polyamorous life, in which one develops loving and longer-term relationships, or a monogamous life, developing the same relationship with one person, is a better fit for this interpretation than a string of casual affairs, whether one does so from the perspective of a single person, or as a person in an open relationship.

To conclude: the four noble truths of Buddhism, particularly the second one which identifies desire as the cause of suffering, makes sexuality a source of danger in the Buddhist worldview. Sexual desire is a strong emotion, and, like some of our other basic and powerful emotions, such as anger and fear, it can overpower us and lead to immoral behavior, which can harm ourselves and others if not appropriately conscribed and controlled. The precepts are the moral guidelines by which one controls how these emotions affect one's behavior (methods for coping with psychological and other effects of these emotions appear in other aspects of Buddhist doctrine). Traditionally, sexuality has been forbidden to those in the monastery, and allowed for the laity, but only within the context of societally approved marriages and for the purposes of procreation. However, alternate interpretations of the third precept are available, and within these interpretations, a non-discriminatory ethics of sexuality can be developed, which can guide anyone, regardless of sexual orientation or tendencies toward polyamory or monogamy, through the complexities which arise when sexuality is not repressed, but rather expressed, and can help one build a moral and fulfilling sex life, no matter one's personal orientation.

NOTES

1. It is worthwhile to note that the first four of these are ones we may and certainly do break; it is impossible, for example, to live a human life never harming another living creature. However, any breach of these precepts is viewed as unethical, and adds to the negative karma one accrues. The fifth precept is meant to be adhered to strictly; intoxicants should never be consumed. Very few Buddhists I am aware of argue that intoxicants can be ingested in moderation, whereas many Buddhists admit that meat can be eaten under certain circumstances. Monks who obtain all of their food through begging, for example, may eat meat if it is given to them. Thus, the third precept too is one we aspire to uphold to the best of our ability, knowing that at times we may fail.
2. See, for example, the Venerable Yin-Shun, *The Way to Buddhahood: Instructions from a Modern Chinese Master*, Boston: Wisdom Publications, 1998; p. 87.
3. "Magga-vibhanga Sutta: An Analysis of the Path," Translated from the Pali by Thanissaro Bhikkhu. <URL= http://www.accesstoinsight.org/tipitaka/sn/sn45/sn45.008.than.html>
4. "Maha-cattarisaka Sutta: The Great Forty," Translated from the Pali by Thanissaro Bhikkhu. <URL= http://www.accesstoinsight.org/tipitaka/mn/mn.117.than.html>
5. For Buddhists, all attachment is seen as less than desirable. For this reason, many Buddhists have chosen a world-denying life, retreating to the monastery or the meditation center, avoiding anything which can cause disruption. Not all Buddhists retreat regularly, however; some are actively engaged and encourage participation in worldly affairs in a whole-hearted manner rather than simply the minimal one necessary to continue one's existence. For engaged Buddhists, limiting attachment is an important task. One can love one's children, for example, but one must recognize that they are not a part of oneself, they are independent creatures whom one cannot control or own.

6. Yin-Shun, *The Way to Buddhahood*, p. 86.
7. Ibid.
8. *Dakini Teachings:Padmasambhava's Oral Instructions to Lady Tsogyal*, tr. Eric Hein Schmidt, Hong Kong: Rangjung Yeshe Publications, 1999; p. 39.
9. Though both specifications are discussed in older Buddhist literature as well.
10. Buddhist literature is wide and vast, however, and I am by no means an expert in Buddhist texts. If I am mistaken about this, I would be very grateful if someone could point out the earlier source.
11. "Dalai Lama urges 'respect, compassion, and full human rights for all,' including gays," *Bay Area Reporter*, Dennis Conkin, June 19 1997. <URL = http://www.quietmountain.org/links/teachings/gayrites.htm>
12. "'According to Buddhist Tradition': Gays, Lesbians and the Definition of Sexual Misconduct," Steve Peskind, *Shambhala Sun*, March 1998. <URL = http://www.shambhalasun.com/index.php?option=-com_content&task= view&id=1977>
13. Ibid.
14. "'According to Buddhist Tradition': Gays, Lesbians and the Definition of Sexual Misconduct," *Shambhala Sun*, March 1998. As the Dalai Lama advocates that one adheres to one's own religion, regardless of which religion that is, as a means to making spiritual progress, I assume this was meant to apply to non-Buddhists as well as Buddhists; i.e., if one has taken religious vows in any religion which forbids same-sex sexual activity, the Dalai Lama would advocate avoiding breaking those vows. As our focus here is Buddhism, however, I wish to focus specifically on this religion, rather than considering what the Dalai Lama might say about a Christian who identified as bisexual and wished to engage in same-sex activity.
15. The blatant preference for activity in line with one sexual orientation over all others seems to me to contradict a fundamental Buddhist principle, that of "loving-kindness." Buddhists are encouraged to develop compassion not only for our fellow creatures on earth, but for ourselves as well. We are all imperfect, and much harm is done to self and others in the search to fight against the aspects of the self we dislike; Buddhists advocate a loving self-acceptance of the whole self, warts and all. Even anger, violence, and greed, very dangerous emotions in the Buddhist world-view, should not be greeted in oneself with self-loathing and flight, but open acknowledgement and compassion. Thus, to include a doctrine according to which one's basic sexual orientation, if it is not the more common one, is viewed as fundamentally immoral, or wrong, and the expression of which is always antithetical to the keeping of the five precepts, seems to encourage an internal struggle in those who wish to be Buddhist but who are queer. This internal struggle is the antithesis of loving-kindness.
16. Yin-Shun, *The Way to Buddhahood*, p. 111.
17. Ibid.
18. Thich Nhat Hanh, *Being Peace*, Berkeley: Parallax Press, 1987, pp 98-99.
19. Ibid.
20. Thich Nhat Hanh, *You Are Here: Discovering the Magic of the Present Moment*, Boston: Shambhala Publications, Inc., 2001; pp 16-17.
21. He discusses Engaged Buddhism in detail, including providing a new set of precepts, in *Being Peace*.
22. Thich Nhat Hanh, *The Blooming of a Lotus: Guided Meditation Exercises for Healing and Transformation*, tr. Annabel Laity, Boston: Beacon Press, 1993; p. 133.
23. For example, Franklin Veaux defines polyamory as "the non-possessive, honest, responsible and ethical philosophy and practice of loving multiple people simultaneously." Elaborations on non-possession mirror Buddhist non-attachment principles, and elaborations on honesty and responsibility within poly relationships address the same concerns Nhat Hanh addresses above. Franklin Veaux, "Polyamory 101," Xeromag.com, <URL = http://www.xeromag.com/poly101.pdf>
24. His Holiness the Dalai Lama, *How to Practice: The Way to a Meaningful Life*, tr. Jeffery Hopkins, New York: Pocket Books, 2002; p. 1.
25. Dhammika, Shravasti, "Damma Musings," August 18, 2008. <URL=http://sdhammika.blogspot.com/2008/08/homosexuality.html>
26. Though, it is worth noting that to my knowledge, the Buddha himself did not address same-sex relationship specifically.
27. I specify "as a lay person" here, as it seems obvious that were one to identify as Buddhist and bisexual and wish to take monastic vows, there is no impediment in either interpretation to doing so. By traditionally specifying that Buddhist ethics apply to actions, and not identities, and by requiring celibacy of all monks and nuns, Buddhism has, to my knowledge, no restrictions on the sexual identities of any of its monastic adherents.

Bi, Buddhist, Activist: Refusing Intolerance, But not Refusing Each Other

JONATHAN ALEXANDER
University of California, Irvine, California, USA
KAREN YESCAVAGE
Colorado State University, Pueblo, Colorado, USA

In this personal essay, the authors reflect on their work as activists for lesbian, gay, bisexual, trangender rights and their attempts to nourish such activism through a Buddhist understanding of mindfulness about the suffering of self and other. Although many figure activism as a kind of 'combat' and 'fight' for equality, the authors want to understand the potential cost of vengeful and poisonous thinking about the other, even when having to show those others how they inflict suffering through prejudice. The authors conclude with some strategies for mindful activism that places the care of the self and mindfulness about all of our suffering at the center of activist practice.

MINISTERING, JUDGING . . . AND THE PATH BETWEEN

We begin with a personal journey. . .

> While I (Jonathan) was assisting family members in Louisiana and Mississippi recover from hurricanes Katrina and Rita, I heard one of my aunts, a fundamentalist Christian, say that Katrina's devastation of New Orleans was "God's wake-up call" for a sinful city, known for its Bourbon Street debaucheries and Mardi Gras hedonism. I, usually pretty talkative with something always on the tip of my tongue, was caught off guard. Foremost in my mind was the all too human suffering surrounding me—homes destroyed, families displaced, loved ones lost. It

> seemed to me that any spiritual tradition would see the human needs and pain and minister to that suffering—not reflect judgmentally on the situation.

At the same time, Jonathan realized that such reflection was part of his aunt's spiritual practice, part of her attempt to make sense of the suffering that surrounded her. Still, as a queer man with ongoing bi-erotic interests, he was cut to the quick by her comments. After all, in her worldview, he might be one of the sinful ones whom her God was striking at by sending Katrina to devastate the Big Easy. Jonathan couldn't quite reconcile her understanding of God with his worldview, grounded in part in a Buddhist understanding of suffering and its cessation. A vengeful God lashing out at those who love differently than the norm seemed to be spiritually far removed from a deep sense of karma, personal responsibility and recognizing and attending to each other's suffering. A vengeful God might set capricious rules, or his followers might rely on ancient and outmoded traditions and injunctions; a more karmic approach requires that we take responsibility for our actions and recognize their effects on others and ourselves. In Jonathan's mind, the injunctions against homosexuality and bisexuality seemed part of that outmoded tradition, one that judged difference before asking who is really being harmed by it, particularly by a form of loving.

Such incidents, when spiritual traditions seem to collide, offer all of us an opportunity to reflect on our differences in beliefs and attitudes—and on what values we might share in common. At a time when fundamentalist movements across the globe are insisting that their adherents have sole access to truth (and justice), such spiritual collision may be inevitable, as one values system encounters another. But such differences may also be extremely useful, providing the opportunity for a deeper understanding and a deeper feeling of what a spiritual practice can bring to our lives.

Such an understanding has become extremely important for both of us, who have been queer and bi-identified activists for over a decade now. We use the term *queer* as shorthand for those involved in promoting a greater understanding of lesbian, gay, bisexual, and transgendered (LGBT) lives. However, we have also maintained identities as people deeply invested in bi eroticism, open to erotic possibilities and intimacies with multiple genders. In that time, we have encountered numerous people of a variety of religious faiths who have condemned not only our activism but also our lifestyles. Fundamentalist Christians, in particular, have often met our claims for social equality and equal rights with indignant claims that we are asking for 'special rights' and that no society based on Christian principles should in any way support our deviant and sinful lifestyles.

On many occasions, we have felt deep anger, even rage, at such comments. We know what it is like to grow up with such religious fundamentalism, and we understand—personally—how such views can lead young queer people to contemplate leaving home, severing ties with family and friends and even suicide. For us, such antiqueer religious attitudes are not only bigoted, but also contribute unbelievably to the suffering of people who are trying to understand how to love others. In the past, we have denounced such attitudes, often publicly, and at times we have wondered how anyone with a compassionate heart can ally themselves with a religious tradition that singles certain people out for condemnation, disdain and even hatred. We only have to remember one of the slogans of a Baptist church in Topeka, Kansas—"God Hates Fags"—to recall our frustration and anger with those who promulgate such a worldview.

Sadly, these messages continue to echo in secular society as well. For example, Gene Shalit, the longtime film critic for NBC's *Today* show, unabashedly interpreted loving actions in the "gay Cowboy" film *Brokeback Mountain* as those of a "sexual predator." We could go on and on with examples; suffice it to say, there is no shortage of antigay rhetoric in U.S. society, in spite of the fact that films like *Brokeback* are winning awards and television sitcoms like *Will and Grace* have become huge successes. Although lesbian and gay representation increases, at least for White queers, hateful sentiments are slower to decline. Thus, we are left with a mixture of emotions.

As we work with our feelings in meditation, we realize that nurturing our own anger and hatred toward those who seemingly hate us is counterproductive and harmful to our own spiritual growth and development. In Melvin McLeod's (2006) *Mindful Politics: A Buddhist Guide to Making the World a Better Place*, the Dalai Lama notes that "[a]nger plays no small role in [many] current conflicts. These conflicts arise from a failure to understand one another's humanness" (p. 23). With such a thought in mind, we strive to become more mindful of the seeds of anger in ourselves, and to how such anger blinds us to the humanness of those around us. We have also seen how such anger, often seemingly justified, can spread from person to person, creating barriers to dialogue and mutual understanding. Our work in queer activist groups has shown us all too clearly how anti-Christian attitudes can grow and flourish, cutting people off from spiritual traditions that might otherwise nurture them. Anger at injustice, though understandable, can also blind us to the suffering of those who practice injustice, to a deeper understanding of how our so-called adversaries have come to their beliefs, how their own suffering might prompt such judgmental attitudes and beliefs.

For instance, when Jonathan faced his aunt in Louisiana and heard her claim Katrina as God's righteous wrath against the sinful, he refrained from responding, observed his anger rising and falling, and then saw his aunt's frustration, anger and grief. She too was suffering and expressing her suffering in the only way she knew how. It occurred to Jonathan that what was needed at that moment was not his own judgment and condemnation of her view, as repugnant as it is, but an understanding of her suffering that might open up a compassionate dialogue about the nature of suffering—and our role in both furthering *samsara*, the seemingly never-ending cycle of suffering, and potentially stepping out of the karmic cycles that keep the wheels of suffering turning. Although some pain is only natural, and though some suffering is certainly systemic, brought on by inequities in our social and cultural systems, much suffering is located in the individual and her perceptions. Attending to those perceptions and becoming mindful of how we interpret the world in ego-driven and grasping ways that only further our own suffering, the Buddha says, is the beginning of the path to enlightenment and the end of unnecessary suffering.

Indeed, what has attracted us as two queer and bi people, educators and activists to the Buddhist path is the many insights that path has given us for rethinking our activism. At this point in our spiritual development as activists, we want to think with others about how attention to suffering may help us open up dialogues across boundaries and borders. We also want to explore how even anger at social injustice, even when understandable and seemingly justifiable, may be a barrier to spiritual growth and achieving social justice. At the very least, it can lead to resentment and burnout. As such, we offer our insights in this article to a variety of activists—those working with AIDS, the intersexed, people of color, women, people with disabilities—hoping to provide others with potential tools and mind-sets to do their work, grow as spiritual beings and practice a productive and enriching Buddhist activism.

BECOMING AN ACTIVIST, BECOMING MINDFUL

Several contemporary Buddhist scholars and thinkers have noted, along with monastics and activists such as Thich Nhat Hanh, the potential ways in which Buddhist approaches and practices can support and nurture social activism. There's much work to be done, particularly in easing the suffering caused by widespread social inequities and social injustices. As queer activists, we have been particularly invested in how lesbians, gays, bisexuals, transgender, and intersexed people are often not afforded the same rights and privileges as others in our society. In fact, many *still* face abuse, harassment, and discrimination on a daily basis. In *The New Social Face of Buddhism: A Call to Action*, Ken Jones (2003) drew particular attention to homophobia, which, along with racism and sexism, Jones calls a form of "cultural violence" with systemic roots (p. 145). Jones saw homophobia as a significant source of suffering, one which practitioners of the Dharma must consider and treat mindfully:

> A sense of gay community has resulted in a deepening awareness of a personal . . . woundedness, amounting in extreme cases to guilt and even self-hatred. Here, then, is a specific form of suffering previously barely

> acknowledged. How is the Dharma to be understood, practiced and internalized as a liberation from this suffering? A variety of gay Buddhist groups have come into being to work through these questions together. (p. 204)

Even more pressingly, David Loy (2003) in *The Great Awakening: A Buddhist Social Theory* argues that because "all of us have the same Buddha-nature," this "implies not only the liberation and empowerment of women but opposition to all gender-based discrimination, including gay, lesbian, and transsexual rights" (p. 38). By *gender-based discrimination*, Loy is referring to all of us who do not quite fit the heteronorm, in either gender performance or the sex of those whom we desire. We, of course, would also add bisexuals to Loy's list, and we applaud his assertion that Buddhists should actively be part of the opposition to queer oppression and in support of "liberation and empowerment" for all, regardless of sexual interest or gender performance.

Certainly, groups such as Q-Sangha in San Francisco or the Diamond Metta Gay and Lesbian Buddhist Society in New York encourage mindfulness about queer people and minister directly to the needs of LGBT people. But Jones' question—how can the Dharma work toward liberating us from the suffering of homophobia?—is a pressing one, particularly in a world in which battles over gay rights, marriage issues and gays in the military still spark—and stem from—widespread fear and hatred of gays, lesbians and bisexuals. Moreover, rising violence against transgendered people, or people whose gender identity is ambiguous, points to suffering inflicted on trans people and suffering lashing out from people who are threatened by those who are simply different.

Given this, the question that some of us as queer activists have been asking is, how can our walk along the Buddhist path lead us to a more profound, peaceful and productive activism?

BODHISATTVAS: ACTIVISM'S SPIRITUAL DIMENSION

Thinking along these lines, we have often asked ourselves a seemingly simpler but more fundamental question: does activist work have a spiritual dimension? In many ways, yes, it does. In some Buddhist traditions, the bodhisattvas are those who have achieved enlightenment but who decide to stay in the human realm until all other people have achieved enlightenment and ended their suffering. Bodhisattvas, by the very choice they make, are activists. How might we follow in their path? One can do this by simply role-modeling pride (as opposed to internalized shame) in one's desires, queer or otherwise. One can also role model (and actively engage in) peaceful resistance, especially for those within the movement who advocate for angry action. Activism can also be seen as a form of teaching, which is considered a noble endeavor on the eightfold path, and that teaching might be a powerful way to role-model awareness and compassion, particularly for those who don't do anything in the face of oppression. If that activism, however configured, focuses on peace and acceptance from within, then it is part of the walk of the path of enlightenment, a truly spiritual practice.

In other ways, though, activism can potentially sidetrack our Buddhist walk. Nothing can give our lives meaning; therefore, one challenge activists face is in becoming more mindful of pride arising from an 'acting out' or 'acting up' against discrimination. There is a profound difference between a healthy self-confidence (a 'gentle pride') and a fierce, angry, and potentially alienating pride that draws boundaries between self and other. The trick may be to protect one's self from discrimination while keeping open to the other. Further, activism should not become more than a 'gentle' passion. Should one erroneously derive feelings of pride and ego satisfaction from this practice, he or she may be ultimately walking a primrose path, albeit a seemingly noble one in many people's eyes.

As difficult as it may be to be an activist—which, for us, ultimately means caring deeply about the world and those in it—we have committed ourselves both to work as queer and bi activists and to exploring what the compassionate practices of Buddhism can teach us, for others and for ourselves as activists.

One of our chief struggles as queer activists is recurrent anger, even rage, at the ways in which queers of all kinds are ridiculed, discriminated against and even killed. Upon hearing of the murder, for instance, of Matthew Shepard, we felt outrage, a profound sense of grief and disillusionment. It is easy for us at times to see the callous brutal killing of young queer people as intimately connected to—even arising out of—the intolerant and hostile attitudes of some fundamentalists, particularly those who claim that their God hates us. Faced with such internal feelings, we have at times wanted to take a radical (and reactionary) approach, challenging Christian fundamentalists to truly live by their values and 'stone us' already. We have wanted to put them on the defensive by demonstrating that they are not abiding by their God's word (in the Old Testament, at least).

One approach that Karen has attempted to rationalize is advocating legislation that would give Christian fundamentalists a taste of their own moral medicine. Specifically, if lesbian, bisexual, and gay people cannot marry because it is deemed a poor moral choice, then heterosexuals should not be allowed to divorce because it too is a poor moral choice, that is, one not supported by (their) God. Fair is fair after all, right? Karen realizes after working herself into a frenzy that these thoughts and potential actions seem not to water the seeds of compassion, but rather those of vengefulness. Even if such activist strategies did influence attitudes, they do little to encourage enlightenment. We feel it in our gentle bones, even those that sticks and stones have sorely bruised. We recall that it is not "do unto others as they have done unto you" but rather, "do unto others as you would have them do unto you"—a guideline we see as transcending, perhaps uniting, Christianity and Buddhism in their deep concern for the other, for being mindful of what kinds of seeds we plant and nourish in our own minds and in the others of others.

We must admit that we don't always feel very compassionate when thinking up such strategies to 'combat' another group's moral values. How can Buddhist practice help us in this regard? Certainly, one powerful way that Buddhism has assisted both of us in our activist work is by providing us meditative space in which to pull back from activism, reflect, explore the ground of our own suffering and work with the wounds inflicted on us by homophobia experienced in the past and, unfortunately, still in the present. This individual spiritual work is crucial—and a key ingredient of activist work of any kind.

LIVING BI THE MIDDLE WAY

Buddhist practice has insights for more engaged queer activist work as well, and this is where our ongoing investment in bi eroticism is important to us. Specifically, our commitment to remaining open to and feeling a variety of erotic possibilities and intimacies goes hand in hand with our openness as Buddhists to other people, to trying to understand and respect the many varied journeys that different people are on. Such openness, a willingness to take life as it comes and to remain engaged, prompts us to engage others in ongoing questioning, of self and values. For instance, perhaps we can try to come to the table to search for shared values, even if such values might have to be very, very broadly defined. Doing so would also allow us to see where each perspective takes us to a fork in the road. Where do we part ways? Can we work our way to seeing where we agree with each other morally? We hopefully would come to find that some of the most fundamental common ground that we might share is a desire not to harm one another. With that in mind, how can we all get along if we are overly invested in telling the other how they should be? Imagine Jesus and Buddha sitting down together for a meal; regardless of whatever differences they might have in either belief or practice, they would probably enjoy the meal they shared and then leave the table, leading by example.

Pushing further, we try to envision how to get along with differing value systems, particularly when those values systems paint ours in a negative light. How can we engage productively with those who see us as disturbed or, at least, disturbing? Why should they trust us when we use the same deficit model to explain them? If we're perverts, then they're bigots . . . and on and on. The war of words continues while people still die of hunger, war and hate.

When we judge the actions of organizations like Focus on the Family as acts of hatred, we build our own walls of judgment, circumventing a chance for communication across the great divide. Should we move to a more defensible critique of their position, namely that creating or endorsing antigay rights legislation is an act of Christian hypocrisy, we still run into difficulties. Although such antigay actions are not compatible with (what we understand to be) Christ's teachings on love, this kind of righteous argument runs into potential deadends. Religious conservatives believe, in many ways, that antigay activity is compatible with their view of love. For instance, if one is a part of a group that sees logic in doing God's work, and saving souls is God's work, then logically speaking, queer activists are Satan's helpers, trying to destroy the very moral fabric of society. We can't really argue with such reasoning. Indeed, here lies the difficulty for us as individuals striving to act compassionately with those with whom we truly feel we cannot argue, if only because all we can say is, "We agree to disagree with the values of our fundamentalist Christian brothers and sisters." In the end, though, we are still interconnected, still living under the same societal roof.
So, what tools are we left with?

We can actually take a productive cue from Christ's own teaching about "turning the other cheek" in the face of hostility or attack. How many times have we failed to "turn the other cheek," or been unable to transform angry comments from, "They're just a bunch of Bible-thumping, ignorant, hateful people who blindly follow 2000-year-old man-made writings," to, "Thank you, you are my teacher because you have shown me that I am not in control of my anger." In such emotionally difficult situations, we are provided an opportunity to transcend the world of dukkha, or suffering, by recognizing—and owning—our own suffering. Our struggle with inequitable systems does not always originate outside of us, specifically in this case, with those who might view us in a less than favorable light, 'morally' speaking. Rather, much suffering begins with our own attachment to a supposed "wounded ego," or to a deep-seated value of equality. Further, when we recognize feelings of moral superiority in ourselves, we are quickly humbled. In such a state (of grace?) we see a different vision precisely because we have turned the other cheek. Instead of snapping back at those who attack us, we remain focused on where we aspire to be spiritually, that is, in control of our anger, without judgment of others or self, and continuing along the compassionate path toward enlightenment. Doing this work, opening ourselves to the other, particularly when the other views us as sinful, even worthy of damnation, is difficult work—but it is work that cuts to the heart of developing and experiencing compassion. And as bi people—people open to our own varied desires and desire for meaningful connection regardless of gender—we attempt to embrace compassion, for self and other. Indeed, what helps us not feel "beaten" is a return to mindfulness of our interconnectedness to all beings.

We have a choice in how we interpret others' actions toward us. If we read antigay legislation as an attempt at caring for our souls, protecting us from what is perceived as evil, that is, homosexuality, then we may be in a better position to manage our emotions than if we take that caring as an insult to our self. When we defend the legitimacy of ourselves, we are experiencing attachment to ego, and that is, the Buddha says, the origin of much suffering. However, if we see the attempt at love and compassion on their part, then we can start talking together about what compassion is—and the possibility for greater dialogue and mutual understanding opens up. Ultimately, we want to role model a truly inclusive value of "judge not," not only for those who presumably seek to "save our souls" but also for those who simply have a strong distaste for the kind of diversity we exemplify. We role model for other queer activists as well who similarly struggle with anger and frustration.

> I (Karen) remember one incident in particular when I had the chance to role model. When a local high school boy was harassed by a group of his male classmates for being openly gay, the Southern Colorado Equality Alliance put together a rally at the County courthouse to both show support for this young victim and to demonstrate publicly intolerance for anti-gay harassment and violence. I had been asked if I would say a few words. As I listened, several people angrily spoke out against the hostile actions directed at this brave young man who dared to be his authentic self in a school setting less than supportive. As I listened to friends and parents speak about this child's innocent suffering, the crowd's collective frustration increased. I did not know this boy personally, nor did I know the boys who did this to him; that is to say, I was not "personally" invested in this situation as so many of the speakers before me were. However, I was deeply invested in working toward a more peaceful coexistence for us all.
>
> When the microphone made its way into my hands, I took a deep breath and silently asked that I have the courage to speak only from the heart. What I found come out were words of compassion—not for the boy who had bottles thrown at him—but for the boys who found themselves unwilling—or unable—to manage their emotions in the presence of their gay peer. I encouraged the people who came out for this rally to understand that while it is incredibly important that we protect our gay youth from antigay epithets and violence, it is equally essential to protect our youth who are raised without the tools needed to coexist with us, for they are the ones facing a felony record for their unchecked homophobic attitudes.
>
> As I spoke, my words of compassion for the perpetrators did not water the mob mentality that was understandably developing; rather, I felt the calmness that I brought to the podium ripple out into the crowd. A fire that had been fueled with comments of righteousness angrily articulating how "these boys deserved to be punished" was now being watered with

> a reminder of our responsibility to care about all our youth, and a call to help especially those so threatened by us that they seek to cause us harm. My activist approach had clearly changed. Where once I would have been caught up in all the emotions surrounding the suffering of "my people," I was now simultaneously less reactionary and more at peace. My words of compassion came from my heart. My heart was sincere in its search to end suffering, all suffering.

Our ultimate challenge as activists and Buddhist practitioners may be to work for social justice without becoming too attached to particular goals or outcomes for that social justice. Such nonattachment to outcomes is useful for our individual practice (less attachment equals less suffering) but also for maintaining energy, strength, and commitment as activists. We can each recall intense periods of burnout from working hard and diligently for LGBT causes and experiencing acute disappointment when our efforts seemed to go unrewarded or unfulfilled. Even apparent success can be draining. When the Supreme Court overturned Colorado's Amendment 2, which allowed discrimination against lesbians, gays, and bisexuals, we were elated and exhausted. Living in Colorado, we had worked to raise awareness of LGBT lives and experiences, so we felt that the overturning of the amendment was, in part, our success too. But Jonathan recalls also feeling drained and even somewhat resentful—resentful if only because we had had to fight such discriminatory legislation in the first place. Indeed, reacting to others takes time away from more productive work. However, when not thinking about it as time away from realizing future goals, we recognize it as but another opportunity to experience heartfelt compassion, in the moment.

Encountering such emotions may be inevitable, part of the experience of living in the realm of *samsara*, the world of continual birth, death and rebirth. However, working with our relationship to such difficult emotions can yield personal insights and reenergize us for further social justice work. Letting go of intense attachments to specific outcomes and expectations can refocus us on working with others in the moment, seeing more clearly the personal and immediate dimensions of the work we do. We will have successes and we will have losses at the level of the institution, and we certainly need to keep in mind the relationship between institutional systems and oppression; we are often oppressed because of and within inequitable systems. At the same time, to ward off burnout, we should continue to work toward institutional change but keep our focus on the individual and his or her suffering. We work for equality and awareness not just to overturn unfair/unnecessary legislation, but to ease the suffering of individuals. Keeping our awareness on that suffering should continually remind us of the importance of the work we do without tempting us to become fixated on outcomes that may or may not come to pass. As in everything, finding the balance—in this case, the middle way between working with awareness of the individual and awareness of the system—is crucial.

What are some pointers for maintaining that balance? We recommend the following, though we recognize that activists everywhere, particularly if they are following a spiritual path, may have (and should have!) their own variations on these guidelines:

> First, be mindful. Be mindful of anger, harmful or prideful attachment to particular goals, and of lingering resentments. Even too much 'pride' in one's identity—as an activist, as a member of the group for which you are an activist—can lead to increasing attachment to particular concrete goals as opposed to cultivating compassion.
>
> Second, work on transforming 'us against them' thinking. It's too tempting at times to demonize those who are working against us. This bipolarity only isolates from others and prevents us from exploring potentially useful common ground. Consider, instead, how we are all interdependent.
>
> Third, to extend the point we just made, be grateful to your enemies. After all, they can teach us much, most particularly, how to evolve spiritually. Those who may at first seem to be working against us actually can offer us unique opportunities to practice compassion and to recognize our common humanity.

WAKING UP...

Ultimately, as queers, as Buddhists, as activists, we want to question the rigidity in ethical and moral systems—in all systems. It is that questioning that makes us queer, that keeps us open to experience and questioning as opposed to simply accepting what others say is 'right' or the 'norm.' However, we believe that it is that questioning, that willingness to explore, that also opens up compassion. When we suspend our expectations for other people's lives, our expectations for how they should behave and what they should believe, then we open up a space for seeing their suffering, their genuine suffering—not filtered through the lens of our own understanding, ideas, or beliefs. Seeing that suffering is the ground of compassion. Or, in Pema Chodron's (1997) words, we realize that "[t]here is nobody on the planet, neither those whom we see as the oppressed nor those whom we see as the oppressor, who doesn't have what it takes to wake up" (p. 113). We practice—as Buddhists—to 'wake up' and to make it possible for others to 'wake up' too. That, we believe, is what makes us activists.

REFERENCES AND RECOMMENDED READING

Brazier, D. (2002). *The new Buddhism*. New York: Palgrave Macmillan.

Cabezon, J. I. (Ed.). (1992). *Buddhism, sexuality, and gender*. Albany, NY: State University of New York Press.

Chodron, P. (1997). *When things fall apart: Heart advice for difficult times.* Boston, MA: Shambhala Classics.

Faure, B. (1998). *The red thread. Buddhist approaches to sexuality.* Princeton, NJ: Princeton University Press.

Jones, K. (2003). *The new social face of Buddhism: A call to action.* Boston, MA: Wisdom Publications.

Leyland, W. (Ed.). (1998). *Queer dharma: Voices of gay Buddhists. Volume I.* New York: Gay Sunshine Press.

Leyland, W. (Ed.). (1999). *Queer dharma: Voices of gay Buddhists. Volume II.* New York: Gay Sunshine Press.

Loy, D. (2003). *The great awakening: A Buddhist social theory.* Boston, MA: Wisdom Publications.

McLeod, M. (Ed.). (2006). *Mindful politics: A Buddhist guide to making the world a better place.* Boston, MA: Wisdom Publications.

Shaw, M. (1994). *Passionate enlightenment: Women in tantric Buddhism.* Princeton, NJ: Princeton University Press.

The Sacredness of Pleasure

A BI SPIRIT CLASSIC
BY STARHAWK

A speech for the National Conference Celebrating Bisexuality, Washington, DC, April 24, 1993

Hello. First let me say how honored and delighted I am to be here at this conference, and to be able to participate in the important events of this weekend.

We are at a crucial moment in history, a crossroads in which we as a society must make decisions that will shape the next millennium. At this vital moment, I would like to speak to you about questions of the sacred. Native Peoples have asserted the need to honor their ancient sacred traditions as integrally woven into the fabric of their cultural survival and land rights.

But most progressive movements have abandoned the terrain of the sacred to Fundamentalists. As a result, we are constantly having to define ourselves against a very narrow view of the spirit.

For centuries, if not millennia, patriarchal religions have held that what is sacred is outside the world, removed from the body, from nature, from material being. The desacralized earth and her human children are thus fair game for exploitation. Although even within the most hierarchical religions there have always been earth-centered currents, the mainstream has defined the realm of the spirit as separate and severed from the earth.

But there is another view of the sacred, one held by indigenous peoples of every continent on earth, one that is probably the earliest human understanding of spirit. In this view, the earth is alive, not an object but a being, in whose life we each participate. The sacred is embodied, in the web of interconnections that sustain life, in air, fire, water, and earth, in animals and plants and humans, in the cycles of birth, growth, death, and rebirth that move through both nature and culture.

I speak to you out of one particular earth-based tradition, the old religion of the Goddess of Europe and the Middle East, called Wicca or Witchcraft. The period of the Witch persecutions of the sixteenth and seventeenth centuries is one of the great undigested traumas of Western culture. They

---

Reprinted, with permission, from *Bisexual Politics: Theories, Queries and Visions*, Naomi Tucker, ed., Haworth Press, 1995.

involved the torture and judicial murder of hundreds of thousands to millions of women and men over a period of 400 years. Eighty percent of the victims were women. Many of the men who were killed were targeted because they were gay.

The burnings can be seen as a war on women, but they were also very much a war on all the remaining cultural and healing traditions that stemmed from the ancient understanding of the earth as living being. And they were a war on sexuality. Most of the charges against Witches were of sexual misconduct and perversion—in the Churches' terms. The infamous Witchhunter's manual the *Malleus Maleficarum* states that "all witchcraft comes from carnal lust, which is in women insatiable." The fear and horror that are still associated with that time have left us with a deep fear of any sexuality that steps outside the narrow bounds defined by the authorities. The burning left us with a fear of women's power, and a half-conscious sense that any woman who takes charge of her own sexuality is dangerous and possibly demonic.

The Burning Times were also the time of the African slave trade and the conquest of this continent with the enslavement and destruction of its native peoples. They too were defined as dangerous and demonic, in need of control and Christianizing even if it killed them. Everywhere the consciousness of the earth as a living being was attacked and nearly but never completely destroyed. Now, 500 years later, when the very life-support systems that sustain all earth's creatures are threatened, we need that consciousness more than ever.

To say that this earth is sacred is to take a very radical position, for what is sacred cannot be defiled or exploited. What is sacred has a value inherent in itself, that cannot be measured by any other standard or weighted by a profit-and-loss accounting system. If we hold the forest sacred, we cannot clear-cut the last stands of old growth, no matter how many short-term jobs that might provide. If we honor the diversity of living things, we must be willing to preserve other species. If the air is sacred to us, we can't sit by and run our air conditioning as the ozone is destroyed. What is sacred is what we are willing to sacrifice for.

This vision of the earth is also integrally connected to our struggles as lesbian, gay, and bisexual people. For if we experience the earth as living being, then in all honesty I think we have to admit that she's an erotic being. How else do we explain fireflies, mangos, the unfurling of ferns? We are part of an erotic being in an erotic universe, whose deepest purposes seem to be served by getting various creatures to rub against each other in a wide variety of ways. Erotic energy holds the universe together. What is gravity but the desire of one body for another?

When we hold the erotic as sacred, we say that our capacity for pleasure has a value in and of itself, that in fact it is one of the ways in which we connect with the deepest purposes of the universe.

I believe that is a position we as bisexuals need to take. For our struggle is not only about affirming our own right to pleasure, but about affirming pleasure, variety, diversity, fluidity, as sacred values worth struggling for.

In a world in which attempts to change our orientation by coercion and force abound, lesbians and gays have necessarily defended the position that homosexuality is inborn and unchangeable. While that is true for a certain percentage of gay people, just as it's probably true for a similar percentage of heterosexual people, those of us who are bisexual, and honest, have to admit that our sexual orientation sometimes seems to change with the phases of the moon, or the level of pollen in the air, or just with propinquity to whoever happens to be around. I honor the lesbian and gay activists who have made their sexual orientation a cornerstone of their identities, and respect the political need for doing so and the strength that comes from that position. But if I'm honest about my own sexual identity, it has something to do with a deep reluctance to be pinned down.

How do we take a firm stand in the shifting sands of our own sexual fluidity? How do we counter the vicious hatred that gets aroused by saying, "I'm gay not because I have to be but because I choose to be, at least today I do, and I have a right to make that choice?" How do we hold solidarity with our lesbian and gay sisters and brothers who do not have the option to pass as straight?

When we say that pleasure is sacred we take a firm stand on ancient sacred ground. When we fight for the right to determine our own erotic choices, we fight for the right of our own lesbian sisters and gay brothers to be who they are. We directly confront our cultural fear and mistrust of pleasure, saying that we do not lack morality, we uphold a different morality: one which says that each human is the keeper of her or his own body, that inherent in our body's capacity for pleasure is our moral authority to determine just what sort of pleasure we want to take. That morality supports our stance as women when we say that by virtue of our wombs we and only we can be the keepers of our bodies' reproductive powers. It supports the struggles of those of us with disabilities to be decision makers about our particular needs and capacities and to participate fully in our culture.

To affirm pleasure is to affirm life in its deepest purposes, to value the intimate connections we make, the moments of ecstasy we experience. When we claim our sacred right to pleasure we are honoring life in its variety, diversity, its endless arrangements and rearrangements. We are acknowledging our participation in the deepest erotic purposes of the universe.

To assert this right is to assert the right of the old-growth forest to remain a forest, not a lumberyard, the right of the sacred mountain to be inviolate, the right of the stream to flow clean and undammed, the right of every human infant to be held in loving arms and nourished by loving breasts.

We must not abandon morality to the Fundamentalists. Instead, we as bisexuals can, out of our own unique experiences, define a new morality based on the honoring of our inner, body-rooted authority, and the integrity of the earth body of which we are each a part. Our issues are linked with all struggles of self-determination being waged by people around the world. We need to envision a new world, one with room in it for whales and howler monkeys and drag queens and grizzly bears and ancient sacred tribal lands and leather dykes and plentiful rain and happily married couples with 2.5 children and people who just can't make up their mind and black-white-red-brown-tan-golden-sepia-chocolate-ivory-ebony and (who knows?) maybe striped and spotted ones of us. And then we need to do the work that will make this vision a reality.

For the last 5 years I've been working on a book that attempts to imagine such a world. It's a novel set in the 21st century, called *The Fifth Sacred Thing* (Starhawk, 1993). I'd like to close by reading just a bit of the manifesto that opens the book, the Declaration of the Four Sacred Things that sets forth the values of that hopeful world:

Declaration of the Four Sacred Things

The earth is a living, conscious being. In company with cultures of many different times and places, we name these things as sacred: air, fire, water and earth. Whether we see them as the breath, energy, blood, and body of the Mother or as the blessed gifts of a Creator, or as symbols of the interconnected systems that sustain life, we know that nothing can live without them.

To call these things sacred is to say that they have a value beyond their usefulness for human ends, that they themselves become the standards by which our acts, our economics, our laws, and our purpose must be judged. No one has the right to appropriate them or profit from them at the expense of others. Any government that fails to protect them forfeits its legitimacy.

All people, all living things, are part of the earth life and so are sacred. No one of us stands higher or lower than any other: Only justice can assure balance: only ecological balance can sustain freedom. Only in freedom can that fifth sacred thing we call spirit flourish in its full diversity.

To honor the sacred is to create conditions in which nourishment, sustenance, habitat, knowledge, freedom, and beauty can thrive. To honor the sacred is to make love possible.

To this we dedicate our curiousity, our will, our courage, our silences, and our voices. To this we dedicate our lives.

"All Cool Women Should be Bisexual": Female Bisexual Identity in an American NeoPagan Community

SUSAN HARPER

Department of Anthropology, Southern Methodist University, Dallas, Texas, USA

This article examines female bisexuality in the Texas NeoPagan community. Based on interviews and participant observation, this article documents and analyzes the various ways in which female bisexuality is performed within a NeoPagan context. The connection between NeoPagan thealogy and bisexuality is addressed. The methods by which female NeoPagan practitioners construct a bisexual identity, the power relations that are negotiated around that identity and the discourse by which practitioners make female bisexuality normative and even idealized within the NeoPagan community are deconstructed and analyzed.

The American NeoPagan movement has long been associated with alternative, radical or so-called deviant forms of sexuality. Strongly influenced by the counterculture of the 1960s, with its ideas of free expression of sexuality, and in the feminist movement and the attendant politicization of lesbian-feminist politics, NeoPaganism has consistently represented a religious movement where those who identify with sexual identities and practices that fall outside the American middle stream have found a safe and welcoming home. Ranging from homosexuality, to bisexuality, to transgendered sexuality, to polyamory, sadism and masochism (S&M), and bondage and beyond, a wide variety of sexual proclivities and practices can be found within the NeoPagan social landscape.[1]

This article examines the presence of one such form of sexuality, female bisexuality, in the Texas NeoPagan community. The methods by which female NeoPagan practitioners construct a bisexual identity, the power relations that are negotiated around that identity, and the discourse by which practitioners make female bisexuality normative and even idealized within the NeoPagan community, are deconstructed and analyzed.

My research and analysis suggests that there is a dance between sexual freedom and sexual objectification at work when it comes to female bisexuality within the NeoPagan community. Through the rhetoric of spirituality and feminism, women are encouraged to explore their sexuality and identify as bisexual. Bisexuality is constructed as the most spiritual, the most natural, choice for women. At the same time that they are encouraged to explore their "true selves" by exploring their bisexuality, however, women are also put in the role of sexual object, or their sexuality is circumscribed by male partners who orchestrate sexual encounters—becoming, as one woman put it, "wank material" for a man fulfilling his fantasy of being with two women at the same time. As such, for NeoPagan women, identifying as bisexual can be liberating and confining. For heterosexual-identified NeoPagan women, the image of the "hot bi Pagan babe" can also be problematic, creating a situation where they may feel it necessary to either skirt the issue of their own heterosexuality or be made to feel guilty, less spiritual or less feminine because they identify as heterosexual.

BACKGROUND AND METHOD

This article is based on research conducted for my larger dissertation project, *Negotiating Gender Identity and Social Identity in an American NeoPagan Community*. Although the scope of the dissertation was much larger than bisexual identity, in the early stages of my fieldwork some distinct trends relating to this issue emerged. I chose to further research these trends as phenomena in and of themselves, and as they related to my larger research questions about the interconnections of gender identity, sexuality and spirituality.

A variety of qualitative and quantitative methods were employed in collecting data for this article. A survey, which was distributed at several NeoPagan gatherings across Texas, provided demographic data. I also conducted participant observation at a number of NeoPagan gatherings, women's Goddess retreats, and NeoPagan community functions. These gatherings and events provided ample opportunity for informal, unstructured interviews as well. The NeoPagan gatherings I attended ranged in size from a few dozen to several hundred participants. Such gatherings feature a mix of rituals, workshops on a wide variety of spiritual and secular topics, community-building exercises and social activities such as drumming, dancing and live music. For many NeoPagans, these gatherings are some of the only contact they have throughout the year with their co-religionists. Women's Goddess retreats are often similar in content—with rituals, workshops and community social activities—but are limited to women and tend to focus on the feminine aspects of the Divine and issues important to women. For the most part, gatherings and retreats are held outdoors and involve camping for a few days. The community functions I attended for this research included open drumming circles, Pagans Night Out socials, services at the local earth-based Unitarian Church and workshops and classes.

In addition to participant observation and informal interviews conducted as part of it, I also conducted 25 structured interviews, via e-mail, with self-identified bisexual NeoPagan women. Interview respondents were located through several Texas-based NeoPagan discussion lists facilitated through Yahoogroups (http://www.yahoogroups.com).

For the survey and the structured electronic interviews, all respondents were self-selected. Because there is no formal membership registry for NeoPagans, it was not possible to use a systematic random sample for this research. However, it is established in the literature that when working with "hidden or difficult-to-find" populations and examining "phenomenological" issues or expressive behavior, random sampling is not necessary (Bernard, 1994). Therefore, I chose to openly solicit for survey participants; I required only that participants be at least 18 years of age and residents of the state of Texas, and that they self-identify as some sort of Pagan or NeoPagan. When soliciting for respondents to the structured electronic interviews, I further stipulated that respondents must be female and self-identify as bisexual.

My sample reflected the demographic trends I found in the larger Texas NeoPagan community. They were overwhelmingly White. Most had completed at least some college, and a handful had postgraduate degrees. Although a range of ages was represented, most respondents were between ages 18 and 35. Despite relatively high levels of education, most indicated their household income was below $30,000. As Orion (1995) noted, this may have to do with the fact that many NeoPagans enter the so-called helping professions—teaching, health care, childcare, to name a few—which are not highly financially rewarded. An overall economic recession during my fieldwork period also affected the financial data; many of my respondents worked in the computer and information technology field, which was hit particularly hard and resulted in widespread layoffs and un- and underemployment. Finally, the relatively young age of most respondents may indicate that they are embarking on careers or choosing professions and thus have not actualized their earning potential as yet. And of course, the fact that women on the whole earn less than do men in many industries in American culture cannot be ignored in this all-female sample.

NEOPAGANISM DEFINED

NeoPaganism is defined as "an informal network of people devoted to Wicca, the Craft, Goddess worship, and other ritual practices inspired by the religions of pagan Europe and the Mediterranean" (Scupin, 2000, p. 330). However, this definition must be hedged round, even from the beginning, with caution and clarification. It only begins to capture the great diversity that exists within the American NeoPagan movement. The label has been applied to a wide range of religions (called "traditions") ranging from modern movements such as Wicca and feminist spirituality to "reconstructionist" movements,[2] to Western occult traditions such as the Golden Dawn (Adler, 1979/1986, 2006). Although these religions have their own, unique practices and theologies, they can be said to share some common symbols and ideals. Among these are a recognition of a Feminine Divine ("the Goddess," sometimes worshipped in conjunction with a male deity, "the God"); belief that humans and nature are interconnected and interdependent; belief that the Divine is inherent in all things, rather than abstract and distant; veneration of the seasonal changes of the earth, around which most ritual calendars are based; and a belief in magic (Adler, 1979/1986, 2006; Luhrmann, 1989; Orion, 1995). Additionally, most NeoPagan traditions assert that they are revivals of pre-Christian religions, particularly those of the Celtic and Teutonic worlds, though they are in fact modern religions that have emerged since World War II (Adler, 1979/1986, 2006; Luhrmann, 1989; Orion, 1995).[3] In addition to drawing on traditions of the ancient European and Mediterranean world, some NeoPagan traditions or groups incorporate Native American, Native Central American, African and Afro-Caribbean practices, as well as modern shamanic exercises, into their rituals.[4]

By far, the most common religious identification in my sample was "Eclectic Pagan," which is an umbrella term for a personalized, often solitary form of NeoPaganism. Eclectics typically employ a structure similar to Wicca in their practice—celebrating the eight Wiccan Sabbats,[5] recognizing a masculine and feminine form of divinity, and practicing ceremonial and folk magick—and use a diversity of mythologies, symbolic systems and other New Age or occult practices such as Tarot card reading, Reiki healing, yoga, channeling, working with crystals and psychic phenomena. Because eclectic Paganism tends to be highly individualized—a common community gloss for *eclectic* is "whatever works" or "whatever feels right"—practitioners typically practice solitary or with a small group of family or friends. Unlike traditional, initiatory, coven-based Wicca (or British Traditional Wicca),[6] eclectic Paganism has no set liturgy or dogma but instead relies on individual experience, exploration and investigation. The personalized nature of eclectic Paganism may help explain the presence of sexual diversity within the community.

It is important to note that I conducted this research, and present these findings, not only as an anthropologist but also as a lesbian-identified bisexual feminist Witch. I found that my own self-identification as NeoPagan, and as a bisexual female, helped rather than hindered my research efforts; respondents seemed far less afraid of being judged for their lifestyle and practices, and as such were more open to participating in the research and doing so openly and honestly. Furthermore, I have been a participant in the Texas NeoPagan community for more than 10 years. My long tenure in the community helped me to be accepted "as a witch" (Orion, 1995), which other researchers have found to be a significant hurdle in researching NeoPagans (Luhrmann, 1989; Magliocco, 2004; Scarboro, Campbell, & Stave, 1994).

BISEXUALITY DEFINED

As Garber (2000) noted, the term *bisexuality* has long been a contested one. The question of what makes one bisexual (or, more problematically a bisexual) has been addressed by sexologists, psychologists, psychoanalysts and anthropologists (Garber). Is bisexuality an identity or a behavior—or both? Is it a middle ground between two poles—gay and straight—or does it instead define a large area along a spectrum of sexuality? Can someone who has never had a sexual encounter with a member of his or her own sex be considered bisexual? Or is bisexuality merely a "phase" on the way to becoming wholly homosexual or wholly heterosexual? (Garber, 2000).

Such questions are largely beyond the scope of this article. For the purposes of the present discussion, I adopted James's (1996) definition of *bisexuality* as "the sexual or intensely emotional, although not necessarily concurrent or equal, attraction of an individual to members of more than one gender" (p. 217). I do not qualify my operational definition with behavior, because in my research I found that it was possible for a person to be attracted to someone (or a class of people) but unable to act on that attraction for reasons of opportunity, prior commitment or shyness, among others.

It is, however, important to qualify the use of *bisexual* in this article by stressing that my sample consists of self-identified bisexuals. To participate in this research, women merely needed to identify themselves as bisexual—it was not necessary that they meet any minimum requirement such as being a "Kinsey 3"[7] or having had a certain number of same-sex sexual encounters to be considered a "real bisexual." In the structured electronic interviews, I did probe further to find out how many of my cultural consultants had indeed had same-sex erotic encounters and found great variation in the frequency and type of behavior, as is discussed in more detail below.

NEOPAGANISM AND SEXUAL DIVERSITY

Adler (2006) asserted that the majority of American NeoPagans self-identify as hetero- or bisexual. Other researchers have similarly found high numbers of nonheterosexuality within the NeoPagan community. In her 1995 ethnography of NeoPagans in the northeastern United States, Loretta Orion posited that the high number of non-heterosexual-indentified NeoPagan practitioners was indicative of

> a greater willingness to discuss unconventional sexual preferences in the uncritical environment of the gatherings, or, even more likely, that individuals having an unusual sexual preference are drawn to this uncritical religion. (p. 62)

Magliocco (2004) found results similar to Orion's, and further stated,

> Many lesbians, gay men, and bisexuals are drawn to Neo-Paganism [sic] because of its accepting attitude toward all sexual orientations ... Also, many Pagans are open to sexual experimentation to the same extent that they are interested in experimenting with new forms of spirituality. They may have sexual partners of both genders over the course of a lifetime, and be more willing to identify as other than heterosexual. (p. 62)

Indeed, the American NeoPagan community is home to tremendous diversity in sexual orientation and sexual practice: In addition to a large number of gay, lesbian, and bisexual-identified people, there is open discussion of transgender and intersex sexuality. Gatherings where I conducted fieldwork featured workshops on transgendered identity and behavior, S&M, bondage practices and sacred sexuality. One gathering even provided a ritual space where participants could receive information about safer sexual practices and engage in alternative/radical sexual practices in sacred space. Even before embarking on my fieldwork, I found the (seemingly) high prevalence of female bisexuality in the Texas NeoPagan community striking. It seemed, as one interview respondent suggested, "Pagan women in Texas are expected to be lesbian or bisexual." The preliminary analysis of my survey data, along with my informal interviews, confirmed a high percentage of female self-identified bisexuals: Out of a sample of roughly 100 respondents, nearly 60% of women identified themselves as bisexual.[8]

It might be expected that a community with well-documented openness to sexual diversity might contain a higher percentage of bisexuals than does the general population. However, this high reporting of female bisexuality was in marked contrast to the nearly nonexistent reporting of male bisexuality. Only two of my male respondents reported themselves as bisexual.[9] In contrast, men seemed far more likely to self-identify as gay or straight; women were more reluctant to identify as lesbian, choosing instead the label *bisexual* or *heterosexual*.[10]

Additionally, the incidence of bisexuality in my sample appears to be higher than that found by other researchers. Orion (1995) reported that 28% of her sample reported as bisexual, whereas Pike (2001) found only 17% of her sample considered themselves bisexual. Unfortunately, neither Orion nor Pike break their demographics of sexual orientation down by gender, which makes it more difficult to draw comparisons between their populations and the one in question in this article.

In seeking to understand the prevalence, and apparent wide acceptance, of female bisexuality within my research sample, I noticed that bisexual and nonbisexual community members engage in discourse that makes female bisexuality a normative, and in some ways ideally Pagan form of sexuality. This discourse draws on four major themes: NeoPaganism's historical links with feminist, and particularly lesbian feminist, politics; the idea that bisexuality represents a rejection of binary or bipolar thinking about gender and sexuality; the interrelationship between NeoPagan images of divinity and sexuality; and the idea (or ideal?) of bisexuality as a "more natural" form of sexuality.

NEOPAGANISM AND FEMINISM

Through the central symbol of the Goddess, NeoPaganism as a whole is very woman positive, and to some degree woman centered (Christ, 1987; Magliocco, 2004). This focus on the Feminine Divine, along with the intertwining of NeoPaganism with feminist politics, is often cited as a factor that brings women to this religious movement (Adler, 1979/1986, 2006; Christ, 1987; Eller, 1993; Orion, 1995). Growing largely out of the countercultural and feminist movements of the late 1960s and early 1970s, American NeoPaganism has long had a feminist flavor.[11] Early NeoPagan writers and activists such as Z. Budapest (1989) declared NeoPaganism and Witchcraft to be "women's religion,"[12] viewing it as the necessary spiritual component to the feminist movement's political aims. Linking NeoPaganism and Witchcraft to largely mythical, primordial matriarchal, Goddess-centered, cultures where women had purportedly enjoyed high status, feminist Witches encouraged women to reclaim this power as their feminine birthright. Furthermore, these activists contended that earth-centered spirituality was a feminist concern because, as the earth was steadily devalued, so too did women's status decline; the state of the earth reflected the state of women, and vice versa. Although recent critiques (Davis, 1998; Eller, 2001) have called into question the historical validity of such claims, they nonetheless play a powerful and important role in the sacred history of Feminist Witchcraft and many NeoPagan groups.

The relationship between political feminism, particularly second-wave feminism, and Feminist Witchcraft, is not unproblematic. Many political feminists felt that pursuit of spiritual goals, even woman-centered thealogies[13] that advocated female power, was merely a distraction from the larger political and social goals of feminism. It was not until the 1980s that there was any widespread acceptance of Feminist Witchcraft (and Feminist Spirituality more broadly) within the larger political feminist movement. Although third-wave feminists are more willing to accept and incorporate spirituality (Baumgardner & Richards, 2000), there is still some tension in the relationship between spiritual feminism and political feminism.

Witchcraft has long been associated with female power—or, perhaps more accurately, the fear of female power—and particularly female sexual power (Eller, 1993; Starhawk, 1979). Feminist Witchcraft furthered this link by encouraging women to use the tools of Witchcraft for political and personal liberation. The 1967 WITCH Manifesto (Women's International Terrorist Conspiracy from Hell) stated:

> WITCH is an all-women Everything. It's theater, revolution, magic, terror, joy, garlic flowers, spells. It's an awareness that witches and gypsies were the original guerillas and resistance fighters against oppression-particularly the oppression of women-down through the ages. Witches have always been women who dared to be: groovy, courageous, aggressive, intelligent, nonconformist, explorative, curious, independent, sexually liberated, revolutionary. Witches were the first Friendly Heads and Dealers, the first birth-control practitioners and abortionists, the first alchemists. They bowed to no man, being the living remnants of the oldest culture of all—one in which men and women were equal sharers in a truly cooperative society, before the death-dealing sexual, economic, and spiritual repression of the Imperialist Phallic Society took over and began to destroy nature and human society.
>
> Witch lives and laughs in every woman. She is the free part of each of us, beneath the shy smiles, the acquiescence to absurd male domination, the make-up or flesh-suffocating clothing our sick society demands. There is no "joining" WITCH. If you are a woman and dare to look within yourself, you are a Witch. You make your own rules. You are both free and beautiful. You can be invisible or evident in how you choose to make your witch-self known.
>
> Whatever is repressive, solely male-oriented, greedy, puritanical, authoritarian-those are your targets. Your weapons surround you: theater, satire, explosions, magic, herbs, music, costumes, candles, bells, Vodou dolls, incense ... Your power comes from your own self as a woman, and it is activated by working together with your sisters. (Morgan, 1982, pp. 428–429)

It is important to note that WITCH was not, and never identified as, a NeoPagan group, or in fact a spiritual group of any kind. It was a street theater and performance group that used the cultural images of witches and dangerous female power (among many others) as a platform for political action. Eller (1993) noted that some groups have incorporated the manifesto into their liturgies, or at the very least into their traditions as a kind of inspirational text. I myself encountered groups who included the manifesto among their key spiritual documents, alongside other inspirational, woman-centered, or woman-positive poems, stories and writings. Although the WITCH Manifesto is not a NeoPagan text, it does invoke the images of witchcraft as a fundamental (and dangerous) power associated with women by virtue of being women, which echoes many of the writings key to the Feminist Spirituality/Feminist Witchcraft movement (Budapest, 1989; Mountainwater, 1991; Stein, 1990, 1991)

The use of the term *Feminist* or *feminist* in relation to NeoPaganism is always tricky. Some assert that all NeoPagan traditions are feminist by virtue of having a Goddess, whereas others rightly point out the fundamentally patriarchal nature of many NeoPagan traditions. Other writers make the distinction that *Feminist Witchcraft* or *Feminist Spirituality* should be applied only to all-female groups that work exclusively with a Feminine Divine. This semantic debate is largely beyond the scope of this article. However, going forward, I use the term *Feminist* (capital *F*) to indicate groups that are composed only of women, venerate only the Goddess, and incorporate feminist themes and concerns into their spiritual practice. I have tended to use the term *Feminist Witchcraft* to indicate the NeoPagan nature of these groups, as there are groups outside of NeoPaganism that can properly be called *Feminist Spirituality*. I have adopted this usage (*Feminist*) because there are many NeoPagan traditions, such as Reclaiming and Covenant of the Goddess, which can properly be called *feminist* because they espouse feminist ideals of equality and consensus, and which incorporate political action into their thealogy and practices. Such *feminist* (lowercase *f*) groups are distinguished from *Feminist* groups because they initiate men and women and tend to work with a multigendered Divine rather than just the Goddess. Interestingly both types of groups—Feminist and feminist—can be met with suspicion and even hostility within the larger NeoPagan community due to the political components and viewpoints.

Many, though far from all, Feminist Witchcraft groups were historically composed of lesbians and "nonpracticing heterosexual" women.[14] Much like the "political lesbian" of the 1970s, who ceased sexual activity with men as a demonstration of solidarity with women (Rust, 1995), women in these groups chose either to identify and live as lesbians, or to at the very least stop having intimate relationships with men, because they felt that it brought "male" energy into "women's religion" (Budapest, 1989). Indeed, some Feminist Witchcraft groups, in addition to refusing to initiate men, refused to initiate women who were practicing heterosexuals, though this was far from universal (Adler, 1979/1986, 2006). The place of bisexual women in such groups was much like the place of bisexual women in the larger feminist movement at the time—they were viewed with some degree of suspicion, if not outright hostility, because of their relationships (or potential to have relationships) with men (Adler, 1979/1986, 2006; Garber, 2000; Rust, 1993).

Adler (1979, 2006), Eller (1993), and Orion (1995) found that all-female NeoPagan or Witchcraft groups still thrive today, though they are less common than they might have been 20 years ago. In my own fieldwork, I found some all-female groups, though like Adler and Orion, I also found that lesbianism was not a requirement for initiation into such a group (Adler, 1979/1986, 2006). References to "the Dianics"—community shorthand for radical lesbian feminist Witches[15] —abounded; however, in the course of my research I met few community members who actually fit this description. More common were groups in which men and women practiced together, and in which there was a significant gay and lesbian population. Although some covens and ritual groups still exist in Texas that are composed entirely of lesbians, they are now the exception rather than the rule. Additionally, I found one ritual group composed entirely of bisexual and gay men, and a thriving community of Radical Faeries (Adler, 1979/1986, 2006) who, though not exclusively male or gay, do honor and celebrate gay male spirituality. I did not find any NeoPagan groups where nonheterosexuals are overtly excluded.

With the emergence of NeoPaganism into popular culture in the 1990s, the feminist flavor of the movement began to change. Instead of "women's religion," the focus became a more egalitarian, balanced, earth-centered religion with a polar image of Divinity—much more similar to the Wicca envisioned by BritTrad patriarch Gerald Gardner than the politically oriented, consciousness-raising, radical feminist Craft of the 1970s. Some previously exclusively female covens began initiating men; mixed-gendered groups and even male-only groups such as some Radical Faeries (Adler, 1979/1986, 2006) began to be more public and common.

Adler (2006) noted and in some ways lamented the decline in feminist political fervor in the NeoPagan movement she saw between her original research and her revisiting of her data (Adler, 1979/1986, 2006). She pointed to the overall decline in the number of all-women's groups, and the reduction of feminist political activism among NeoPagans more broadly. Although some argue that this means NeoPaganism has become less feminist, this is not necessarily universally true. Traditions which espouse feminist ideals, such as the Reclaiming Tradition, the Reformed Congregation of the Goddess, and the Covenant of the Goddess, have strong presences in the Texas NeoPagan community and in the American NeoPagan community more generally. These groups are explicitly feminist and are not exclusively female. Reclaiming, in particular, not only espouses feminist principles of equality and social justice, but also on many instances engages in political and social activism on behalf of humanitarian and ecological causes. Although Salmonsen (2002) questioned whether Reclaiming groups live out the feminist ideals they espouse, my experience has been that

Reclaiming groups represent the principle, though not sole, feminist voice in the NeoPagan community. In terms of gender and sexuality, Reclaiming espouses gender equality as a feminist value, rather than the exclusion of men. Although there may be less argument about NeoPaganism as "women's religion" today, and though (in keeping with a larger cultural trend) many practitioners may be reluctant to identify as feminists, most NeoPagans and NeoPagan groups do include among their core values such feminist principles as gender equality.[16]

However, if NeoPaganism lost some of its feminist flair, feminism did not necessarily lose its NeoPagan bent. Jennifer Baumgardner and Amy Richards (2000) noted that early on in their feminist explorations, they employed Wiccan circle castings as part of their meetings; third-wave feminists, in particular, have incorporated Goddess imagery, alternative healing methods, and NeoPagan forms of worship into their own political and spiritual lives. Although some of this may be attributed to young feminists' growing up with NeoPaganism "in the water" (to borrow Baumgardner and Richards' phrase), it is undeniable that for many feminists the idea of woman-centered politics and woman-centered religion is in some way intertwined. Indeed, some feminist Jewish and Christian groups have begun to incorporate feminine imagery and even earth-centered imagery, into their services (Christ & Plaskow, 1979/1992; Gross, 1979/1992).

In much the same way as claiming a female godhead has been construed as an overtly feminist act, so too can the act of claiming the identity as one who loves other women be seen as feminist. However, in contrast to the political lesbian of the 1970s, Baumgardner (2007) and Baumgardner and Richards (2000) contended that exploring sexual relationships with women and identifying as bisexual is becoming something of a rite of passage for young feminists; because both parties in a same-sex relationship "go through life experiencing the prejudices and perks of being female" (Baumgardner & Richards, 2000) such relationships may be more egalitarian than those between alternate-sex partners. Bisexual identity may also be seen as a feminist choice in that the discourse of "loving the person and not the gender," which was often invoked by my respondents in talking about their own bisexuality, echoes feminist rhetoric about gender inclusivity. The feminist aim of equality for the sexes, it would seem, extends even to one's choice of sexual and romantic partners. Baumgardner (2007) further argued that young women of the third wave bring "gay expectations"—of equality and mutual independence and respect—even to heterosexual relationships.

Explicitly feminist and woman-centered thealogies give women permission to express nonheterosexual forms of sexuality, in much the same way that the larger feminist political movement gave voice to women's political and social concerns. Ellen T. Brenner, a bisexual Unitarian Universalist minister, (2000) stated:

> Feminist thealogies [sic] gave me permission to seek wholeness, to tear down the boundary between body and mind/spirit instilled in me by society, and celebrate my embodied woman-self as the incarnation of God/dess herself. (p. 241)

REJECTING POLARITIES, EMBRACING DIVINITY

In contrast to exclusively Goddess-centered forms of NeoPaganism, many NeoPagan traditions recognize a masculine and a feminine godhead.[17] The polarity of the God and Goddess is at the heart of these traditions; it is the through the unity of the polarities that creation is believed to occur. Although the polarities are spiritually important, at the same time the goal of most practitioners is to integrate these polarities into themselves. Most NeoPagans speak of the unity of the whole, of the optimal balance between masculine and feminine. Bisexual female NeoPagans often conceptualize their sexuality as a way to shatter the either/or, male/female gender polarity at work in NeoPaganism and in larger American culture. Because they are capable of loving a person regardless of his or her gender, they contend, they can fully know masculine and feminine experience—or, perhaps more accurately, the full spectrum of gendered experience—and thus journey closer to the "wholeness" which is, explicitly and implicitly, the spiritual goal of many NeoPagan rituals and practices.

Pashta MaryMoon (2000) described the relationship between her bisexuality and her Wiccan spirituality thus: "[N]owhere have I found a spiritual home base that honors the both/and, the polarity of the Divine and Its firstborn child, as I have in Wicca" (p. 89).

The honoring of the polarities inherent in each person, the "bi parts" or the "masculine parts" and the "feminine parts" (Ault, 1996b), that is found in NeoPagan theaology is uniquely suited to bisexual identity, according to some practitioners. Fae,[18] a 33-year-old Eclectic Pagan, stated, "I think [my bisexuality] allows me to experience both of my male and female aspects better."

Ault (1996b) analyzed the way in which bisexual women consider their bisexual identity as a method of shattering the binary assumptions that underlie American notions of sex and gender. By refusing to be "either" homosexual "or" heterosexual—"smack in the middle of 'lesbian' and 'straight,'" to quote one of Ault's informants—bisexual women see themselves as shattering the dualistic paradigm of gender and sexuality that most Americans take for granted. As Garber (2000) has contended, bisexuality can be a form of resistance by questioning the notion of sexual duality as normal. Although, much as Ault also discovered, I found that in the process of "shattering" gendered dualities, my bisexual informants also reified that same polarity—"male side" and "female side," "bi side," "God and Goddess"—it was evident in the electronic interviews that women did see bisexuality as a way of resisting an either/or vision of sexuality. Laura, 39, said, "Being bisexual to me is like being neither matriarchal or patriarchal, but a balance of both. I feel much more comfortable in my witch skin now than I did before I discovered this side of myself."

In discussing the duality-shattering nature of bisexuality, however, NeoPagans often construct other dualities that bisexuality appears to reify. Most common is the construction of a duality between NeoPaganism and "more mainstream religions" (by which most community members appear to mean Christianity). NeoPaganism is constructed as "more accepting" of sexual diversity, as "not discriminating against anyone based on their sexual orientation," and as more tolerant toward people of nonheterosexual orientation. Christianity, by contrast, is cast as sexist, repressive of sexual expression and generally hostile to nonheterosexuals. Christians "just don't understand or accept" nonheterosexuals, according to one woman, but "Pagans do without question. Pagans are more open to different people, sexualities and beliefs." Trish, 42, stated that NeoPaganism "has broadened my mind and opened me to all forms of love and sexuality," which she contrasts with her Christian upbringing. Similarly, 23-year-old Maria (who was raised Catholic) said, "I am not ashamed of my own sexuality. It has shaped me in a lot of ways, and I enjoy my uniqueness. I feel free knowing that my spirituality embraces that belief."

The construction of a NeoPaganism universally accepting of sexual and gender diversity—and Christianity as universally hostile to the same—is a bit simplistic. Although overt homophobia or gender discrimination runs counter to expressed NeoPagan values, and though I did not see expressions of such sentiment widely professed, neither is the NeoPagan community as free from bias as the above comments from practitioners might make it seem. Like all religious practitioners, NeoPagans operate within a larger cultural context, and the American cultural context is far from free of homophobia or gender bias. As operators within the American cultural context, NeoPagans at times may display evidence of internalized homophobic attitudes, and it can be argued that the historical focus of many NeoPagan rites and rituals on a heterosexual model of God and Goddess is in and of itself homophobic or at least serves to make sexual and gender diversity invisible (Adler, 2006). Individual groups may be more-or-less welcoming of sexual and gender diversity as well. On the other hand, there are numerous Christian groups that are open and affirming of sexual and gender diversity, far from the monolithic homophobia my interviewees might have indicated was present within the Christian context (Thumma & Gray, 2004).

Garber (2000) noted, that bisexuality "messes up the neat double columns of straight and gay." A duality between bisexuality and monosexuality[19] also emerged in the interviews with bisexual-identified women in the community. The theme of balance was invoked by women who declared their sexuality "more balanced" than monosexuality; others declared bisexuality "freeing" in the sense that it allowed them to explore "all kinds of love for all kinds of people." An image of monosexuality as a restrictive form of sexual expression that "limited [one] to loving only half of the human race," or denies one the chance to know the full breadth and depth of human emotional and sexual expression, emerged in the informal and electronic interviews. Moira, 30, said her bisexuality has allowed to her recognize and honor "the many-ness at the root of all things," and that an important aspect of this recognition has been "being able to love and lust for many different people, of different ages, genders, ethnicities, and other 'divisions'." Some women even stated that monosexuality has negative spiritual repercussions for NeoPagans, holding that bisexuality affords a more complete experience of the Divine, which is typically envisioned as male and female. Moira said, "Similarly, loving many people, including women, allows me to understand the different deities, including the goddesses, in a more intimate way. Every person I love becomes a different facet of the God and Goddess, for me."

"ALL ACTS OF LOVE AND PLEASURE": NEOPAGANISM AND SEXUAL EXPRESSION

NeoPaganism supposes an immanent Divine, and, as such, practitioners' experiences, rather than scripture, are considered the ultimate authority. Bodily experiences and sensuality are seen as manifestations of the immanent Divine, and, as such, are things to be celebrated as sacraments rather than shied away from or hidden. The construction of NeoPaganism as a religion that is embracing of sexual expression in all its myriad forms—often contrasted to the stricter sexual mores of mainstream religions such as Christianity—is one way in which practitioners construct female bisexuality as a form of sexuality that is uniquely suited to NeoPagan religiosity. Invoking NeoPaganism's vision of a dualistic deity composed of male and female aspects, and NeoPaganism's acceptance of diversity, many practitioners contend that is bisexuality is not only a way of exploding dualities or integrating male and female aspects of the self, but also is a natural progression for NeoPagans to embrace bisexuality based on their theological principles: that, in the words of MaryMoon (2000), "I am the Goddess and the God, therefore I am bi."

Sex as a way to "pray with your body," and as a result fundamentally pleasing to the Divine as NeoPaganism envisions it, was a theme in the informal and electronic interviews conducted as part of this research. To "love all the people you love freely" (Adler, 1979/1986) is one of the fundamental NeoPagan values cited by practitioners in the course of my research. The primacy given to individual choice, and the free expression of that choice, is one of the most common reasons community members give for their conversion to NeoPaganism from more conventional forms of religion.[20]

The Charge of the Goddess, credited to Doreen Valiente (1989), is possibly one of the best known, most quoted (and misquoted) pieces of NeoPagan literature. Best known for the line "All acts of love and pleasure are my rituals," the Charge is seen by many practitioners to be the encapsulation of the NeoPagan idea of sacred sexuality. The Charge was quoted by many of my interview respondents as they discussed the relationship of their bisexuality and their spirituality. Mar, 42, explicitly invoked one of the many versions of the Charge in her response:

> I believe that sex is an expression of the divine—a creative and conscious way to pray with your body and share loving energy with another person. I was strongly drawn to paganism [sic] in part because sexuality was accepted and honored. As it says in the Charge of the Goddess, ". . . make music and love, for all acts of pleasure are ritual unto me."

Thalia, 23, similarly sees sex and sensuality as pleasing to the Divine, stating"[O]ne of my personal gods is Aphrodite and my belief is that loving consentual [sic] sex of all types honors her . . .. [S]ex, when done consentually [sic], is pleasing to the harmony of the universe and not just my gods."

Sex as a "gateway to the Divine" is also a common theme in practitioners' discussion of the interrelationship between sexuality and NeoPagan spirituality. Arachne, 48, said,

> Sex is one of the Gateways—very easy (at least in theory, but it takes practice) to raise power and focus it, more practice to actually direct and use that power with precise Will—language is slippery after all. I am a spiritual being having a physical experience, and sexuality represents and accesses many of the "peak experiences" available in this form.

The synthesis of NeoPagan values of inclusiveness, along with the NeoPagan vision of deity as bi- or multigendered and the idea that sex can be one way to commune with the Divine in all its forms, results in a conclusion for many practitioners that NeoPagans are particularly well suited to bisexuality. This conclusion appears bolstered by the fact that the vast majority of women I interviewed for this research came to identify as bisexual only after they came to identify as NeoPagan. For some, this may be a function of coming to NeoPaganism, with its openness to sexual variety, and discovering that their feelings had a name or a place—several respondents said they had had same-sex attractions since childhood or adolescence, but only after coming to NeoPaganism did they "know there was a name for" those desires—rather than uncovering a double conversion whereby practitioners convert to bisexuality as they convert to NeoPaganism.

However, for other women I interviewed, this type of double conversion appears to be exactly what occurred. After spending some time in the NeoPagan community, they adopted a bisexual identity. Some reported that NeoPaganism gave them a context for same-sex feelings that had been present in their lives before. Others found the adventurous sexual culture of NeoPaganism appealing, and though they may not have entertained same-sex desires before, found themselves (in the words of Aurora, 32) "suddenly liking girls as much as [they] liked boys." And for still others, a combination of the idealization of female bisexuality in the NeoPagan community and pressure from fellow practitioners and the male partners in their lives seems to have led them to identify as bisexual.

HOT BI PAGAN BABES: FEMALE BISEXUALITY AS THE IDEAL

Upon learning of my own bisexual identity, one of my informants responded with, "So glad to hear you're bi—I think all cool women should be." This idea—that "all cool women should be bi"—was pervasive in the interviews I conducted in the course of this research, and in the settings where I conducted participant observation. There is a coexistence of what Moira called the "fetishization of the hot bi Pagan babe," a male-dominated encouragement of same-sex performances between women in public spaces such as festival fires, and a construction of monosexuality as deviant and bisexuality as normative. The image of the hot bi Pagan babe, in fact, is so ubiquitous that it has even made it into a song by well-known NeoPagan band Gaia Consort, who use it as a refrain in their song "The Perils of Poly."

The construction of female bisexuality—but notably, not male bisexuality—as the ideal within the NeoPagan community is conducted in ways that are overt and covert. Bisexuality is characterized as a natural progression, couched in secular humanist terms of the genderless soul of all humans. Many times throughout the research process, women employed various forms of the "I fall in love with/am attracted to the person, not the package" rhetoric which has also been noted by other researchers of bisexuality (Garber, 2000). Storm, 30, stated,

> I believe that the human soul is sexless or perhaps contains all sexes. Therefore our bodies are just what we ride around in. So often, it's more than just looks that attract me to any person . . . it's behavior, personality and so on. So it just makes sense that I would find both men and women sexually attractive.

Nova, 25, similarly said, "I fall in love with the spirit and soul not with the carrying case." MaryMoon (2000) called bisexuality the extension of the love of the Goddess and God to "Their humyn [sic] representatives, femael [sic] and mael [sic]."

While expressing openness to sexual encounters with women, interview respondents were split on the question of whether they would consider having an exclusive romantic relationship with a female partner. Most said they would consider a woman as their primary or only romantic partner if the "right woman" came along. Others said they would not consider such a relationship, from reasons as varied as a standing committed relationship with a man, to the fact that women are "crazy and unstable," to the simple fact that "I really like penises!" Of the 25 interview respondents, all had had at least one sexual experience with a woman.[21] However, only two respondents had had steady female partners at any point in their lives, and none was currently partnered with a woman. Those involved in polyamorous or open relationships might have a female partner somewhere in the arrangement—Nova stated she is "dating a married couple," and Moira has a "long-distance female partner," for instance—but none had a woman as their primary romantic or life partner. Most were, in fact, currently either married to or partnered with a man. In conducting informal interviews and participant observation, I found this trend to hold true on a community level. Bisexual-identified women tended to have other women as sexual partners but to choose men as their life partners and to build their primary relationships with men. Sexual activity with women appears to be a side activity. Several of my interview respondents reported never having had a one-on-one sexual encounter with a woman; a man was always present in their encounters with other women, most often in a triad or threesome arrangement.

The construction of female bisexuality as an ideal identity also seems to be at work even among women who have never had a sexual experience with a woman. In my participant observation, I met many women who identified as bisexual but who had never had a sexual experience with a woman. I do not mean to negate the authenticity of these women's identity—coming from the standpoint that sexual identity is just that, an identity rather than necessarily a behavior, I believe that it is very much possible for one to have same-sex attractions without acting on them. Some women did not act on their attraction to other women because of shyness, lack of opportunity or because they were in a committed relationship with a man that did not allow for either partner to have outside sexual relationships. However, in the course of my participant observation I did notice a certain sense of "compulsory bisexual identity," in which women who had not had a sexual experience with a woman felt the need to identify as bi and state that they had not had an experience with a woman yet.

Although it is seldom overtly articulated, there appears to be a sense that bisexual identity makes a woman "more Pagan" than a monosexual woman. This is sometimes overtly articulated—some heterosexual-identified women I spoke to in the community reported having been accused of being "repressed," "hanging on to Christian moralities" or "deluding themselves" by not identifying as bi. However, more often this attitude is conveyed through discourse that positions bisexuality as a natural outgrowth of NeoPagan theologies—as if, as a NeoPagan practitioner, one could not be anything but bisexual. MaryMoon (2000) articulated it thus:

> To love the Divine, then, is to feel the most intimate of bondings, sexually enacted or not, with both the Goddess and the God potentials within the Whole. It is to see, and to choose to touch and to intercourse with, both essential expressions of Divinity within our bi gendered world. For me, personally, then, how could I not be open to the deepest of intercourse with the soul/spirit, with both gendered forms, with female and with male? (p. 90)

This discourse takes the "why limit yourself to one half the human race?" and "fall in love with the person, not the gender" rhetoric often employed in the larger bi community and adds a layer of spiritual significance to bisexual identity. In so doing, monosexuality is implicitly and explicitly constructed as somehow less holistic, less healthy, and somehow "less Pagan" than bisexuality.

In her 1986 interview with Adler (1979), American Witch Sharon Devlin put forth the following opinion on bisexuality and NeoPaganism:

> I consider bisexuality, by and large, a higher state than simply homosexuality or heterosexuality because it offers a greater number of alternatives. You should be able to love all the people that you love freely. If you desire to give physical expression to that love, that should be permitted. If men choose to make love to only men, and if women choose to make love to only women, that's fine, but they should remember that it is just as limiting as restricting yourself to a member of the opposite sex. (p. 179)

Although Devlin characterizes homo- and heterosexuality as equally limiting, I did not find this sentiment in much of the community where I conducted research. Rather, it is (female) heterosexuality that is indicted as "limiting," "repressive," or restrictive. Lesbianism, though also a form of monosexuality, does not come in for the same criticism. This is likely largely rooted in the NeoPagan value of openness to nonmiddlestream forms of sexuality. Some interview respondents made mention of the antipathy of lesbians toward bi women—antipathy rooted in the idea that bi women are "traitors to the cause" of women's spirituality, or that they are untrustworthy, deluded and promiscuous (Ault, 1996a). However, with the exception of occasional jabs at "the Dianics," my respondents did not seem to characterize lesbianism as a limiting or "less Pagan" form of sexuality in the same way that they did heterosexuality.

Ault (1996b) analyzed the strategies by which bisexual-identified women construct straights and lesbians as somehow the "perverted" ones, while constructing bisexuality as a more natural or normal form of sexuality. This discourse, overlaid with the spiritual implications discussed above, is at work in ways subtle and blatant within the NeoPagan community. Adding another dynamic is the NeoPagan ideal of openness and nonjudgmentality, which is held up as one of the primary reasons why NeoPaganism is a more appealing religion than Christianity. It is interesting to note that few of my informants remarked on the intolerance often faced by heterosexual-identified NeoPagan practitioners. However, heterosexual-identified practitioners do seem to pick up on the ethic that bisexuality (at least for women) is an ideal and idealized identity, and that there is perhaps something wrong or at least "less spiritual" about those women who identify as heterosexual.

One of the most overt ways in which this manifests itself within the community is in heterosexual-identified practitioners' apologetic stance in relation to their own heterosexuality. Consistently, heterosexual-identified NeoPagan women I encountered in my research stated they were "straight, but had no problem with bis or gays." More common was the statement that "Maybe I just haven't met the right woman yet," implying that they had the openness and ability to change their identity to bisexual if the right opportunity presented itself. Other women chose to not commit to either heterosexual or bisexual identity, instead choosing to label themselves "80% straight, 20% bi," "only 85% het," or similar constructions that made allowances for their primary (or sole) sexual relationships with men while also allowing them to claim some of the bisexual privilege at work in the community. Two women I interacted with in the course of my research were part of a polyamorous relationship between two couples—the two women and their husbands engaged in partner-swapping and group sex, and the two women (but not the two men) engaged in one-one-one sexual activities. Neither woman identified as bisexual, instead claiming heterosexual identity. However, when they were together in NeoPagan contexts such as festivals, the women made it clear to all around them that they were in a sexual relationship through referring to each other as "my girlfriend" and engaging in public displays of affection. Even while refusing the label of *bisexual*, these women seemed to also want to access the status and privilege afforded to bisexual women within the community, while perhaps avoiding some of the stigma attached to heterosexual-identified women.

The stigma attached to heterosexual identity for NeoPagan women is something that many women in the community feel, regardless of their own sexual identity. Heterosexual-identified women who did not engage in the strategies outlined above that would have allowed them a "bi out" were quick to make clear that they sometimes felt looked down upon for their heterosexuality. Some even stated that they felt "bad" or "guilty" because they couldn't "get past" their heterosexuality. Heterosexual-identified women are often perceived of (and spoken about) as prudish or somehow less free than their bisexual-identified sisters in the community. Heterosexuality is seen by some as something to be overcome; bisexuality is seen as a higher stage of spiritual evolution, something that will come "in time," by many community members.

While at a women's Goddess retreat, one woman reported to me that she was "afraid she might be straight" because she was finding herself less attracted to women since her marriage to a man. She had identified as bisexual since her late teens, and she and her husband had had a polyamorous relationship that allowed them to take partners of both sexes. After a less-than-satisfying sexual encounter with another woman, she was now questioning her bisexuality. She "felt bad" about it and was clearly in great consternation as she contemplated the possibility of being a NeoPagan heterosexual-identified woman.

The reluctance of this woman to relinquish her bisexual identity, as well as the maneuvering of some heterosexual-identified women to have "one drop" of bisexual "blood" reflects the status that identifying as bisexual affords women with this NeoPagan community. Karlen (1988) noted that "in some circles the word *bisexual* is used often and loosely; for a woman it carries no stigma and may even raise her status" (p. 480). Throughout my research, I found this to be largely the case. Bisexual-identified women are sought after by many NeoPagan men, and the archetype of the hot bi Pagan babe is one of considerable power within the community. Bisexual woman are "at the top of the sexual food chain," as one discussion board participant put it. Implicit in bisexual identity in many circles, including the NeoPagan community in which I worked, is nonmonogamy; polyamory in various forms (swinging, open relationships, threesomes) was the norm among my interview respondents and in my overall sample, which gives some credence to the idea that at least for NeoPagans bisexuality and nonmonogamy exist side by side. One interview respondent said that hot bi Pagan babes are often sought after by heterosexual men in the community to act out their own fantasies; a woman's stock goes up, so to speak, if she identifies as bisexual.

The power of bisexual privilege within the community was persuasive. In the course of my research, I met one heterosexual-identified woman who, upon entering a new relationship with a partner who was outspoken about his desire for a bisexual girlfriend, began engaging in sexual relations with women. She quickly became as outspokenly bisexual as she had been outspokenly heterosexual, declaring her former heterosexual identity a "delusion."

Many bisexual-identified women speak of "coming to realize" or "coming to accept" their same-sex attractions, implying that they (and perhaps all?) women are bisexual by nature, and it is simply culture or Christianity that represses these desires. NeoPagan women who come to identify as bisexual in this way are typically rewarded with status and a great deal of attention from NeoPagan men. Although it seems somewhat counterintuitive that this would be so desirable in a religion that incorporates feminist values and perspectives, for many women it appears that the approval of other women in the community, and the approval and desire of men, is an important aspect of adopting a bisexual identity.

Although it has been conjectured (Baumgardner & Richards, 2000) that adopting a bisexual identity is often a feminist act, the inverse seems to be at work for many NeoPagan women. There is sometimes great pressure from their male partners for women to not only identify as bisexual and pursue sexual experiences with women, but also to do so either in public spaces such as festival fires or in situations where the male can either participate or watch.

The stereotype of a male partner who "likes to watch" while two women make love is perhaps too simplistic, and at the very least is adolescent. Many interview respondents, though, found themselves in this situation precisely. Although their relationships with male partners were negotiated in such a way to allow for their bisexuality and exploration of that bisexuality, any same-sex encounters were circumscribed in such a way that the male partner was included. Trish, for example, stated that her husband is "fine [with her bisexuality] as long as he can watch or participate." Others acknowledged that their male partners found their bisexuality "sexy," "hot" or "exciting." Some women cited this as evidence of their partners' tolerance for their bisexuality; others seemed intrigued by the status and power that their bisexuality, and their partners' excitement in it, gave them in their relationships. A number of interview respondents reported that their only same-sex sexual experiences had been facilitated by a male partner who orchestrated the situation. Although it is unlikely that the women had no say in such an arrangement, and even more unlikely that they were coerced, it was through the initiative of a man (and possibly for his benefit) that these encounters took place. Similarly, most interview respondents stated that most or all their sexual encounters with women had taken place in the context of a threesome or group where a man or men was present, rather than one on one between the women themselves. Moira stated that this is "not by her choice," something echoed by other respondents. In conducting informal interviews and participant observation, I noticed similar trends. Male partners seemed to be the driving force behind their female partners' sexual escapades with other women and on the whole orchestrated these encounters so that all parties participated. Storm stated that her partner has encouraged her to seek out females for one-on-one encounters, but up to the time of her interview all her encounters had involved him "joining in" at some point. This trend seems to follow the larger one of same-sex encounters being supplemental to primary relationships with men, even in polyamorous arrangements.

This fetishization of female bisexual identity extends to public spaces as well. Within the sexually open setting of the NeoPagan festival, bisexual-identified women are also encouraged to engage in public displays of sexuality and sensuality with other women. Many women I spoke to feel that the festival environment is among the safest environment in which to engage in sexual experimentation, and as such many bisexual-identified women (and indeed practitioners of various sexualities) feel comfortable engaging in sexual behavior within the festival environment. Encounters appear to be exclusively consensual, and the festival environment is constructed in such a way that boundaries are typically respected and any violation of those boundaries is swiftly dealt with. In the course of my participant observation, however, I noticed that a significant portion of the same-sex displays of affection between women are encouraged by their male partners (or in some cases male friends and bystanders) and seem to be performed as much, if not more, for the benefit of the male observers than that of the female participants.

This dynamic is especially interesting not only in light of NeoPaganism's feminist overtones, but because NeoPagan ideals of gender tend to be fairly egalitarian. NeoPagan women cite equality between the sexes as one of the main reasons they were attracted to NeoPaganism; they enjoy the perceived lack of sexism within the NeoPagan community, which appears to also include the right of women (and men) to freely and safely explore their sexuality. Men and women within the NeoPagan community stated that they value the importance placed on equal partnership between all parties in romantic and committed relationships, and the presence of strong women and compassionate men (while somewhat stereotypical, perhaps) is often mentioned as one of the most appealing aspects of the NeoPagan community as a whole. Therefore, it is interesting to see the encouragement of displays of same-sex sexuality between women by men; whereas some of this encouragement is done in good fun, and certainly not all women feel coerced or demeaned by this behavior, at the same time it can be interpreted as objectification, something that seemingly runs counter to NeoPagan ideals of gender and individual freedom.

Some women clearly stated that they feel that such behavior is an objectification of women and their sexuality, and they object strongly to it. At a large festival where I have conducted participant observation, an incident of two women doing "body shots" off of each other before a whooping audience of men drew criticism from many women (and men). Similarly, at the same festival, various revel fire dancers were offended by the presence of a couple who trolled the fire with cans of whipped cream, randomly squirting women's breasts so that the female member of the couple could then suck them clean; the behavior was described as "sleazy" and seen as not only an exploitation of women's sexuality for the titillation of a male, but as a violation of the spirit of sexual play that is inherent in the revel fire (Pike, 2001).

Other women, however, not only do not object to the fetishization of female bisexuality (and female bisexuals, by extension). Rather, they actively engage in the construction of the hot bi Pagan babe, who is largely considered to be promiscuous as well. In listening to bisexual-identified women speak about other women, I heard language that ran counter to what some of the same women had just told me about gender ideologies. Although these women enjoyed the respect for women that is present in NeoPaganism, they also laughed about "watching chicks" with their male partners; "getting some pussy" at the revel fire; and loving being bisexual because "there is eye candy everywhere!" By and large, these women identify as feminists. Even as they participated in a religion that asserts the right of women to shape their own lives, these bisexual-identified women were engaging in the same type of objectifying language that much of feminism has taken on.

Although not true of all (or probably even a majority) of bisexual-identified NeoPagan women, there was nevertheless a palpable sense that many such women have internalized the idealized (or fetishized) image of the nonmonogamous, promiscuous, adventurous hot bi Pagan babe. Only a few of my interview respondents report being in a monogamous relationship, polyamory is far more common. (Polyamory is more common in my sample overall, which may skew this picture somewhat.) Perhaps in keeping with the theme of not limiting oneself to lovers of one gender, NeoPagans seem to also reject limiting oneself to one lover at a time. In some ways, this buttresses the stereotype that bisexuals cannot be happy unless they are actively engaged in relationships with a partner of each sex; although not universal, this stereotype does seem to hold some truth within the community where I conducted my research. In keeping with the ideal/stereotype of the bi Pagan woman as sexually open to many partners, many of the bisexual-identified Pagan women I spoke to seemed to view all women as potential sexual conquests; one even went so far as to declare that "all the bi women need tags" so she could know which women it was acceptable to approach sexually. (The implication, of course, was that she didn't want to "waste" time talking to women who weren't potential threesome participants.)

BI WAY OF ANALYSIS

The idea that "all cool women should be bi," and the image of what that "bi-ness" looks like, within the Texas NeoPagan community is omnipresent and complex. Bisexuality is seen as a way for women to get closer to the Divine and as a way for them to achieve a certain type of status within the NeoPagan community. Using discourse that is explicit and subtle, NeoPagans construct an image of the bisexual female as an ideal to be aspired to and an object to be pursued.

Ault (1996b) examined the way in which "doubly deviant" individuals construct identity, and in doing so construct their own identities as normative. Bisexual-identified NeoPagan women appear to engage in the same type of negotiation. They are "doubly deviant" in that their religious identity and their sexual identity fall outside the mainstream—defined as Christian and heterosexual. As they negotiate the NeoPagan landscape and the larger American landscape in which it exists, NeoPagans create a world in which Christianity and heterosexuality are set up as "other"—in essence, NeoPaganism and bisexuality become the norm and Christianity and heterosexuality become the "queer."

Christianity becomes associated with restrictive mores, suffocating dualities, intolerance and repression. NeoPaganism, in contrast, is seen as welcoming, freeing, holistic and tolerant. Christianity relegates people to the realm of passive follower and conformist. NeoPaganism is constructed as a religion of personal choice and determination. And that choice extends to sexuality. Heterosexuality, seen as compulsory only because the dominant Christian culture makes it so, is for NeoPagans a limiting and self-denying form of sexual expression. Bisexuality, on the other hand, is associated with an ability to truly know divine love and to explore all the possibilities that exist in the realm of sensuality. In a very real way, then, heterosexuality becomes equated with Christianity for many NeoPagans. Because they are resisting Christianity, they also resist heterosexuality.

The picture is somewhat skewed, however, when we realize that it is only women who seem to be expected to be bisexual within the NeoPagan community. Presumably, if bisexuality were really being constructed as an ideal, it would apply to members of both genders. On the ground, this is not the case. Although male NeoPagans freely identify as gay or heterosexual, few identify as bisexual. The distaste for male bisexuality is sometimes as palpable as the clamoring for female bisexuality. As one male NeoPagan put it, "Female bisexuality is beautiful and expressive—not at all like male-male [sex]." Certainly some of this can be chalked up to the homophobia that is often pervasive in American culture, and particularly in the American South where my research is located. However, the inequity in the expectation of bisexuality may also point to something larger.

CONCLUSION

Like all forms of sexual identity and sexual behavior—indeed, all forms of human expressive behavior—female bisexuality within a NeoPagan context is complex and nuanced. It can be easy to dismiss bisexual NeoPagan women who seem to perform sexually for the benefit of male partners as subordinate or at the very least playing into dominant cultural structures of the male gaze and male privilege. In light of the generally woman-positive and gender-inclusive nature of NeoPagan thealogy and practice, the jarring disconnect between ideals of equality and free will and seemingly coerced sexual expression can leave the observer feeling disenchanted, even bereft. Certainly that is what I felt upon first observing the phenomenon I document in this article: a sense that women who had left one set of confining religious conventions had simply entered another, similiarly confining, environment that bore the window dressing of equality and freedom.

Feminist criticism of bisexual women who take their relationships with women less seriously than they do their relationships with men (Ault, 1996a; Garber, 2000; Rust, 1992; Weise, 1992)—what one early reader of this piece termed the philosophy of "woman as side dish"—is worth examining here. The situation of female bisexuality within NeoPaganism in some ways turns lesbian and feminist criticism on its head by positioning straight women, rather than bi women, as suspect or somehow deviant. However, many of the assertions of these critics, particularly that bisexual women may tend to play fast and loose with the emotions of other women for either their own enjoyment or the pleasure of men, do appear to be played out in this situation. It would be unfair, however, to tar all the bisexual women I interviewed and observed for the current study with the same brush. Certainly, there were cases where sexual experiences with other women were pursued primarily for the benefit of men, and the male gaze did seem to dominate many settings in which same-sex interactions between women took place. Some women were conscious of this dynamic, and either played into it—seeking out women because their male partners found it "hot"—or accepted it reluctantly as a cultural norm, and as a type of price to pay for getting to explore their same-sex attractions. Other women, however, rejected this notion that bisexual activity should be done for the benefit of men and instead viewed it as a way to claim (or reclaim) sexual autonomy and power over their own bodies. This attitude is perhaps more in keeping with the third-wave feminist ideals that many young women in the NeoPagan community have grown up with and internalized (Baumgardner, 2007; Baumgardner & Richards, 2000).

At first blush, the situation of female bisexuality with a NeoPagan context can seem (forgiving the pun) straightforward. It can alternately be interpreted as women reclaiming sexuality through a feminist and sex-positive religious community, or viewed as a fetishization of female sexuality and a reification of the male–female power dynamic often at work in the larger American culture. To choose either analysis whole cloth, however, is to essentialize not only the women and men in question, but also NeoPagan thealogy and practice itself. My own inclination, at first, was to see bisexual NeoPagan women as not only exploited by their male partners but, to some extent, also complicit in their own exploitation. Although I still contend that there are instances where women are exploited—by male partners, or by other women—in their same-sex encounters, I now see it as too simplistic to assume this is true of all women or all encounters. Sexual experience, and the construction of sexual and gender identity, is fundamentally dynamic and complex. As women, and men, try to negotiate the different sexual and gender boundaries at work in the NeoPagan context, new power relations will likely result even as old power dynamics from the dominant culture need to be confronted.

NOTES

1. It is important to note that the NeoPagan movement in Europe and America has a long history going back much further than the 1960s. Indeed, roots of the NeoPagan movement can be found in the 19th century Romantics, and also in the occult movements of the 1930s such as the Order of the Golden Dawn. Similarly, the NeoPagan movement has not always been particularly feminist or sex positive, and indeed sectors of it are still markedly patriarchal and less tolerant of sexual diversity. However, as Adler (1986, 2006), Pike (2001), and others have noted, American NeoPaganism has drawn much from the 1960s counterculture and feminist politics.

2. Reconstructionist movements, such as Asatru, Theod and Celtic Reconstructionism, are religious movements that purport to reconstruct (hence the name) religious practices of past cultures, most typically Norse and Celtic, though Greek, Latin and Egyptian reconstructionist groups do exist, among others. Many adherents to these traditions reject the NeoPagan label, asserting that they are instead working with traditions with deep history and not creating something new. Adler (2006) provided an excellent portrait of reconstructionist movements and their place within the larger NeoPagan community.

3. I use the terms *NeoPagan* and *Pagan* interchangeably in this article, reflecting the community standard of usage. Few of the people who I have worked with in this project refer to themselves as *NeoPagan*, preferring the more generalized *Pagan*. The difference is really one of semantics. In the scholarly literature, *NeoPagan* is used to distinguish the modern religious movement from the historical (*Pagan* or *pagan*) traditions of cultures like ancient Rome or Greece. For modern day practitioners, the term *Pagan* is often preferred because they do not like the implication that their religion is new or "Neo."

4. There is robust debate within the NeoPagan community about whether or not such practices can properly be called Pagan or NeoPagan, which is beyond the scope of this article.

5. The eight Wiccan Sabbats mark the two Solstices, two Equinoxes, and four "cross-quarter days" in the year. They are Samhain (October 31), Yule/Winter Solstice (December 21), Imbolc/Candlemas (February 2), Ostara/Spring Equinox (March 21), Beltaine (May 1), Midsummer/Summer Solstice (June 21), Lammas/Lughnasad (August 1) and Mabon/Fall Equinox (September 21). There may be some variation in names or dates for these observances in various NeoPagan traditions, but this is the most common ritual calendar.

6. *British Traditional Witchcraft* refers to initiatory, coven-based Wiccan traditions that base their heritage in Great Britain and on the teachings of Gerald Gardner and his intellectual descendents, including Gardnerian, Alexandrian, and Georgian Wicca (Adler, 2006). In community usage, it is sometimes shortened to "BTW" or "BritTrad."

7. This refers to the Kinsey scale employed by Kinsey in his famous research on American sexual behavior. A "Kinsey 3" is someone whose attractions and behaviors locate them in the exact center of the bipolar, 7-point scale between homo- and heterosexual.

8. It is important to note that the sample size is small. It is possible that the small sample size "queers the pitch," so to speak, although based on my informal interviews and participant observation, I do not believe this to be the case.

9. The Texas NeoPagan community reflects the trend of the wider American NeoPagan community in that it is roughly 60% female. However, I do not believe that gender disparity alone accounts for the difference in male and female bisexual identification.

10. A few women qualified their identity as "bicurious" or "having bi tendencies," which they saw as qualitatively different from identifying as bisexual. The lack of bisexual-identified males may have much to do with the overall American cultural trend of being less accepting of male bisexuality or sexual fluidity. Garber (2000) and others have noted a greater tolerance for female bisexuality in American culture. Certainly larger cultural attitudes and internalized homophobia play a part.

11. This is an important difference between American NeoPaganism and European NeoPaganism. European traditions, and those American traditions that trace their heritage to such traditions such as British Traditional Witchcraft traditions, are markedly less feminist. In fact, the principle British traditions—Gardnerian, Alexandrian, and Georgian—were all founded by and named after men, and have a markedly patriarchal flavor. Such groups do not typically engage in political activity of any kind, and have more in common with the occult movements of the late 19th and early 20th centuries than the American counterculture of the 1960s. Adler (1979, 2006) and others have pointed out this difference between NeoPaganism on opposite sides of the Atlantic.

12. This idea lives on in the distinction of "Women's Spirituality" or "Feminist Spirituality" from more generalized "Wicca" or "Paganism" used by community members.

13. I follow the lead of feminist writers such as Carole Christ (1987, 1992) and Starhawk (1979) in using *thealogy* rather than *theology* to connote the fundamentally feminine and Goddess-focused nature of such systems of thought.

14. Community stereotypes often hold that all such groups are made up only of lesbians, but that appears to have been the exception, even at the height of the Feminist Witchcraft movement.

15. This is, in fact, a largely inaccurate usage of the term. Although some Dianic groups are composed largely of lesbians and do (or have in the past) espouse separatism, this appears to be the exception rather than the rule. Using the term in this way ignores Dianic traditions, such as the MacFarland Dianics, that do initiate men and women. The majority of Dianic groups do not limit their membership to women or necessarily require lesbianism or separatism of their members (Adler 1979/1986, 2006). It is unclear to me exactly how the term *Dianic* came to be used in the way I describe above—as a largely pejorative term implying misandrony, separatism and a certain degree of thealogical purity—but over the course of my 15 years in the Texas community, I have heard it used in this context almost exclusively. Some community members do recognize that groups such as the MacFarland Dianics do not conform to the stereotype associated with the term, but the usage endures nonetheless. Interestingly, women who espouse thealogies that use only a female godhead or who overtly incorporate feminist political concerns in their NeoPagan practice also become tagged with the term *Dianic*, whether or not they are initiated into the tradition. (I myself have been labeled as such, though I have never taken a Dianic initiation of any kind.)

16. This is not to say the NeoPaganism is a utopia of gender equality. As Salmonsen (2002) noted, there can be a marked disparity in the values espoused by some groups and behavior. Additionally, not all NeoPagan groups advocate gender equality—some are markedly patriarchal, including those that draw from the Western Mystery Tradition. I found the greatest gender disparity among Reconstructionist groups, where so-called traditional gender roles (women as mothers, men as breadwinners) were a key component of theology and community life.

17. Although this is far from universal to all NeoPagans, it is perhaps the most common point of belief, after the sacredness of the earth, in an incredibly diverse community. Not all NeoPagans conceive of divinity as dual, polar, gendered or even anthropomorphic. However, such conceptions are common enough that they do inform the issues in this article.

18. All names used for the women who participated in my research are pseudonyms. All participants were aware that they could be quoted for this article, and that neither their legal names nor their "Craft names" (names that many NeoPagans employ rather than their legal names) would be used.

19. The term *monosexual* refers to one who is attracted to only one sex, whether it be the same or an alternate sex. I use it because it is more streamlined than using hetero/homosexual.

20. In keeping with the trends noticed by Adler (1979, 2006), the majority of my informants had converted to NeoPaganism from varying forms of Protestant Christianity. Most converted when they were in late adolescence or early adulthood.

21. When it comes to same-sex behavior, operationalizing *sex* can be tricky. I chose to define *sex* as "physical intimacy beyond kissing: that is, fondling, heavy petting, mutual masturbation, oral sex, manual sex, or overt genital sex. Basically, if you wonder if it was 'real sex,' it probably was!" This definition, which I did not arrive at easily, was in keeping with the "two or more people, one or more orgasm" definition that many community members mentioned as their definition of *sex*.

REFERENCES

Adler, M. (1986). *Drawing down the moon: Witches, druids, goddess-worshippers, and other pagans in America today*. New York: Beacon Press. (Original work published 1979)

Adler, M. (2006). *Drawing down the moon: Witches, druids, goddess-worshippers, and other pagans in America today* (rev. and updated ver.). New York: Penguin.

Ault, A. (1996a). Hegemonic discourse in an oppositional community: Lesbian feminist stigmatization of bisexual women. In B. Beemyn & M. Eliason (Eds.), *Queer studies: A gay, lesbian, bisexual and transgender Queer studies: A gay, lesbian, bisexual and transgender* (pp. 204–216). New York: New York University Press.

Ault, A. (1996b). The dilemma of identity: Bi women's negotiations. In S. Seidman (Ed.), *Queer theory/sociology* (pp. 311–330). Cambridge, MA: Blackwell Publishers.

Baumgardner, J. (2007). *Look both ways: Bisexual politics.* New York: Farrar, Strauss and Giroux.

Baumgardner, J., & Richards, A. (2000). *Manifesta: Young women, feminism, and the future.* New York: Farrar, Strauss and Giroux.

Bernard, H. R. (1994). *Research methods in anthropology: Qualitative and quantitative approaches* (2nd ed.). Walnut Creek, CA: AltaMira Press.

Brenner, E. T. (2000). From minister to sex radical: Further (mis)adventures of a lesbian-identified bisexual fag hag. In D. R. Kolodny (Ed.), *Blessed bi spirit: Bisexual people of faith* (pp. 239–248). New York: Continuum.

Budapest, Z. (1989). *The holy book of women's mysteries.* Oakland, CA: Wingbow Press.

Christ, C. P. (1987). Why women need the goddess. In C. P. Christ (Ed.), *Laughter of Aphrodite: Reflections on a journey to the goddess* (pp. 17–32). San Francisco, CA: Harper and Row.

Christ, C. P., & Plaskow, J. (Eds.). (1992). *Womanspirit rising: A feminist reader in religion.* San Francisco, CA: HarperCollins. (Original work published 1979)

Davis, P. G. (1998). *Goddess unmasked: The rise of neopagan feminist spirituality.* Dallas, TX: Spence Publishing.

Eller, C. (1993). *Living in the lap of the goddess: The feminist spirituality movement in America.* San Francisco, CA: HarperRow.

Eller, C. (2001). *The myth of matriarchal prehistory: Why an invented past will not give women a future.* Boston, MA: Beacon Press.

Garber, M. B. (2000). *Bisexuality and the eroticism of everyday life.* New York: Routledge.

Gray, E. R., & Thumma, S. (Eds.). (2004). *Gay religion.* Walnut Creek, CA: AltaMira.

Gross, R. M. (1992). Feminist God language in a Jewish context. In C. P. Christ (Ed.), *Laughter of Aphrodite: Reflections on a journey to the goddess* (pp. 167–173). San Francisco, CA: Harper and Row. (Original work published 1979)

James, C. (1996). Denying complexity: The dismissal and appropriation of bisexuality in queer, lesbian, and gay theory. In B. Beemyn & M. Eliason (Eds.), *Queer studies: A gay, lesbian, bisexual and transgender anthology* (pp. 217–240). New York: New York University Press.

Karlen, A. (1988). *Threesomes: Studies in sex, power, and intimacy.* New York: William Morrow.

Luhrmann, T. M. (1989) *Persuasions of the witch's craft: Ritual magic in contemporary England.* Cambridge, MA: Harvard University Press.

Magliocco, S. (2004). *Witching culture: Folklore and neopaganism in America.* Philadelphia: University of Philadelphia Press.

MaryMoon, P. (2000). I am goddess and God, therefore I am bi. In D. R. Kolodny (Ed.), *Blessed bi spirit: Bisexual people of faith* (pp. 89–100). New York: Continuum.

Morgan, R. (1982). WITCH: Spooking the patriarchy during the late Sixties. In C. Spretnak (Ed.), *The politics of women's spirituality: Essays on the rise of spiritual power within the feminist movement* (pp. 428–429). New York: Anchor.

Mountainwater, S. (1991). *Ariadne's thread: A workbook of goddess magic*. San Francisco, CA: The Crossing Press.

Orion, L. (1995). *Never again the burning times: Paganism revived*. Prospect Heights, IL: Waveland Press.

Pike, S. M. (2001). *Earthly bodies, magical selves: Contemporary pagans and the search for community*. Berkeley, CA: University of California Press.

Rust, P. C. (1993). Neutralizing the threat of the marginal woman: Lesbians' beliefs about bisexual women. *Journal of Sex Research, 30*(3), 214–228.

Rust, P. C. (1995). *Bisexuality and the challenge to lesbian politics: Sex, loyalty, and revolution*. New York: New York University Press.

Salomonsen, J. (2002) *Enchanted feminism: Ritual, gender, and divinity among the reclaiming witches of San Francisco*. New York: Routledge.

Scarboro, A., Campbell, N., & Stave, S. (1994). *Living witchcraft: A contemporary American coven*. Westport, CT: Praeger.

Scupin, R. (Ed.). (2000). *Religion and society: An introductory text*. San Francisco, CA: HarperRow.

Starhawk. (1979). *The spiral dance: The rebirth of the religion of the great goddess*. San Francisco, CA: HarperRow.

Stein, D. (1990). *Casting the circle: A women's book of ritual*. Freedom, CA: Crossing Press.

Stein, D. (1991). *The women's spirituality book*. Minneapolis, MN: Llewellyn Publishers.

Valiente, D. (1989). *The rebirth of witchcraft*. London: Hale.

Weise, E. R. (Ed.). (1992). *Closer to home: Bisexuality and feminism*. Seattle, WA: Seal Press.

BI BOOK REVIEW

Gaia and the New Politics of Love: Notes for a Poly Planet, by Serena Anderlini-D'Onofrio

REVIEWED BY YEHUDIS (HUDI) SCHORR

Gaia and the New Politics of Love: Notes for a Poly Planet, by Serena Anderlini-D'Onofrio. Berkeley, CA: North Atlantic Publishing, 2009, 272 pages, paperback.

Our world is in crisis amid wars.

Military wars are robbing mothers' of their children, and people of their land. Political wars are pitting the people of our nation against one another, forcing them to take positions that may make the boundaries between those who have and those who cannot afford to have, more clear and defined than ever before.

Religious wars are abundant around the globe, attempting to justify the denial of basic rights of freedom as the word of God. The Earth has been catapulted into a state of chaos; the wars that we are waging upon her have taken their toll. Never before have we witnessed such levels of increased poverty and environmental degradation. In our time, the human species has acquired the capability to destroy human life and the biosphere that hosts it.

Gaia and the New Politics of Love: Notes for a Poly Planet is a masterpiece by Serena Anderlini-D'Onofrio that offers us a chance to transform crises into opportunity. Using science and nature as her backdrop, Anderlini-D'Onofrio constructs a new politics of Gaian symbiosis that affirms love as the force with which we must affect change in our universe, if we, as a species, are to survive our current state of environmental and political chaos.

In three sequential and interconnected parts Anderlini-D'Onofrio outlines a practical strategy to combat the toxic forces we have inflicted upon our planet. Using feminist ecological epistemology she offers an entirely new way of thinking about love, based upon teachings learned from bisexual and polyamorous communities that can offer a fresh perspective with which we can begin to repair the damage done to the biota that currently sustains us. If we are to survive the trauma to the Earth that we have caused, we must rethink our current conceptions of what that Earth is and the forces that we use to negotiate our way through it. We must expand beyond our currently limited definitions of love and family to include entire communities and the ecosphere that we inhabit. If we continue on our path of obsessive consumption of resources without regard to the harm we are causing, the biota will transform and survive, while our species will become one of the many extinct species that have at one point inhabited her live body.

Anderlini-D'Onofrio ominously warns us: if we continue to mistake Gaia for an assemblage of useable resources, we will kill ourselves, not her. It is now more than ever that we need her messages of warning, and instructions of repair.

GAIA IN FEMINIST SCIENCE

Anderlini-D'Onofrio begins by placing her Gaian philosophy within a framework of feminist ecology. Ecofeminism postulates that Gaia, the Earth, has a life of its own. It has a consciousness like an animated, self-regulating organism. In ecofeminism, subject and object are largely the same, and control is replaced by more symbiotic dialogue and collaboration. This feminist epistemology effectively defeats the logic of either/or and embraces a more inclusive logic of both/and. In this way, feminist ecologies debunk the myth of distinction between that which is "human" and that which is "nature." A Gaian philosophy implies giving up our sense of entitlement as a species deluded to thinking that the biota is a resource to be exploited by us.

> If we humans can come back to viewing ourselves as a resource among other resources with no special entitlement to occupying the position of subject in opposition to a "natural world" that becomes objectified as existing for the sole purpose of meeting our needs, then we can find again forms of coexistence with each other and the planet that hosts our lives. (p. xxii)

Symbiotic reason indicates that though there are no mere resources, every cell in Gaia's body can function as a resource for another cell. Symbiosis is the practice of sharing bodies in which both symbionts, the host and the guest, benefit. We only have to look to nature to see examples all around us: the cow who hosts the bacteria to make her food, the womb that hosts the fetus to nurture its survival. All parts of the equation are beneficiaries of the give-and-take relationship, without losing their individual identities in the process. We—humans, animals, minerals, the very Earth herself—are all part of the greater whole of Gaia, the process of life. The pain we inflict on nature is in fact pain we experience as a species, the growth we experience as individuals affects the world at large. A symbiotic logic requires us to view this bigger picture and begins to develop lines of communication between the now-disparate pieces that make up Gaia to find a more symbiotic harmony amongst them.

Symbiotic reason is more apt than individual reason to understand life as an interrelated web in which each individual is a small node that exists thanks to others' presence. The author points to the behavior of growth among trees and roots. Our ecosystem contains two kinds of intricate growth processes among vegetation. There are the arborescent plants: treelike growths organized as individual trees that sprout from a seed and grow vertically by sinking their roots deeply in the soil, and the rhizomes, such as gingerroots and potatoes that operate as subterranean root networks that grow sideways, store resources within the soil, and intermittently sprout interrelated plants across the terrain where the rhizome is present. A tree species may have strong individuals who grow to be taller and more powerful than any plant sprouting from a rhizome, but the rhizome in itself is more resilient to adversity and ecological changes due to their numerous points of entry. For Anderlini-D'Onofrio, the rhizome can represent the Gaian principle of evolution by symbiogenesis, the symbiotic process by which a species acquires the genes of its symbionts into its own DNA. This process is more horizontal. Anderlini-D'Onofrio argues that all life is symbiotic because biology shows that without exchanges between interrelated beings, there would be no life at all. It is within this reasoning that she has developed her new politics of love.

POLITICS OF LOVE

Anderlini-D'Onofrio's politics of love is new way of looking at love that draws from ancient teachings of a sacred feminine to postmodern understandings of health. Our current notions of health are monopolized by allopathic discourse that views health as the absence of disease and medicine a war against its attacks. It ignores the fact that perhaps disease is not a foreign attack on the body, rather a part of the body itself, crying out for repair. Holistic discourse on the other hand realizes a symbiotic alignment of an ecosystem's dynamic parts. Disease is viewed as a message from the body that demands a change in its ecology. Gaian awareness compels us to shift our current paradigms of health from an overwhelming allopathic discourse to more holistic notions of health, all the while invoking symbiotic reasoning to encourage dialogue between the allopathic and holistic health collectives.

The AIDS crisis played a massive role in positioning love on the side of disease. Through criminalizing loving communities, a rhetoric of fear was born, which produced a social energy that linked erotic expression with fear. A new politics of love seeks to reverse this trend by transforming its negative social energy into a positive one that reconnects erotic expression with safety and well-being. Hypothesizing Gaia helps the world shed needless fears from current dogmas of love as a crime or a disease.

In a holistic perspective, players are encouraged to enhance the health practices that strengthen their immunity and hence their health. This follows the Gaian principle that the health of Gaia's body is proportionate to the health of each of her cells. Conventional allopathic medicine tends to attack the symptoms that express the body's problem, and may neglect to seriously investigate its causes (p. 63). As Anderlini-D'Onofrio posits: if an individual is a cell in a super organism, his or her disease cannot be a foreign agent, for all agents are part of the larger entity of which that individual is an element. Disease in the elements of a super organism is a force that manifests a crisis in its life. Disease is thus read as a message that can help the living ecosystem deal with the crisis and reconfigure itself (p. 71).

The AIDS epidemic can be read as a crisis within Gaia, and as such, a signal for systemic change. Excessive emphasis on allopathic hypotheses in sexual health has kept the world stuck in a mode of fear. Anderlini-D'Onofrio's Gaia hypothesis postulates that the planet Earth is a web of interconnected organisms with a life of its own, a postmodern perspective that reverberates with indigenous, ecofeminist, premodern and symbiotic cultural elements (p. 102). In Gaian post modernity, "sex" is an erotic expression, the joy of taking and giving, and the orgiastic revitalizing pleasures of bacteria. It is the art of loving that lives in the wider space of the arts of healing, and as an art, is shy of any normativity (p. 110). Western masculinity emphasizes control over intimacy. It acts like a cultural imperative that dominates modern philosophical discourse reflected in Western modernity's obsession with the mastery of nature. The idea that humans can master nature is but a myth of modernity. The reality is that humans cannot master nature, and there is no reason why they should (p. 113).

Reconfigured as ecological erotic orientations, the love styles that correspond to former perversions are found to have a positive effect on Gaia's health for various reasons: They multiply the possibilities of love, they help expand the boundaries of the loving arts, and they contribute to establishing regimes of love that help in the sharing of resources and the creation of sustainable emotional communities (pp. 123–124). Love is free, and it can be multiplied at will. Anderlini-D'Onofrio defines it as "a renewable resource that saves one from the trappings of useless consumerism" (p. 125). The healing arts emphasize practices of the body that redeem people from modernity's secular materialism. They are effective in empowering people and communities to heal themselves by creating a more symbiotic understanding of us as individuals, without losing the connectivity to each other and our Mother Gaia. As Anderlini-D'Onofrio so eloquently writes, "this may not instantly resolve all global problems, but the perspective it puts things in vastly improves the prospects for healthy global ecologies" (p. 127).

THE ARTS OF LOVING

In this part of her book, Serena Anderlini-D'Onofrio articulates why she feels that bisexual and polyamorous communities provide the framework to actualize a Gaian awareness of living. Bi/poly communities generate areas of stability of erotic awareness and emotional sustainability that free the imagination from needless fears and create the emotional and ecological abundance that Gaia needs (p. 152). Because of their heavy reliance on touch, connectedness, nonviolence and a subtle knowledge and practice of intimacy, the styles of love invented by poly and bi people promote the activation of the hormonal cycle of Oxytocin (p. 137). Oxytocin is the hormone responsible for states of emotional calm and connectedness that often fills the aural and inner spaces of bi and poly societies. Oxytocin becomes a social lubricant within these communities where playfulness is key. It is the gentle playfulness produced by these arts of loving that enable emotional negotiations and agreements that would otherwise be impossible in an environment without it.

The styles of love practiced in bi and poly communities help build the trust necessary to overcome fears and are often intentionally designed to break down people's defensive identities, body armors and egos, so that all players can enjoy the free circulations of amorous energies. It is this symbiotic reason that transforms scarcity into abundance.

Consumer society can be visualized as an extensive orgy inasmuch as it is organized as a continuum orgiastic display of material temptations that induce desire for things we often don't need or want (p. 163). Anderlini-D'Onofrio writes that the combined practices of bi and poly love have the power to allow individual players to become part of the "flow of the orgy," to consciously navigate its flow and become consensually immersed into the movement of the symbiotic energy generated by our aural, astral and physical bodies at play (p. 163). This results in sustainability, balance and renewability of resources for all involved, and it maximizes a player's ability to give and receive love. She writes:

> As players learn to navigate this emotional/erotic space, the dialogue between the emotional and erotic realms enables them to maximize the love energy they can share. This sharing of emotional resources generates symbiotic energy fields between players, and enables the creation of emotional sustainability that result in symbiotic plateaus of enhanced awareness. These plateaus involve crises that manifest at certain points in the network, and whose collective management can productively turn them into opportunities for deeper levels of symbiosis. This growth and change can move the entire network on a higher level of awareness that enables more focused and productive experiments in the management of shared emotional resources and the symbioses therefore. The network

> thus functions like a sustainable ecosystem for all of these interpersonal energies. It generates the sustainability, balance, and renewability of resources for all involved. (p. 165)

Applied on a global scale, this turns scarcity into abundance, fear into hope, and hatred into love. This transformation happens when we players lose our intense sense of entitlement to the resources that surround us in our ecosphere. The tools of this transformation can be found in the schools of bisexual and polyamorous philosophy where intentional communities are formed by people who consciously choose to live by a shared utopian vision, motivated by Gaian principles. They share an expansive sense of love and sexual expression that involves consensual sharing of emotional and erotic resources and can be learned at their schools (p. 154).

Anderlini-D'Onofrio proposes a journey to these schools to learn the tools of the loving arts, regardless of one's orientation or identity. These philosophies of both/and/all include and cherish all points in every continuum. They celebrate our diversities and encourage us to recognize each other and harmonize ourselves with Earth's symbiotic ecosystem. If we can take from them the ability to think of love as an art whose forms of expressions is infinite, then perhaps we can incorporate those healing and loving arts to stave off ecological catastrophes caused by our irresponsible behavior as a species.

IMAGINE A BETTER WORLD

We must begin to imagine a world that is better than the current one we inhabit, where wars are being waged, and fear is abundant. Serena Anderlini-D'Onofrio has directed us upon a path that might open our imagination to new and thrilling ideas that, if we allow ourselves to be open enough to consider them, can restore our planet to a place of homeostatic symbiosis; a world where we give and take from what and whom is around us instead of stripping all of their available resources and leaving desolation in our wake. *Gaia and the New Politics of Love* offers us a glimpse as to what a world without animosity, soaked in selfish consumption might look like: a place where differences and individuals thrive together while dedicating themselves to the health of Gaia, that which came before us and will sustain herself after we pass.

Perhaps with this new model emphasizing nonviolent, loving sustainability we might do our part in ending the wars and restoring Gaia to her harmonic balance, thus ushering in the new era of planetary peace and health, based on mutual respect and love, that our world surely needs today.

Index